NUCLEAR DECOLONIZATION

NEW DIRECTIONS IN RHETORIC AND MATERIALITY
Wendy S. Hesford, Christa Teston, and Shui-Yin Sharon Yam, Series Editors

NUCLEAR DECOLONIZATION

INDIGENOUS RESISTANCE TO HIGH-LEVEL NUCLEAR WASTE SITING

Danielle Endres

THE OHIO STATE UNIVERSITY PRESS
COLUMBUS

Copyright © 2023 by The Ohio State University.
All rights reserved.

Library of Congress Cataloging-in-Publication Data
Names: Endres, Danielle, author.
Title: Nuclear decolonization : Indigenous resistance to high-level nuclear waste siting / Danielle Endres.
Other titles: Indigenous resistance to high-level nuclear waste siting | New directions in rhetoric and materiality.
Description: Columbus : The Ohio State University Press, [2023] | Series: New directions in rhetoric and materiality | Includes bibliographical references and index. | Summary: "Offers an account of how Western Shoshone, Southern Paiute, and Skull Valley Goshute peoples and nations prevented the construction of two high-level nuclear waste sites on their lands and how two sets of rhetorical tactics—Indigenous Lands rhetorics and national interest rhetorics—played an important role in these efforts"— Provided by publisher.
Identifiers: LCCN 2023030011 | ISBN 9780814215562 (hardback) | ISBN 0814215564 (hardback) | ISBN 9780814283172 (ebook) | ISBN 0814283179 (ebook)
Subjects: LCSH: Indians of North America—West (U.S.)—Social conditions. | Radioactive waste sites—Nevada—Yucca Mountain. | Radioactive waste sites—Skull Valley Reservation (Utah) | Rhetoric—Political aspects—Nevada. | Rhetoric—Political aspects—Utah. | Gosiute Indians. | Southern Paiute Indians. | Decolonization.
Classification: LCC E78.W5 E43 2023 | DDC 978.00497—dc23/eng/20230807
LC record available at https://lccn.loc.gov/2023030011

Other identifiers: ISBN 9780814258910 (paperback) | ISBN 0814258913 (paperback)

Cover design by Susan Zucker
Text design by Juliet Williams
Type set in Adobe Minion Pro

CONTENTS

List of Illustrations	vi
Acknowledgments	vii
Preface	ix
INTRODUCTION Indigenous Rhetorics and Nuclear Decolonization	1
CHAPTER 1 From Nuclear Colonization to Nuclear Decolonization	27
CHAPTER 2 The Indigenous Lands of Yucca Mountain and Skull Valley	60
CHAPTER 3 Indigenous Lands Rhetorics	88
CHAPTER 4 Indigenous National Interest Rhetorics	130
CONCLUSION Decolonization Tactics for Survivance	175
Bibliography	189
Index	213

ILLUSTRATIONS

FIGURE 1	Portion of a Western Shoshone permit	28
FIGURE 2	Participants in a 2007 Mother's Day demonstration walking toward the gates of the Nevada Test Site	29
FIGURE 3	Skull Valley with the Cedar Mountains in the background	61
FIGURE 4	Traditional territories of Great Basin and Colorado Plateau Indigenous peoples	66
FIGURE 5	Entrance to the Skull Valley Goshute Reservation	73
FIGURE 6	Map of Skull Valley Goshute Reservation	74
FIGURE 7	Federal Lands in Southern Nevada	79
FIGURE 8	Contemporary Indigenous governments in relationship with Yucca Mountain	81
FIGURE 9	Western Shoshone Lands in Crescent Valley	90
FIGURE 10	A sign erected by the state of Utah expressing opposition to storing high-level nuclear waste within Skull Valley	171

ACKNOWLEDGMENTS

This book has been a long time in the making and, therefore, builds from years of support from a variety of relations with people, institutions, organizations, places, and more-than-human beings. I want to start by recognizing the two scholarly institutions that have most directly enabled me to do this project: the University of Washington, from which I received my doctorate, and the University of Utah, where I have been a faculty member since 2005. My first trip to Las Vegas to use the archives at the Department of Energy's Yucca Mountain Information Center was supported by a small grant from the Department of Communication at the University of Washington. A variety of entities at the University of Utah provided subsequent support for the project, including the Department of Communication, Environmental Humanities Program, College of Humanities, Vice President for Research Office, and Tanner Humanities Center. Most recently, I am grateful for the support provided by The Ohio State University Press. In particular, Tara Cyphers's support for the project despite the tumult caused by the COVID-19 pandemic and other difficulties gave me confidence to complete this work.

This book would not have been possible without the decades of dedicated work by Indigenous organizations and peoples who produced the texts upon which my analysis is based, engaged in collaboration with me, participated in the oral history project, invited me to events, and welcomed me on Newe and Nuwuvi Lands. Key organizations include the Western Shoshone

Defense Project, Indigenous Environmental Network, Native Community Action Council, Honor the Earth, Ohngo Gaudadeh Devia, and National Environmental Coalition of Native Americans. I am forever grateful for the individuals who directly and indirectly participated in this project, including Carrie Dann, Mary Dann, Margene Bullcreek, Corbin Harney, Ian Zabarte, Kim Townsend, Julie Fishel, Jennifer Viereck, John Haddar, Judy Treichel, and Steve Frishman. In particular, I want to specifically express gratitude for four elders who devoted their lives to protecting Western Shoshone and Skull Valley Goshute Lands and cultures and who have since passed on: Carrie and Mary Dann, Margene Bullcreek, and Corbin Harney. I also want to thank Newe and Nuwuvi Lands—including all of the living beings that make up these places—that I visited and formed relationships with to do this research, specifically Crescent Valley, Las Vegas, Skull Valley, and Yucca Mountain.

Many people in academia have supported my research on nuclear colonization and nuclear decolonization, starting with my mentors from the University of Washington: Leah Ceccarelli, Barbara Warnick, and Gerry Philipsen. Colleagues who have supported me and my work include Mark Bergstrom, Jason Black, Laura Black, Brett Clark, Ashley Cordes, Ann Darling, Andrea Feldpausch-Parker, Marouf Hasian, Chris Ingraham, Jeffrey McCarthy, Tarla Rai Peterson, Phaedra Pezzullo, Madrone Schutten, Leah Sprain, Mary Stuckey, and Steve Tatum. Of course, there are many more who remain unnamed, including the two reviewers of this book as well as many reviewers of past research papers and conference presentations, whose keen constructive criticism improved my research and writing. I am grateful for the help of the graduate and undergraduate research assistants who contributed to this project over the years: Jessie Chaplain, Cory Robinson, Samantha Senda-Cook, Joaquin Torre, Bryan Wallis, and Paul Whisman. My writing support system—including my writing group with Samantha Senda-Cook, Bridie McGreavy, and Stacey Sowards and my Friday morning writing partner, Maria Blevins—provided the support, wisdom, and guidance I needed to finish this book.

Finally, Isaac Gottesman has been a part of this project since the beginning and continues to be my academic rock. My family is a source of endless support and love, including Wayne, Rosa, Owen, Sammy, my mom, and Nick. This book is dedicated to the memory of my dad, Richard L. Endres.

PREFACE

This book recounts stories of Indigenous activism from the 1980s to 2010s to prevent two high-level nuclear waste storage facilities from being built within Indigenous Lands[1]: the Yucca Mountain high-level nuclear waste repository within Western Shoshone and Southern Paiute Lands and the Private Fuel Storage (PFS) interim high-level nuclear waste repository within Skull Valley Goshute Lands. Within this continent—known as North America by settlers and Turtle Island by some Native peoples—Indigenous peoples and nations disproportionately bear the burdens and harmful effects of the nuclear production process, in most cases imposed by settlers. Indigenous antinuclear activists, environmentalists, protectors, peoples, and nations use *radioactive colonization* and related terms—*nuclear colonialism, nuclear colonization*—to describe a form of environmental injustice that works in the intersection of settler colonialism and nuclearism and has disastrous effects for Indigenous Lands, peoples, and nations.[2] But nuclear colonization is not the whole story,

---

1. In gratitude to Max Liboiron, I use *Lands* to refer to the entire ecology of beings present in Indigenous territories. The term is based in Indigenous knowledges and relationships with the more-than-human world. Liboiron, *Pollution Is Colonialism*.

2. See, for example, Endres, "Rhetoric of Nuclear Colonialism"; Kuletz, *Tainted Desert*; LaDuke and Churchill, "Native America," *Journal of Ethnic Studies*; and Indigenous Environmental Network, "Indigenous Anti-Nuclear Statement." Note: I have made the difficult decision to include Ward Churchill's work in my book. Much of the initial research on radioactive or nuclear colonialism in the US context was coauthored by Ward Churchill and Winona

nor the most important story. Indigenous peoples and nations have consistently engaged in nuclear decolonization to protect their sovereignties and Lands from nuclear technologies, including thus far preventing high-level nuclear waste from being relocated and, temporarily or permanently, stored in contemporary reservation, treaty-guaranteed, and sacred Lands.[3] These efforts can be celebrated as successes. Beyond the instrumental goal of stopping these two high-level nuclear waste sites, there are additional ways to define success by and for these movements, including constitutive enactments of self-determination, sovereignty, radical resurgence, survivance, and presence as well as forms of refusal that insistently remind the US federal government and non-Indigenous peoples that Native peoples and nations are still here, and protecting Lands is possible.[4]

In this book, I offer an account of rhetorical tactics used by Western Shoshone, Southern Paiute, and Skull Valley Goshute peoples and nations to prevent the Yucca Mountain and Skull Valley PFS sites from opening. The actors in this story are Indigenous environmental and antinuclear protectors[5]—sometimes working within and sometimes working against their own governments, sometimes working with non-Indigenous allies, and sometimes exploiting disruptions created by non-Indigenous opponents—who resisted high-level nuclear waste siting and nuclear colonization on their Lands. West-

---

LaDuke. Churchill has been identified as a person who claimed an Indigenous identity without sufficient evidence to support his claim. Moreover, he faced charges of plagiarism and academic misconduct at the University of Colorado Boulder. The academic misconduct findings report does not indict Churchill's work on radioactive colonization. Subsequent independent research has substantiated the phenomenon of radioactive colonization. LaDuke and Churchill's collaborative work on this topic continues to be valuable research that describes a phenomenon that extends well beyond their original work. Despite the controversy over Churchill, Winona LaDuke continues to be a key force in frontline Indigenous environmental justice activism. I want to amplify LaDuke's work. While I have limited my use of Churchill's research throughout this book, I have decided not to omit it completely because to do so would have the consequence of omitting LaDuke's contributions and would risk erasing a terminology and set of research that is still useful to and used by Indigenous activists. For more on the academic misconduct finding, see University of Colorado Boulder, *Report*.

3. Low-level and other forms nuclear waste are stored within Indigenous Lands, most notably the Waste Isolation Pilot Plant facility within Mescalero Apache Lands in what settlers named New Mexico.

4. Lake, "Enacting Red Power"; A. Simpson, *Mohawk Interruptus*; L. Simpson, *As We Have Always Done*; and Vizenor, *Survivance*.

5. In line with contemporary Airs, Waters, and Lands protector movements that seek to self-determine and reframe their work from protest to protection, I use this terminology to describe those Western Shoshones, Southern Paiutes, Skull Valley Goshutes, and members of other Indigenous peoples and nations who resisted high-level nuclear waste sites. However, this is not a term that was used by the actors themselves, perhaps because these struggles predated the widespread use of the term *protectors*.

ern Shoshone, Southern Paiute, and Skull Valley Goshute rhetors employed a range of nuclear decolonization tactics to make their agency and presence known in decision-making processes about high-level nuclear waste siting.

ORIGINS OF THE PROJECT

This project began before I set foot in graduate school and learned about rhetorical studies. It emerged from my interests in environmentalism and environmental justice, nuclear technologies, and Native social movements. Nuclear waste siting within Indigenous Lands is a nexus of these concepts. This book is the culmination of twenty years of research and writing, and even more years of active engagement with learning about the relationships between Indigenous peoples and nations and the life cycles of nuclear technologies. I began this project with nuclear colonialism, focused on the various strategies through which nuclear colonialism has been and continues to be perpetuated. The book was initially meant to be an extension of the work I have already done to expose the significance of rhetoric in nuclear colonialism. While I did my best to avoid a story in which Indigenous peoples and nations are passive victims of nuclear colonialism, my previous work mainly centered the strategies of nuclear colonialism, a form of criticism of settler colonial rhetorics. A commitment to studying structures of oppressive power is a crucial step in understanding nuclear colonialism as a complex set of interconnected rhetorical strategies. Yet, as I began to work on this book, influenced by a series of prods by reviewers, audience members at talks, and new research in Native American and Indigenous studies, I decided I wanted to retell the story of the relationship between high-level nuclear waste and Indigenous peoples and nations from a different vantage point, highlighting the modes of decolonization, survivance, resurgence, and self-determination that undergirded efforts to protect sacred Lands from the harms of nuclear waste. I wanted to do more to center Indigenous voices, to amplify tactics of decolonization, to tell a story of survivance and success. While nuclear colonialism continues to hold power as a structure that perpetuates nuclearism at the expense of Indigenous peoples, nations, and Lands, I write this book from a different starting place: the power of nuclear decolonization.

A shift from studies of colonization to studies of decolonization works against the re-centering of imperialism, white supremacy, and power. It works against narratives that lock Indigenous peoples and nations into a position of "dominated others upon whom history was enacted."[6] As Jodi Byrd wrote: "It

---

6. Byrd, *Transit of Empire*, 76.

is time to imagine indigenous decolonization as a process that restores life and allows settler, arrivant, and native to apprehend and grieve together the violence of U.S. empire."[7] While I do not believe that it is possible to separate nuclear decolonization from nuclear colonization as they are so inherently intertwined—they are always reacting to each other—I wanted to shift my lens from deriding the strategies of nuclear colonization, a form of rhetoric largely used by non-Indigenous peoples, to celebrating the tactics of nuclear decolonization, a form of rhetoric largely enacted by Indigenous peoples, nations, and their allies. The research presented in this book still treats the concepts as interconnected. And, at times, I assert causal or temporal arguments about how certain tactics of nuclear decolonization respond to certain strategies of nuclear colonization. I try, however, to envision nuclear decolonization as the through line, as a story that centers Indigenous modes of relationality and survivance that link past, present, and future. This book is my best attempt to amplify and appreciate the rhetoric of Indigenous peoples and nations who successfully protected their Lands. In this way, the book assumes, as Michael Lechuga contends, that "social movement activism is not an object of study but, rather, a source of knowledge akin to theory."[8] My role is not only to learn from the brilliance of a movement that I have engaged with for many years but also to learn from missteps in my previous work.

I would not have been able to write this book nearly twenty years ago when I started my research on Western Shoshone and Southern Paiute resistance to the Yucca Mountain site. At least two key developments have helped me to shift my gaze. First, in the last twenty years, there has been a significant shift in Native American and Indigenous studies research paradigms. This is not to say that Native American and Indigenous studies work did not exist or did not inform my previous work. Rather, the scholarly conversations over the past twenty years have, as one would expect, changed and deepened, in part due to a growth of Indigenous scholars doing the work of developing Indigenous theories and methodologies.[9] This book is particularly inspired by the nuancing of decolonization, settler colonialism, and Indigenous knowledges. Over the course of a particularly productive sabbatical, I delved into scholarly conversations that changed the way I thought about nuclear colonialism and nuclear decolonization. Likewise, my own discipline of communication has seen a shift in thinking about anticolonialisms, postcolonialisms, and deco-

---

7. Byrd, 229.
8. Lechuga, "Anticolonial Future," 378.
9. See, for example, Wilson, *Research Is Ceremony*; Kovach, *Indigenous Methodologies*; and L. Simpson, *As We Have Always Done*.

loniality that opened doors for my shift in focus from nuclear colonization to nuclear decolonialization as the central framework of the book.

Second, tangible successes in the Yucca Mountain and Skull Valley PFS cases have allowed me to think reflectively on the factors that contributed to these outcomes. When I began my research on both high-level nuclear waste sites, decisions had not yet been made and, though I fought alongside those opposing both sites, I believed that both sites would ultimately be built. That both the Yucca Mountain and PFS high-level nuclear waste sites were stopped was a surprise to me. This surprise may very well reflect my positionality as a white settler woman who had lost hope, who had not personally experienced the power of survivance. Viewing these as successful moments in a larger struggle has allowed me to move my research in new directions. My long-standing commitment to Indigenous decolonization coupled with my conviction that *when I stop learning I cease to be a scholar* contributed to my ability to stay open, revise past work, and keep learning. Indeed, I imagine that I may look back on this book in twenty years and see all of the ways my thinking has changed and evolved alongside both scholarly and activist movements.

A NOTE ON TERMINOLOGIES

There are a variety of terms to collectively describe the original inhabitants of what settlers now call the United States: *Indigenous, Native, Native American,* and *American Indian.* As a general practice, I use the terminology that Indigenous peoples and nations use to describe themselves, particularly in sections where I rely on quoting them. Otherwise, I use *Indigenous* and *Native* somewhat interchangeably throughout the book. *Indigenous* refers to the original inhabitants of a place and is a global terminology that exceeds my specific focus on Indigenous inhabitants of the part of the North American continent that settlers call the US (First Nations and Indigenous peoples living within Mexico are beyond the scope of this project but are also Indigenous inhabitants of this continent). *Native* is a newer term that drops *American* and functions similarly to *Indigenous* in that it is a terminology that can be applied outside of the North American context. *Indigenous* and *Native* can express the solidarity, similarities of experience, and coalition-building among the many Indigenous/Native peoples and nations worldwide. I also sometimes use *Native American, American Indian,* and *Indian*—terms that are used by Indigenous peoples and nations in texts I analyze—to describe the Indigenous inhabitants of what settlers now call the US. All three of these terms can be problematic because they use settler terminology for this place (*America*) or because they rely on a misnomer for this place assumed by the first Europeans who encountered this place (*India*). Moreover, while *Indigenous, Native, Native American, American Indian,* and *Indian* can be useful when describing a form of solidarity that has emerged in postcontact times, they can also simplify, overgeneralize, and essentialize the experiences of the 574 federally recognized Indigenous nations that survive in the US, suggesting "a cultural and racial homogeneity that does not exist."[10] While Indigenous peoples and nations sometimes engage in specific and strategic efforts to make similar the experiences of Indigenous peoples and nations in what is now called the US, these terms can have the effect of erasing the differences between and the specificity of distinct Indigenous nations and cultures. Yet, these terms remain in use among Indigenous peoples and nations, underscoring the limits of language.

I use specific names for Indigenous peoples and nations whenever possible. While Western Shoshone, Southern Paiute, and Skull Valley Goshute peoples and nations are the specific focus of this book, I am careful to use the specific names for other Indigenous peoples and nations that come up in the story of nuclear decolonization. When possible, I also introduce the terms used by Native peoples to describe themselves, such as *Newe* (Western Shoshones and Skull Valley Goshutes) and *Nuwuvi* (Southern Paiutes).

The terms *Indigenous peoples and nations* or *Native peoples and nations* reflect my decision to demonstrate that those engaged in nuclear colonization and nuclear decolonization may be speaking from the position of Indigenous nationhood or may be speaking from the position of an individual, a member of an Indigenous activist/protector group, or with a coalition of people from different Indigenous nations. My use of *Indigenous peoples* is not meant to erase the realities of Indigenous sovereignty and nationhood or assimilate Indigenous peoples as an ethnic minority group within the US. That said, since many of the actors in this story are not speaking as representatives of or from the perspective of their Indigenous nation(s), it would be limiting to rely only on the term *Indigenous nations*. I do not use the term *tribe*, unless in direct quotes or following the wishes of Native participants, because *tribe* can be derogatory and result in deemphasizing sovereign status. As David Wilkins and Heidi Stark note,

> What complicates matters, of course, is that there is no single term that is acceptable to all indigenous people all the time, and even people within

---

10. Beyond the 574 federally recognized nations, there are also state-recognized nations and nations not recognized by the federal government (in some cases, as a result of termination policies). Byrd, *Transit of Empire*, 73.

specific native communities sometimes disagree vigorously on what name they prefer (e.g., Navajo or Diné; Chippewa, Ojibwe, or Anishinaabe; Iroquois or Haudenosaunee) and on whether they would rather be identified as tribal communities (which emphasize their kinship affiliation) or as national entities (which, while not discounting kinship ties, tends to place greater emphasis on an independent political character and a right to engage in diplomatic relations with other nations or states, like the United States or other polities).[11]

Communication scholars like myself know well that language is fraught and often imperfect, even more so when writing about Indigenous peoples and nations in a colonizer's language. As a result, I have paid close attention to my language and terminologies throughout the book along the lines I have described in this section.

MY STORY

As this book recounts Indigenous peoples' and nations' stories of nuclear decolonization—a form of Indigenous research methods based in relationalities—it is important to tell you about myself. I am a white settler woman, with German, Scandinavian, and Anglo roots, living in what is now called the US. My ancestors came to this continent well before me, arriving as early as the 1600s and continuing through the 1700s and 1800s from Germany, Sweden, Norway, England, Ireland, and Scotland. Although initially settled in the Northeast and Midwest regions of this continent, my relatives have settled and dispersed across many places as they arrived, homesteaded, followed jobs, ventured away from family roots, and made lives on this continent. I grew up and lived eighteen years of my life in the homelands of the Ramaytush Ohlone. My pursuit of higher education brought me to live and work in the homelands of Kumeyaay, Kalapuya, and Duwamish peoples. I also spent two years living and working in a small rural town on the main island of Nihon (Honshu), called Kozagawa.[12]

Today, I live in Goshute, Shoshone, Paiute, and Ute Lands. What is now called the Salt Lake Valley, east of the Great Salt Lake, remains a gathering place for Indigenous peoples as well as being the ancestral and traditional

---

11. Wilkins and Stark, *American Indian Politics*, xviii.
12. Kozagawa is not part of the traditional homelands of the Ainu or Ryūkyūan people (who are Indigenous to the northern region of Honshu and Hokkaido and to Okinawa, respectively).

homelands of Goshute, Shoshone, Ute, and Paiute peoples and nations.[13] About sixty thousand American Indian and Alaska Native peoples live in what is now called the state of Utah, named after the Ute nation. Eight distinct Indigenous nations border Utah, and in some cases also border the states of Colorado, Nevada, Arizona, and New Mexico. There are 2.45 million acres of Indigenous trust Lands in Utah, which is about 4.5 percent of the total land base of Utah (as of 2009).[14] I own property and work at a university that occupies a portion of these Lands, both of which afford me privileges as a settler and represent forms of complicity within settler colonialism.[15] The University of Utah uses the *Utes* name for its sports teams with permission from the Ute Indian Tribe of the Uintah and Ouray Reservation.[16] While I still consider my homeplace to be Ohlone Lands, I have developed a strong sense of place and affection for this high desert place where I intend to continue to live and work for the foreseeable future.

I learned from my engagement with Western Shoshone, Southern Paiute, and Skull Valley Goshute Lands protectors how important it is to always know where I am, on whose Lands I am working, and how those places are entangled with systems of power. Beyond my personal history of movement and emplacement within this continent, this book project is also grounded in particular places. The project started when I lived in Duwamish Lands and has continued in my time in Ute, Paiute, Shoshone, and Goshute Lands. My home and campus offices as well as the many coffee shops where I wrote are within these occupied Lands. This project also entailed numerous visits to Western Shoshone, Skull Valley Goshute, and Southern Paiute Lands, including visits to Yucca Mountain and the proposed PFS site on the Skull Valley Goshute Reservation. Visiting these places greatly enhanced my ability to do this work, not only because it facilitated conversations with participants but also because I was able to see, feel, and be with the Lands proposed to host high-level nuclear waste. My engagement with these places gave me a perspective that I could not have acquired through written accounts, photos, and maps. Engaging in place mattered for my ability to see why Western Shoshone, Southern Paiute, and Skull Valley Goshute peoples and nations worked so hard to protect these Lands.

---

13. University of Utah, "Indigenous Land Acknowledgement."
14. McGinty, "Land Ownership of Utah."
15. I use the Western notion of ownership of property here to recognize my complicity within a system founded on stolen Lands, despite my desire to see Lands as entities that cannot be owned.
16. "Memorandum of Understanding between the Ute."

As a white professor in a field of study that is built on white supremacy and settler colonialism, has very few Indigenous scholars, and marginalizes Indigenous knowledges, I write this book from a position of privilege. There were many times that I thought about not writing this book, out of coupled desires to resist complicity in a system of higher education that still has far too many white settler "experts" on Indigenous peoples and nations and to resist adding another publication to my CV on a topic I have researched for many years.[17] Yet, I persisted in writing this book because of a feeling of accountability to those who collaborated with me over the years as well as a strong desire to retell these stories in ways that better center Indigenous agencies and voices in a successful campaign of Lands protection. This book represents my attempt to do good work in a good way with a good heart,[18] guided by the tenets of Indigenous research methods.[19] I have worked to support Indigenous struggles for Lands, sovereignty, and survivance, not just in the written products of my scholarship but also in the activist work that I have done throughout this scholarly project, particularly in the early years of my research. I came to this research and book-writing process with a stance of self-reflexivity, humility, and an open ear ready to listen and learn. I have committed to a process of engagement with anticolonial work, Indigenous knowledges, and Indigenous struggles for Lands in a way that respects the Indigenous peoples and nations involved. I cannot promise that I have never made mistakes (who can?), but I have worked to engage in a never-ending process of reflexivity, stay in relation with Indigenous research methods, and ultimately learn from the rhetorical tactics of decolonization I will amplify in this book.

My commitment with past work and this book is to critique nuclear colonialism and amplify nuclear decolonization efforts. I am not claiming that this book or my scholarship are forms of decolonization. Rather, this book shows the power of decolonization movements. I hope that the book will contribute to anticolonial struggles within and outside the academy by sharing the stories and successes of Western Shoshones, Southern Paiutes, and Skull Valley Goshutes with the audiences I can reach.

I believe that this story needs to be told and I am in a position to tell it. More so, I feel a responsibility to tell it. Since I first began this research, several of the elder collaborators who so generously contributed to my project have passed away. Sharing the wisdom, theories, and brilliance of Margene Bullcreek, Carrie Dann, and Corbin Harney and doing my part to carry forward their ideas served as a motivation. Further, my relationships, experiences with

---

17. Wilson, *Research Is Ceremony*.
18. Riley-Mukavetz, "Developing a Relational Scholarly Practice."
19. Wilson, *Research Is Ceremony*; and Powell et al., "Our Story Begins Here."

Lands, conversations, participation in protest events, and much more constantly remind me of the stakes of this work. Stopping out of fear of not getting it right would disrespect the many relations that shared their knowledges and theories with me in the hope that I would share them with others. While this retelling will benefit me in terms of my own career, I have also written it in a way that I hope can contribute to Indigenous peoples and nations fighting high-level nuclear waste and engaging in other forms of Lands protection by getting the story out to different audiences—mainly students and academics. My writing is necessarily different from firsthand storytelling, research, and writing by the Indigenous peoples and nations involved in these struggles. My goal is to use my skills as a rhetorical scholar to find similarities across those stories and describe successful tactics of decolonization that link these cases. I hope that this book will put this story on the radar of scholars and students in my field and outside my field, that it will encourage more research, and that it will ultimately contribute to better scholarship and engagement with Indigenous peoples and nations in relation to nuclear technologies, in the field of communication and beyond. Working alongside the insights of Tiara Na'puti, Ashley Cordes, B. Liahnna Stanley, Dalaki Livingston, Anthony Sutton, Andrea Riley-Mukavetz, Michael Lechuga, and others, it is imperative that the fields of communication and rhetoric better attend to Indigenous rhetorics, Indigenous knowledges, Indigenous perspectives on decolonization, and the continued role of communication scholarship in upholding settler colonialism.[20]

---

20. Na'puti, "Speaking of Indigeneity"; Lechuga, "Anticolonial Future"; Riley-Mukavetz, "Developing a Relational Scholarly Practice"; Stanley, "Pubic Scarves"; Stanley, "Returning Home"; Sutton, "Farming, Fieldwork, and Sovereignty"; Livingston, "Upward Journey and Sunwise Path"; Cordes, "Meeting Place"; and Cordes and Sabzalian, "Urgent Need."

INTRODUCTION

Indigenous Rhetorics and Nuclear Decolonization

Over a series of five years, Margene Bullcreek—a Skull Valley Goshute elder—graciously hosted students from my environmental humanities class within her people's reservation Lands.[1] She spoke to us about her actions to resist the Skull Valley Goshute government's decision to pursue a partnership with Private Fuel Storage (PFS) for temporarily storing high-level nuclear waste on the reservation Lands. Of course, each trip was slightly different and occurred at different moments in her efforts to prevent nuclear waste from coming to what she described as sacred Lands. On one visit, a group of students and I gathered in a circle around Margene on a cold spring day—pockets of snow still on the ground, a sharp winter wind blowing through the desert landscape—so we huddled close. As we listened, Margene told us about her desire to share her story with non-Native people and her calling to navigate the space between two roads—the red road and the white road. She told us about the divide within the Skull Valley Goshute nation over whether to pursue storing nuclear waste as a form of economic development. She was firmly opposed to a nuclear waste site and told us how she had devoted years of her life to this work. She told us about the tensions between her and Leon Bear, the chair of

---

1. Following Liboiron, I capitalize *Lands* to signal the entire ecology of relationships with more-than-human beings in a place, including Waters and Airs. Chapter 3, which is focused on Indigenous Lands rhetorics, offers a fuller definition of *Lands*. Liboiron, *Pollution Is Colonialism*.

the Tribal Council at the time, noting the close proximity between her house and his on the small reservation.

On another trip, while we spoke with Margene, we noticed a large, new, black truck driving up. The truck pulled up right next to where we stood. The passenger side window opened and the driver—the Skull Valley Goshute chairperson—looked at our group and asked what we were doing on the reservation. I have never been in a moment that better encapsulates the old adage that one could cut the tension with a knife. I do not recall and did not record the rest of the conversation, which lasted only a minute or two. But years later, I can still remember how that moment felt—the tension in the way Margene and Leon Bear looked at each other, the discomfort I felt, and the worry of potentially putting our host at risk by allowing us to visit her on the reservation. Margene and I never talked in great detail about this incident in subsequent interactions, but it was clear to me that she had taken a risk by letting us visit the reservation and telling her story to a group of mostly white environmental humanities students. This moment highlights the personal stakes of decolonization work, especially work that entails advocating against the wishes of one's own government and seeking out allies among settler environmentalists.

Decolonization, in all of its variety, entails courageous but also risky engagements in protecting Indigenous Lands, ways of knowing and being, and traditional lifeways. This book engages with collective, but not homogenous, efforts by Indigenous peoples and nations to resist high-level nuclear waste siting within Native Lands. It relays how Western Shoshone, Southern Paiute, and Skull Valley Goshute peoples and nations—along with allies, strategic coalitions, and other actors—successfully prevented two high-level nuclear waste repositories from being sited within Newe and Nuwuvi Lands in the Great Basin.[2] It offers a story of nuclear decolonization.

Nuclear decolonization refers to Indigenous-led efforts to enact sovereignty and self-determination toward protecting relationships with Lands, lifeways, and sacred practices from nuclear technologies. It is a mode of survivance and radical resurgence.[3] It is an envisioning and enacting of futures for Indigenous peoples and nations without the harms of nuclear technologies, in this case, nuclear waste. It is not only a set of actions but also an Indigenous theory of social change. Nuclear decolonization is a counterstory to nuclear

---

2. *Newe* is a Western Shoshone and Skull Valley Goshute word for "the people." *Nuwu* or *Nuwuvi* is a Southern Paiute term for "the people."

3. Vizenor, *Survivance*; and L. Simpson, *As We Have Always Done*.

colonization—also termed *nuclear colonialism* and *radioactive colonization*[4]—a concept created by Native Lands protectors to describe how convergences of systems of nuclearism and settler colonialism disproportionately harm Indigenous peoples, their Lands, and their lifeways throughout the life cycle of nuclear technologies. To fully comprehend the power of nuclear decolonization and its connection with nuclear colonization involves a multifaceted set of inquiries into the historical, material, cultural, spatial, embodied, physical, and rhetorical aspects of nuclearism, settler colonialism, and Indigenous survivance. No one scholarly investigation can retell the full story of how nuclear decolonization and nuclear colonization have played out in what settlers named the US, let alone the rest of the world. This book, therefore, focuses on nuclear decolonization within the specific context of high-level nuclear waste siting in the US. Using a rhetorical lens, that is, a lens focused on the role of language and other symbol systems, this book demonstrates and amplifies rhetorical tactics of nuclear decolonization in contests over nuclear waste siting within Western Shoshone, Southern Paiute, and Skull Valley Goshute Lands.[5] While a rhetorical lens offers an inevitably incomplete account of nuclear decolonization efforts, it underscores the importance of how actors perform, practice, and engage in nuclear decolonization using rhetoric.

While nuclear decolonization is an ongoing mode of Indigenous survivance, in the case of high-level nuclear waste siting, Western Shoshone, Southern Paiute, and Skull Valley Goshute nuclear decolonization tactics worked, contributing to stopping the storage of high-level nuclear waste within Yucca Mountain and Skull Valley. This is an impressive accomplishment, but one that is not unprecedented. As Leanne Simpson notes,

> It is not happenstance or luck that Indigenous peoples and our lands still exist after centuries of attack. This is our strategic brilliance. Our presence is our weapon, and this is visible to me at every protest, every mobilization, every time a Two Spirit person gifts us with a dance at our powwows, every time we speak our truths, every time we embody Indigenous life.[6]

---

4. For example, Kuletz, *Tainted Desert*; LaDuke and Churchill, "Native America," *Critical Sociology*; LaDuke, *All Our Relations*; and Endres, "Rhetoric of Nuclear Colonialism." See footnote 2 in the preface for information about my use of Ward Churchill's research on radioactive colonization.

5. My use of tactics is a deliberate reference to Michel de Certeau's distinction between strategies and tactics. De Certeau, *Practice of Everyday Life*.

6. L. Simpson, *As We Have Always Done*, 6.

Examples of successful resistance such as this are not a perfect or utopian end—they are not the culmination of nuclear decolonization—but moments within an ongoing process that involves wins and losses, constant vigilance, and reflection.[7] That is, while we ought to celebrate and collectively remember successes—such as preventing two high-level nuclear waste sites from being built within Indigenous Lands—we must not forget that both the struggles and the moments of success are temporary. Rebecca Solnit writes, "It's always too soon to go home. Most of the great victories continue to unfold, unfinished in the sense that they are not yet fully realized, but also in the sense that they continue to spread influence."[8] Western Shoshone, Southern Paiute, and Skull Valley Goshute peoples and nations enacted moments of decolonization and succeeded in significant ways, even if struggles for nuclear decolonization in other situations continue. Yet, recognizing, amplifying, and learning from moments of success not only is a form of anticolonial solidarity but more importantly offers opportunities for informing future Lands, Waters, Airs, and Skies protection movements.

Although this book is focused on the struggles against the proposed Yucca Mountain and Skull Valley PFS sites, it is important to recognize that there have been other important enactments of nuclear decolonization that have resulted in the creation of nuclear-free zones on Native reservation Lands, a uranium mining ban on Diné Lands (Navajo Reservation), termination of a proposed high-level nuclear waste site on Mescalero Apache Lands, and decades of resistance to nuclear weapons testing on Western Shoshone and Southern Paiute Lands. My focus on the Yucca Mountain and Skull Valley PFS sites, then, is not meant to overshadow these other stories or claim that there have only been two successes in the decades of resistance to nuclear colonialism on this continent. Rather, by deeply delving into these two cases, this book presents the vibrancy, persistence, and effects of nuclear decolonization as an ongoing set of tactics that prevent nuclear colonialization from becoming complete.

Using this book to amplify the successes of Indigenous decolonization is more important to me than critiquing the rhetoric of settler colonialism.[9] This is not to say that scholars and activists should not critique settler colonialism. Indeed, any celebration of nuclear decolonization is already a critique

---

7. See Rebecca Solnit for more on resisting the temptation to treat social activism wins as ends. Solnit, *Hope in the Dark*.

8. Solnit, 63.

9. For more on the importance of amplifying marginalized voices, see de Onís, *Energy Islands*.

of colonization. While acknowledging the complex relations between nuclear decolonization and nuclear colonization, this book is an attempt to move away from a damage-centered research approach that lingers on trauma to a desire-centered approach focused on "the hope, the visions, the wisdom of lived lives and communities."[10] Throughout decades of Indigenous resistance to nuclear waste siting one can, of course, see the tendrils and damages of settler colonialism and nuclear colonization (and I have done some of that research), but more importantly one can also see self-determination, inherent sovereignty, enactment of Indigenous ways of knowing/being, Lands protection, and resurgences of traditional practices. In short, a focus on nuclear decolonization in this book is a story of hope, survivance, and decolonial futures from the perspective of Indigenous agents of change. What rhetorical tactics contributed to preventing the Yucca Mountain and Skull Valley PFS nuclear waste sites are central questions guiding this book, within a larger framework of appreciation for how Western Shoshone, Southern Paiute, and Skull Valley Goshute peoples and nations used rhetoric to contribute to stopping high-level nuclear waste sites within their Lands. Although this focus on successful rhetoric represents a departure from much critical work in rhetorical studies, it is crucial for rhetoricians to linger on successful resistance rhetorics because of the potential value for ongoing struggles for justice, decolonization, and sovereignty. By highlighting specific rhetorical tactics of decolonization, this book resists a narrative of one-way colonization of Indigenous peoples and nations and offers a story of resilience, endurance, and survival through tactics of decolonization.

Nuclear decolonization is the subject of chapter 1, in which I further describe it as a rhetorical/material phenomenon that is a form of Indigenous praxis and theory. In the remainder of this introduction, I begin by introducing the significance of high-level nuclear waste siting and Western Shoshone, Southern Paiute, and Skull Valley Goshute peoples' and nations' engagements with the proposed Yucca Mountain and Skull Valley PFS nuclear waste sites. This is followed by a discussion of the methodological approach as well as the specific method tools that guided the research presented in this book. I then provide an argument for why a study of nuclear decolonization matters. Finally, I offer a précis of the remaining chapters in the book.

---

10. Tuck, "Suspending Damage," 417.

YUCCA MOUNTAIN AND SKULL VALLEY PFS NUCLEAR WASTE SITES

Nuclear waste is the by-product of nuclear technologies. While there are any number of nuclear technologies—including X-rays, food irradiation, and more—nuclear weapons and nuclear power are the main nuclear technologies that produce the forms of high-level nuclear waste discussed in this book.[11] The entire life cycles of nuclear weapons and nuclear power technologies produce various low- and high-level nuclear wastes that, while they vary in intensity and harmfulness, are dangerous to human and more-than-human health for, in some cases, up to 1 million years. High-level nuclear waste, the most radioactive and dangerous form, is often referred to as the thorn in the side of nuclear technologies, though, for me, that metaphor incorrectly assumes that the technologies themselves are unequivocally positive like a rose. Regardless of one's stance on nuclear weapons and nuclear power production, nuclear waste is undoubtedly a negative consequence. Nuclear waste is a material legacy of nuclear technologies that must be safely contained, but nuclear waste is also entangled with rhetoric through the justifications and arguments used to engage in decision-making about what to do about the legacies of nuclear technologies.[12]

There has been a decades-long movement by Native peoples and nations to prevent forms of nuclear waste from being stored and contained within their Lands, whether those proposals came from the settler government, the nuclear industry, or Indigenous nations. Of course, to write this belies the reality that the entire continent is Native Lands stolen by settlers and, therefore, all nuclear waste currently being stored at nuclear energy plants and government sites is within Indigenous Lands. Yet, there is an important distinction in the campaigns that prevented high-level nuclear waste from being relocated to Western Shoshone, Southern Paiute, and Skull Valley Goshute Lands for interim or permanent disposal. The Yucca Mountain and Skull Valley PFS sites are the two proposed high-level nuclear waste sites that came closest to fruition. In the controversies over siting within Yucca Mountain and Skull Valley, there are a wide range of arguments for and against the sites; these arguments come from the federal government, the nuclear industry, citizens of the states of Nevada and Utah, Native nations, and US publics. Yet,

---

11. Primarily nuclear power, which produces highly radioactive spent-fuel rods that need to be stored for thousands of years to prevent damage to people and ecology. There are some by-products from nuclear weapons that are also classified as high-level nuclear waste and slated for storage at a national nuclear waste repository.

12. Kinsella, "Nuclear Boundaries."

this book is specifically focused on Indigenous peoples' and nations' arguments against these two sites not only because other scholars have told the story from other perspectives that marginalize Indigenous contributions[13] but also because rhetorical scholars, environmental studies scholars, Native and Indigenous studies scholars, and nuclear studies scholars can learn from Indigenous theories and tactics of nuclear decolonization.

I approach nuclear waste siting as an issue of environmental justice. Although some fear that Not-In-My-Back-Yard (NIMBY) and Build-Absolutely-Nothing-Anywhere-Near-Anyone (BANANA) responses will prevent ever having a solution to high-level nuclear waste, characterizing concerns about nuclear waste siting decisions as NIMBY or BANANA are inaccurate and elide the real concerns raised in struggles against nuclear waste sites. Of course, the US needs a solution to high-level nuclear waste. Those resisting nuclear waste sites generally do not deny this. Rather, they argue for a break from patterns of injustice wherein marginalized and underrepresented communities are disproportionately selected for waste sites, in this case, Indigenous peoples and nations. It is possible to do a better job of pursuing justice in the US government's process for deciding where to store high-level nuclear waste. Even though the US needs a solution, should the US ask Indigenous peoples, nations, and Lands to carry this burden? This is a central question nuclear decolonization raises, and it is one with which everyone living in the US must contend.

Although not the only focus of nuclear decolonization efforts, resistance to high-level nuclear waste sites within Indigenous lands is an important focus of analysis for several reasons. First, high-level nuclear waste is the worst by-product of the nuclear production process in terms of its long half-life, high level of radioactivity, and potential for harming local and global ecologies.[14] Second, all of the major sites that were under consideration for high-level nuclear waste storage (not including on-site storage) are disproportionately located on or near Indigenous lands.[15] Beyond Yucca Mountain and Skull Valley, high-level nuclear waste has intersected with Indigenous nations, peoples, and Lands through, for example, the federal government's monitored retrievable storage (MRS) program that targeted Indigenous nations as potential hosts as well as the contemporary controversy over a privately developed

---

13. Vandenbosch and Vandenbosch, *Nuclear Waste Stalemate*; and J. Walker, *Road to Yucca Mountain*.
14. US Nuclear Regulatory Commission, "NRC: Backgrounder on Radioactive Waste."
15. Although this book is focused on the US context, there is scholarship to suggest that nuclear colonialism is also an international nuclear waste siting phenomenon. See, for example, Fan, "Nuclear Waste Facilities"; and G. Johnson, *Deliberative Democracy*.

interim high-level nuclear waste site in New Mexico. Third, as already noted, nuclear decolonization resistance to high-level nuclear waste siting has largely been successful, meaning that it offers an opportunity to reflect on nuclear decolonization tactics that contributed to achieving the goal of preventing disposal within Indigenous Lands.

Yucca Mountain Site

The proposed Yucca Mountain high-level nuclear waste repository site is located in Newe and Nuwuvi Lands in the Great Basin, or a portion of what settlers named Nevada, about one hundred miles from Nevada's most populous city, Las Vegas. After Congress passed the Nuclear Waste Policy Act, which administers the government's responsibility to store high-level nuclear waste from nuclear power and nuclear weapons, the Yucca Mountain site became the only national repository site seriously considered. Had the Yucca Mountain project gone forward, at least seventy thousand metric tons of existing high-level nuclear waste from the nation's ninety-three nuclear reactors at fifty-five power plants in twenty-eight states would have been transported to the Yucca Mountain nuclear waste repository forever.[16] With the completion of the Yucca Mountain project, it would have become the largest accumulation of high-level nuclear waste in one place. Western Shoshone and Southern Paiute peoples and nations contest the federal government's ownership and use of their traditional and ancestral Lands for nuclear waste storage. The Western Shoshone National Council, the Duckwater Shoshone Council, and the Chemehuevi Indian Tribe (Southern Paiutes), for example, passed formal resolutions in opposition to the site, while the Moapa Band of Paiutes passed a resolution concerning how to properly address Southern Paiute cultural resources within Yucca Mountain.[17] According to former Western Shoshone National Council leader Raymond Yowell, "Yucca Mountain is a sacred site in our sovereign territory of the Newe Sogobia. The Bush administration has not consulted with our people on this serious issue that could endanger the future of our tribal nation."[18] Likewise, Edward Smith, former chair of the

---

16. These numbers are accurate as of April 2022. Although the Nuclear Waste Policy Act legislated the official capacity of Yucca Mountain at seventy thousand metric tons, many have speculated that the capacity would likely be expanded beyond seventy thousand both because of space within the mountain and because of the unlikelihood of designating another US repository site. US Energy Information Administration, "Nuclear Explained."
17. Fowler, *Native Americans and Yucca Mountain*.
18. Indigenous Environmental Network, "Yucca Mountain Nuclear Waste Storage."

Southern Paiute Chemehuevi Indian Tribe, argues that multiple nations share Yucca Mountain as part of their homelands.[19] Western Shoshone and Southern Paiute peoples and nations, along with Native allies from other nations, protested, spoke out at public hearings, and filed court cases based on the Treaty of Ruby Valley to prevent the Yucca Mountain site from opening. Resistance began in the 1980s and held firm throughout the past forty-something years on the grounds that the facility would violate the Treaty of Ruby Valley, limit Indigenous relationships with Yucca Mountain, violate spiritual and cultural beliefs about the more-than-human world, and irrevocably harm Lands and Native lifeways.

Western Shoshone and Southern Paiute governments and peoples were not the only opponents of the Yucca Mountain site. When I talk to non-Indigenous people about my research, they are often much more familiar with the opposition from Nevada's congressional delegation (particularly former senator Harry Reid), Nevada state and local government entities, Nevada residents, and antinuclear and environmental groups; indeed, some are surprised to learn about Western Shoshone and Southern Paiute opposition to the site. Yet, this book argues that Western Shoshone and Southern Paiute opposition to the Yucca Mountain site not only played a key role in stopping it but also demonstrates the vitality and power of Indigenous sovereignty and Lands protection movements. This book highlights the significant time and effort Western Shoshone, Southern Paiute, and other Native peoples and nations put into stopping the Yucca Mountain site. Although success cannot be solely attributed to Western Shoshone and Southern Paiute Lands protectors, it is a mistake to overlook the success of their nuclear decolonization tactics.

Skull Valley PFS Site

Private Fuel Storage—a private corporation made up of a consortium of energy companies facing a crisis with on-site storage of spent fuel—proposed a plan to the Skull Valley Goshute nation to lease land from them for a temporary high-level nuclear waste site that would operate within Skull Valley Goshute Reservation Lands, about seventy miles from what settlers named Salt Lake City, Utah.[20] The Skull Valley PFS site was intended to be a privately run interim waste site to manage waste until the federal government opened the permanent high-level nuclear waste site mandated by the Nuclear Waste

---

19. "Yucca Mountain Project Comments," 23.
20. Spent fuel is one type of high-level nuclear waste and represents the majority of what is designated for storage in a national facility.

Policy Act. PFS did not approach the Skull Valley Goshute nation out of the blue; rather, there were already indications that the government might support a high-level nuclear waste site. The Skull Valley Goshute nation's engagement with the possibility of nuclear waste storage began during the Office of the Nuclear Waste Negotiator's MRS program that sought to build a series of government-run interim storage sites to hold waste while a national repository was being selected.[21] The Skull Valley Goshute government expressed interest in the MRS process and proceeded until the program expired in 1994 when Congress did not reauthorize the Office of the Nuclear Waste Negotiator.[22] Following the discontinuation of the MRS program, PFS sought to create their own interim high-level nuclear waste storage facility to remove spent fuel rods from on-site pools and casks until a national repository could be opened. PFS approached the Skull Valley Goshute nation, after which PFS and the Skull Valley Goshute government moved forward with submitting a license proposal to the Nuclear Regulatory Commission (NRC) to build and operate a temporary site. In 1997 PFS signed a lease with the Skull Valley Goshute government to store nuclear waste on forty acres of the reservation. With promises of up to 2 million dollars for each of the approximately 120 Skull Valley Goshute citizens, many Skull Valley Goshute people viewed the PFS proposal as a boon for the nation and one of the only viable economic development opportunities for a reservation surrounded by toxic waste.[23] According to former Skull Valley Goshute chair Leon Bear:

> People need to understand that this whole area has already been deemed a waste one by the federal government, the state of Utah, and the country.... Tooele Depot, a military site, stores 40% of the nation's nerve gas and other hazardous gas only 40 miles away from us. Dugway Proving Grounds ... is only 14 miles away, and it experiments with viruses like plague and tuberculosis. Within a 40-mile radius there are three hazardous waste dumps and a "low level" radioactive waste dump. From all directions, north, south, east, and west we're surrounded by the waste of Tooele County, the state of Utah, and U.S. society.[24]

---

21. This MRS program, created by 1987 amendments to the Nuclear Waste Policy Act, is no longer active. The US Department of Energy is currently pursuing MRS through a different program.

22. Vandenbosch and Vandenbosch, *Nuclear Waste Stalemate*.

23. Ishiyama, "Environmental Justice"; Clarke, "Goshute Native American Tribe"; and Peeples, Krannich, and Weiss, "Arguments."

24. As cited in Churchill, *Little Matter of Genocide*, 338.

Even though the site received a license from the NRC in 2006, it was never built due to continued political action that eventually resulted in PFS withdrawing from the plan in 2012.[25]

While the Skull Valley Goshute government supported the PFS site, a portion of this small nation's citizens opposed the proposal and worked to defeat it, including allying with environmentalist groups and government officials in Utah (which borders the Skull Valley Goshute Reservation on all sides). A small cadre of Skull Valley Goshute peoples—primarily Margene Bullcreek and Sammy Blackbear—fought the decision of their nation's government based on claims the Skull Valley Goshute government was misusing its sovereignty and on spiritual mandates to protect their Lands from nuclear waste, arguing the site would "damage our plant life, water, air, and spiritual atmosphere as well as future generations."[26] Margene Bullcreek formed Ohngo Gaudadeh Devia to unite opponents of the site. Ohngo Gaudadeh Devia worked with other Indigenous peoples and nations (including Western Shoshone and Southern Paiute peoples and nations) and with Indigenous environmental and antinuclear organizations (such as Honor the Earth, the Indigenous Environmental Network, and the National Environmental Coalition of Native Americans, or NECONA) to oppose the Skull Valley PFS site.[27] For the Skull Valley Goshute peoples who opposed the site, the fight to protect sacred Lands was mainly a fight against their own nation's government but also included efforts to persuade the NRC and Department of the Interior to cancel the project.

The proposed interim high-level nuclear waste site within the Skull Valley Goshute Reservation complicates the story of nuclear decolonization beyond the case of Yucca Mountain. Nuclear decolonization efforts, in this

---

25. Decisions by the Bureau of Indian Affairs (BIA) and the Bureau of Land Management (BLM) blocked construction of the PFS site. PFS and the Skull Valley Goshute government sued the US federal government to reverse the rulings, and in July 2010, a federal judge ruled against the Department of the Interior's BIA and BLM rulings. Although the Department of the Interior stated they would not fight the federal court ruling and the Skull Valley Goshute government expressed support for reviving the PFS project, PFS indicated soon after that they would no longer pursue the Skull Valley site. Bulkeley, "Goshute Leader"; Fahys, "Goshute Says Feds, State"; and Fattah and Struglinski, "Pressure Used."

26. Margene Bullcreek, as cited in LaDuke, *All Our Relations*, 105.

27. Indigenous antinuclearism is in some cases overlapped with Indigenous environmentalisms, particularly in cases where the Indigenous Environmental Network, Honor the Earth, and other Indigenous environmental groups are involved in supporting resistance to nuclear colonialism. The term *Indigenous environmentalism* is itself somewhat controversial given ecological Indian stereotypes, environmentalisms' appropriations of supposed Indigenous practices, and the possibility of imposing the term *environmentalism* on Indigenous peoples who would not use the term. Yet, as Kyle Whyte argues, there are many self-identified Indigenous environmental movements that actively seek to connect Indigenous issues with environmental issues. Whyte, "Indigenous Environmental Movements."

case, involved working against an Indigenous government. Noriko Ishiyama suggests the Skull Valley PFS siting controversy has a complicated relationship with environmental injustice because of its intersection with sovereignty and a history of colonialism and economic depression on Skull Valley Goshute Lands.[28] In this case, while stopping the site was a win for the contingent of Skull Valley Goshutes who opposed the site, the Skull Valley Goshute government viewed it as a loss. The government viewed opposition to the PFS site—especially from non-Native environmentalists and the state of Utah—as an environmental injustice and affront to its sovereignty. The Skull Valley Goshute government was also making efforts toward decolonization through their defense of sovereignty and self-determination for Indigenous nations. This is a prime example of the double binds Indigenous peoples and nations face within a system of settler colonialism, or more specifically nuclear colonialism. The complicated story of the Skull Valley PFS site will unfold in this book with a primary focus on the nuclear decolonization efforts of those Skull Valley Goshute peoples who opposed the site.

There are several differences between the Yucca Mountain and PFS sites that demonstrate the complexity of nuclear decolonization and nuclear colonization. First, while the Yucca Mountain facility was proposed to be a government-run national permanent repository, the Skull Valley PFS site was a private industry-run interim site. Second, the decision-making and participation processes were different for each facility. The Yucca Mountain site was subject to community and stakeholder engagement policies outlined in the Nuclear Waste Policy Act and run by the Department of Energy (DOE), as well as supplemental participation processes in line with National Environmental Policy Act and NRC regulations. Community participation in the Skull Valley PFS site decision included local participation during the development of an environmental impact statement and through the NRC licensing decisions. Third, while Yucca Mountain was proposed to be within Western Shoshone and Southern Paiute homelands under the Treaty of Ruby Valley, the PFS site was to be located on the Skull Valley Goshute nation's own reservation Lands. Finally, while many of the Western Shoshone and Southern Paiute governments officially opposed the Yucca Mountain project, the Skull Valley Goshute government officially supported the PFS project. No Native nation is univocal, meaning that there could be Western Shoshone, Southern Paiute, and Skull Valley Goshute individuals taking any number of positions in the respective controversies. However, while there was only minimal vocal support for the Yucca Mountain site by Western Shoshone and Paiute

---

28. Ishiyama, "Environmental Justice."

peoples,[29] Skull Valley Goshute peoples engaged in an acrimonious dispute about whether to support the PFS proposal.[30]

A RHETORICAL APPROACH

Rhetorical theory and criticism offer resources for understanding, evaluating, and critiquing everyday and extraordinary rhetorical acts that influence, persuade, confront, and perform. While nuclear decolonization and nuclear colonization are intersecting material phenomena worthy of study from a variety of vantage points, both fundamentally rely on rhetoric. When I first began to research this topic, the preponderance of research on nuclear colonization was focused on research that empirically supported the reality that Indigenous nations and peoples are disproportionately negatively affected by the nuclear production process. This incredibly valuable research involved mapping, interviews, and archival research to confirm nuclear colonization was indeed happening, as a material reality. My initial research focused on highlighting the intersecting *rhetorical* dynamics that underlaid and created conditions for the perpetuation of nuclear colonization.[31] The rhetorical and material are always connected, and I argue that nuclear decolonization is a rhetorical/material phenomenon; yet, there was and continues to be a need to shine a light on the uniquely rhetorical elements of the multifaceted and complicated relationships between nuclear technologies and Indigenous peoples and nations that both nuclear decolonization and nuclear colonization highlight.

This book highlights embodied and emplaced rhetorical tactics that are not just informed by but also have influence on material conditions for human and more-than-human beings. It also shows the rhetoric of places and more-than-human beings within nuclear decolonization (sometimes called material rhetoric). I take Indigenous knowledges about and lived experiences with places, Lands, and more-than-human beings as my starting point for this engagement. I choose to trace my argument through Indigenous knowledges and theories as much as possible. As Zoe Todd has pointed out, when considering Indigenous knowledges, there is nothing new in new materialisms and the ontological turn.[32] I seek to uplift a rhetorical perspective on materiality

---

29. Kuletz, *Tainted Desert*.
30. Clarke, *Native Americans and Nuclear Waste*; Clarke, "Construction"; Clarke, "Goshute Native American Tribe"; and Peeples, Krannich, and Weiss, "Arguments."
31. Endres, "Rhetoric of Nuclear Colonialism"; Endres, "Sacred Land"; Endres, "Animist Intersubjectivity as Argumentation"; and Endres, "From Wasteland to Waste Site."
32. Todd, "An Indigenous Feminist's Take."

rooted in Indigenous knowledges and decolonization efforts. This works against the ways rhetorical studies is, as Tiara Na'puti argues, a "system of knowledge that has overwhelmingly perpetuated erasure and effacement of Indigenous work."[33] This book, then, offers a perspective on the intertwined material and rhetorical facets of nuclear decolonization, engaging with Indigenous knowledges and theories as lenses for recounting Western Shoshone, Southern Paiute, and Skull Valley Goshute rhetorical tactics.

My analysis relies on texts I gathered over the many years I have researched this topic and these cases.[34] Some of the already documented texts that contribute to my analysis include DOE and NRC public hearing transcripts, government documents, websites, archival collections, books, and newspaper articles. In addition to these documented texts, I used rhetorical fieldwork to gather and document other texts.[35] This includes interviews my research assistants and I collected for the Nuclear Technologies in the American West oral history project and participant observation with tours of Yucca Mountain and the Nevada Test Site (now called Nevada National Security Site), gatherings on Western Shoshone Lands hosted by the Western Shoshone Defense Project and Indigenous Environmental Network, gatherings

---

33. Na'puti, "Speaking of Indigeneity," 496.

34. I use the term *text* loosely to expand beyond the notion of text as a written already documented rhetorical artifact. Rather, I use *text(s)* to mark written, visual, aural, oral, sensorial, embodied, and emplaced moments of rhetorical invention, recognizing that to use *text(s)* for these multimodal forms of rhetoric goes against the strict definition of the term. However, rhetorical critics do not yet have a good word for the multitude of rhetorics we study beyond the commonly used: *text, archive, artifact,* or *object of study*. Because *artifact, archive,* and *object of study* risk entrenching the notion that Indigenous peoples and nations are historical objects of study and not contemporary surviving peoples, I have chosen *text* as what I perceive to be the least problematic term and have, along with others, taken the liberty of expanding it to encompass a diversity of rhetorical forms. Following Conquergood, my use of *text* rejects text-centrism, or the notion that written and documented texts are privileged over oral, embodied, emplaced, and sensorial performances. If rhetoricians redefine *text* to encompass the many underprivileged forms of rhetorical action, then we can avoid the text-centrism primarily associated with written and documented forms of privileged and sanctioned rhetoric. Conquergood, "Performance Studies."

35. I use the term *rhetorical fieldwork* as a broad umbrella for the various approaches to combining rhetorical analysis with qualitative methods, particularly in order to access, document, and analyze more-than-verbal embodied and emplaced rhetorics that would otherwise remain undocumented. I have written about this methodological approach elsewhere, as have many others in the field, and encourage readers to look to the rich literature on these approaches. See, for example, Endres and Senda-Cook, "Location Matters"; Middleton, Senda-Cook, and Endres, "Articulating Rhetorical Field Methods"; Middleton et al., *Participatory Critical Rhetoric*; McKinnon et al., *Text + Field*; Hess, "Critical-Rhetorical Ethnography"; Hauser, "Attending to the Vernacular"; Pezzullo, *Toxic Tourism*; Pezzullo and de Onís, "Rethinking Rhetorical Field Methods"; Endres et al., "In Situ Rhetoric"; and Rai and Druschke, *Field Rhetoric*.

on Western Shoshone Lands near the Nevada Test Site, and class field trips to the Skull Valley Goshute Reservation with students.[36] Taken together, they reflect a multifaceted set of embodied and emplaced moments of rhetorical invention observed in the moment, based on recollection in oral history, and documented by others. While this combination of texts does not offer a complete account, it provides a rich and complex set of texts, allowing me to analyze a wide variety of rhetorical tactics of nuclear decolonization.[37]

Collectively, these texts demonstrate how Indigenous Lands protectors and allies produced rhetoric for public audiences and, in doing so, engaged in forms of rhetorical sovereignty and rhetorical decolonization.[38] My research did not involve gaining access to private information, such as private strategy sessions by Indigenous activists or private spiritual practices. Rather, I attended public events that were designed to raise awareness, share rhetorical messages as widely as possible, build alliances with non-Indigenous communities, and openly protest decisions being made by the federal government about Indigenous Lands.[39] I collected documents from government and activist archives, newspapers, and public hearings that feature Indigenous peoples and nations speaking and writing to various public audiences about their opposition to the Yucca Mountain and Skull Valley PFS sites. Further, my research assistants and I communicated to those who participated in oral histories that their interviews would be stored in an archive at the J. Willard Marriott Library, and they were given opportunities to review their transcripts and make changes before archiving and withdraw from the project at any time

---

36. As a research assistant, Samantha Senda-Cook collected some of the interviews for the Nuclear Technologies in the American West oral history project. My fieldwork visits include a tour of Yucca Mountain in September 2004, two Western Shoshone Defense Project Gatherings in Newe Lands (Crescent Valley, Nevada) in May 2004 and May 2006, a Mother's Day Gathering and Protest at the Nevada Test Site in May 2007, an Indigenous Environmental Network Protecting Mother Earth Conference in So Ho Bee Newe Sogobia (a.k.a. Lee, Nevada), a tour of the Nevada Test Site in March 2008, and five field trips with my environmental humanities class to the Skull Valley Reservation hosted by Margene Bullcreek from 2006 to 2013. Most of these visits are covered under an Institutional Review Board exemption from the University of Utah.

37. It is crucial to linger on the fact that some practices of observation, participant observation, interviewing, and fieldwork with Indigenous peoples and nations have been critiqued as forms of imperialism, exoticization of difference, extraction, and part of the settler colonial project. The purposes, motivations, and methodological choices that guided my research have been informed by these critiques. A. Simpson, *Mohawk Interruptus*; and L. Smith, *Decolonizing Methodologies*.

38. Lyons, "Rhetorical Sovereignty."

39. The University of Utah Institutional Review Board reviewed and determined that my fieldwork at public nuclear events was exempt.

(which some interviewees did decide to do).[40] Although rhetorical scholars are trained to be wary of intent since it can be assumed instead of verified, the rhetorics I collected and analyzed were intended to be public and shared widely. The publicity of these texts, however, does not exclude them from ethical considerations.

I strived to engage in relationships with participants and texts informed by Indigenous research methods and decolonial methods, standard ethical protocols for qualitative research, and standing with Indigenous peoples and nations as a comrade.[41] This was an evolving process over the course of the nearly twenty years I have been working on high-level nuclear waste siting within Indigenous Lands. I take to heart Audra Simpson's ethnography of refusal in the sense that I have made choices about what not to write about and what to exclude from the book, especially considering moments less public and more private, and the ways that reporting on my research might harm the overall cause of Indigenous decolonization, self-determination, and sovereignty as defined by participants.[42] In one example, I struggled with how to talk about and conceptualize the tensions that existed within the Skull Valley Goshute nation over the proposed nuclear waste site, to resist simply characterizing one as good and one as bad, one as decolonizing and one as complicit. I made decisions about how to tell the story of the Skull Valley PFS site that reflect my desire to highlight the double binds Indigenous peoples and nations face within systems of nuclear and settler colonialism while also focusing my attention mainly on the perspectives of those Skull Valley Goshute people who opposed the PFS site. In addition to my engagements with refusal, my research approach relied on seeking permission and informed consent in gathering texts. I gained permission from individual Indigenous people I interviewed and let Indigenous groups know about my research and that I would use what I learned from their public events in my research.[43]

---

40. This oral history project was acknowledged by the University of Utah Institutional Review Board and followed the best practices of the Oral History Association. Copies of the interviews can be found on my website: https://www.danielleendres.com/nuclear-west-oral-histories.

41. Given my long-term engagement with this research project, it is important to note that some of my research and fieldwork predates important recent advances in Indigenous research. Some examples include Denzin, Lincoln, and Smith, *Handbook*; Mihesuah, *So You Want*; Younging, *Elements of Indigenous Style*; L. Smith, *Decolonizing Methodologies*; Kovach, *Indigenous Methodologies*; Wilson, *Research Is Ceremony*; and Dhillon, "Notes on Becoming a Comrade."

42. Simpson, "On Ethnographic Refusal."

43. Because of my focus on public Indigenous antinuclear-waste texts, I did not seek permission from Western Shoshone, Southern Paiute, or Skull Valley Goshute governments but rather from the groups and people who hosted events and participated in my project. The practices of permission and relationship-building that I engaged in with individuals and groups are informed by the focus of my project on public texts produced for wide distribution.

My relationships were grounded in conversations about doing academic research on the topic while making clear my political commitments to the cause. Finally, throughout my research process, I prioritized finding ways to contribute to the peoples and groups with whom I worked. This book, as well as my past research, teaching, community engagement practices, and publicly oriented writing constitute one way that I have contributed to sharing the stories, information, and messages that the events I attended and the individuals I encountered sought to distribute to broader audiences. I chose to do oral history interviews instead of qualitative interviews specifically because I could archive them for future use by those I interviewed, organizations, and other researchers.[44] Beyond these forms of distribution, I also engaged in a variety of actions to support participants, such as recording events and providing groups with a copy for archival purposes, assisting with research, helping create slide presentations, volunteering in the ways requested of participants in events (camp cleanup, etc.), inviting people to speak to my classes, and providing compensation when possible. These are not the only ethical choices I made during this research process and the relationship-building it entailed, but they represent some examples of how I navigated my interactions within this research project focused on analysis of public texts.

My commitment to working with texts that are designed for public and non-Indigenous audiences constitutes an anticolonial research strategy that challenges dominant models of research while promoting deep listening to Indigenous rhetorics. Focusing on the texts and narratives that Indigenous peoples and nations produce on their own terms, this approach accesses, documents, and analyzes vernacular Indigenous rhetorics that might otherwise remain marginalized, and in some cases undocumented.[45] Relying on public texts allows for amplifying and analyzing Indigenous resistance rhetorics in a way that does not ask for more time, energy, and knowledge and guides researchers in making deliberate and careful choices about when an interview is needed to serve the project's, individual's, or organization's goals. Seeing these public texts as forms of Indigenous knowledge and theory opens the possibility for developing interpretations with an eye to supporting Indigenous decolonization and resurgence.[46] Participating in public events created by Indigenous rhetors allows critics to engage in multiperspectival judgment by yielding some critical judgment to rhetors and audiences in the moment of rhetorical invention.[47] My positionality as a settler, a non-Indigenous white person, inevitably contours my research and this rhetorical analysis, as I

---

44. Endres, "Environmental Oral History."
45. Middleton et al., *Participatory Critical Rhetoric*.
46. Lechuga, "Anticolonial Future."
47. Middleton et al., *Participatory Critical Rhetoric*.

discussed in the preface. My goal in writing this book is not to speak for Indigenous peoples and nations but to consider the potential and real rhetorical effects of the nuclear decolonization tactics used by Western Shoshone, Southern Paiute, and Skull Valley Goshute peoples and nations in resistance to high-level nuclear waste siting on their Lands. I consider myself to be one audience of the public rhetorical texts produced by those opposing the Yucca Mountain and Skull Valley PFS sites, and I use my skills as a rhetorical scholar to reflect on how those texts successfully enacted nuclear decolonization.

NUCLEAR DECOLONIZATION MATTERS

Nuclear decolonization is not well-known among academics and publics alike. This book, therefore, seeks to amplify those who have sought to raise awareness of this phenomenon for years and calls explicit attention to Indigenous decolonization efforts. Primarily focusing on the rhetorical practices of Western Shoshone, Southern Paiute, and Skull Valley Goshute peoples and nations who resisted nuclear waste siting on their Lands contributes to the project of localizing and particularizing structures and practices of decolonization in specific contexts. Here I highlight some of the key reasons that this study of the rhetoric of nuclear decolonization matters.

First, this book highlights the role of rhetoric in nuclear decolonization. A key argument of this book is that nuclear decolonization is significantly rhetorical, meaning that scholars, publics, and Lands protectors cannot account for the full picture of nuclear decolonization without attention to its rhetorical dynamics. My analysis provides insight into nuclear decolonization as a distinct form of Indigenous rhetoric that is antinuclear, focused on environmental justice, and rooted in protecting specific peoples and places. Studies of Indigenous rhetorics and settler colonial rhetorics in what settlers call North America (or the US and Canada) have a long but sporadic history within rhetorical studies.[48] This research can be roughly categorized into analyses of settler colonial rhetorics and analyses of the rhetorical theories and practices employed by Indigenous peoples and nations. There is, of course, overlap in these categories and some studies do both. On the one hand, the analyses of settler colonial rhetorics, loosely following anticolonial criticism, critical rhetoric, or ideological criticism, critique the rhetorical strategies that uphold

---

48. Due to white supremacy and settler colonialism in the system of higher education, the preponderance of past scholarship in this area has been conducted by non-Indigenous settler scholars (myself included). But this is changing as more Indigenous peoples are making space in the field.

settler colonialism, such as forms of rhetorical exclusion and naming that position Indigenous peoples and nations as savage, vanished, subhuman, or assimilated into US multiculturalism.[49] Much of my own previous work on the rhetoric of nuclear colonialism fits this category.[50] Amplifying nuclear decolonization intervenes on a focus on critiquing the strategies of nuclear colonialism and settler colonialism more broadly, which is undoubtedly important work but not work that centers Indigenous rhetorical innovations.

On the other hand, Indigenous rhetorics include analysis of historical and contemporary forms of rhetoric invented by Indigenous peoples and nations. While early research began with generalizations about Native oratorical practices that elided the specificity of the now 574 federally recognized peoples in the US and 643 First Nations in Canada,[51] much of this research focuses on the rhetorical theories and practices of particular Indigenous peoples and nations (including Pasifika peoples) or of coalitional Indigenous groups like the American Indian Movement, Idle No More, and Dakota Access Pipeline Water Protectors.[52] Randall Lake, in his early work on the rhetorics of the American Indian Movement, argues rhetorical analyses of Indigenous rhetorics ought to center Indigenous epistemologies and purposes. He argues that while Western-centric theories of instrumental rhetoric might have evaluated Red Power movements as ineffective, centering Indigenous perspectives shows that these movements were enactments of what Scott Lyons calls rhetorical sovereignty.[53] The field did not immediately follow Lake's model;

---

49. A few examples include Buescher and Ono, "Civilized Colonialism"; Na'puti and Dionne, "Settler Colonialism on Display"; Stuckey and Murphy, "By Any Other Name"; R. Morris and Stuckey, "'More Rain'"; Kelly, "Orwellian Language"; Engels, "'Equipped for Murder'"; and T. Johnson, "Dakota Access Pipeline."

50. Although these studies include analysis of Indigenous rhetorics, the main focus was on identifying rhetorics of nuclear colonization. Endres, "Rhetoric of Nuclear Colonialism"; Endres, "From Wasteland to Waste Site"; and Endres, "Sacred Land."

51. G. Kennedy, "North American Indian Rhetoric."

52. Some examples include Black, "Native Resistive Rhetoric"; Black, *American Indians*; Cole, "Writing Removal and Resistance"; Cushman, "Toward a Rhetoric of Self-Representation"; Lake, "Enacting Red Power"; Lake, "Between Myth and History"; R. Morris and Wander, "Native American Rhetoric"; Wieskamp and Smith, "'What to Do'"; Yagelski, "Rhetoric of Contact"; Lyons, "Rhetorical Sovereignty"; Powell et al., "Our Story Begins Here"; Powell, "Rhetorics of Survivance"; Kelly, "Détournement"; Kelly, "'We Are Not Free'"; Johnson, "'Most Bombed Nation"; Na'puti, "From Guåhan and Back"; Na'puti, "Archipelagic Rhetoric"; Na'puti, "Disaster Militarism"; Torre, "Tattooing"; McCue-Enser, "Genocide"; Mays, "Decolonial Hip Hop"; Privott, "Ethos of Responsibility"; Stanley, "Pubic Scarves"; Clary-Lemon, "Gifts, Ancestors, and Relations"; J. Smith and Gleason, "Knowledge Is like Food"; and Nijdam, "Recentering Indigenous Epistemologies."

53. Lake, "Enacting Red Power"; Lake, "Between Myth and History"; and Lyons, "Rhetorical Sovereignty."

in many cases, Indigenous rhetorics continued to center Western theories. Tiara Na'puti, therefore, calls for more engagement with Native American and Indigenous studies in Indigenous rhetorics scholarship to center Indigenous knowledges and theories.[54]

By highlighting the unique rhetorical tactics of nuclear decolonization among Indigenous peoples and nations and seeing those tactics as theory, readers may learn more about ongoing theorization of rhetorics of decolonization and decoloniality. Unsettling the foundations of ongoing settler colonialism and centering Indigenous knowledges in scholarly conversations about post/neo/anti/de-coloniality/colonialism/colonization is important. This is not new, as scholars in Indigenous studies have been making these arguments for years. Yet, still too few scholars, especially those in fields of study based on settler colonialism, attend to amplifying Indigenous voices and the specificities of Indigenous modes of decolonization. Scholars must not ignore Indigeneity or the centrality of Indigenous peoples to any theorization of postcolonialism, colonialism, and neocolonialism. As Jodi Byrd argues, for example, postcolonialism often functions at the expense of Indigenous peoples, contributing to their erasure.[55] Within rhetoric scholarship, Tiara Na'puti calls for a focus on Indigeneity that resists conflating colonization with race.[56] As I have argued with Taylor Johnson, one starting point for challenging settler colonialism within the field of rhetoric, in particular, is through bringing Indigeneity into our conversations about colonialisms and anticolonialisms.[57] This move does not require displacing important anticolonial or antiracism work in rhetorical studies, but it does require understanding colonialisms and anticolonialisms to be complex webs of theory and practice that play out differently within particular times, places, and peoples. While recognizing that there may be incommensurabilities between Indigenous enactments of decolonization and those of other groups engaged in decolonial/decolonization struggles, this research recognizes the importance of seeing similarities and opportunities for solidarity in specific anticolonialisms.[58]

Second, nuclear decolonization rhetoric is different from that of mainstream antinuclear and environmental movements. It is a form of antinuclear Lands protection that is based in an Indigenized perspective on environmen-

---

54. Na'puti, "Speaking of Indigeneity."
55. Byrd, *Transit of Empire*.
56. Racism and the construction of racial identity is certainly interconnected with colonialization, but colonization is not only about race. Na'puti, "Speaking of Indigeneity."
57. T. Johnson and Endres, "Decolonizing Settler Public Address."
58. O. M. Olaniyan is doing this important work, and I am grateful for what I have learned from them.

tal justice.⁵⁹ Nuclear decolonization should not be conflated or subsumed within the broader antinuclear movement because it is not primarily an antinuclear fight, as traditionally conceived by the antinuclear movement. It is primarily a movement to protect and preserve Indigenous Lands and life. Indigenous resistance to nuclear sites on their Lands is part of a much longer and broader history of resistance to settler colonialism and Lands protection, which in this case links with resistance to the harmful effects of nuclear technologies for Native peoples and nations. Indigenous antinuclearism, then, is a distinct form of Indigenous decolonization movement work. Identifying the rhetorical tactics of nuclear decolonization exceeds studies of the relationship between nuclear technologies and the environment or nuclear technologies and society, as is common in nuclear communication and broader interdisciplinary studies. Nuclear decolonization, rather, insists that nuclearism is not just an issue of national security and weapons but also of the ecological, cultural, and political health of Indigenous peoples and nations. This focus on nuclear decolonization engages in conversation with nuclear communication and interdisciplinary studies of nuclear technologies, particularly the small group of studies about nuclear de/colonization in the North American context and beyond.⁶⁰

Nuclear decolonization is also different from mainstream environmentalisms. The stories in this book are first and foremost Indigenous decolonization stories that relate to particular, localized struggles over Lands and the ecological and cultural degradation that nuclear waste could bring to them. This book, therefore, contributes to ongoing conversations about the uniqueness of environmental (in)justices within Indigenous communities and of Indigenous environmentalisms. As Dina Gilio-Whitaker argues, conceptions of environmental (in)justice need to be Indigenized to account for what makes Indigenous peoples and nations different from other marginalized groups: their sovereignty, nationhood, and treaty-based relationships with the settler government.⁶¹ More broadly, Kyle Whyte contends that settler colonialism is an environmental injustice because it seeks to break Indigenous peoples' and nations' connections with Lands and more-than-human ecologies.⁶² The tactics of nuclear decolonization that are the focus of this book are, in part,

---

59. Gilio-Whitaker, *As Long as Grass Grows*.
60. For example, Kuletz, *Tainted Desert*; Kuletz, "Invisible Spaces, Violent Places"; Fan, "Nuclear Waste Facilities"; Fan, "Environmental Justice"; Danielsson and Danielsson, *Poisoned Reign*; Edwards, "Nuclear Colonialism"; Johnston, "Nuclear Disaster"; Keown, "Waves of Destruction"; LaDuke and Churchill, "Native America," *Critical Sociology*; Runyan, "Disposable Waste"; Schwartz, "Matters of Empathy"; and Hecht, *Being Nuclear*.
61. Gilio-Whitaker, *As Long as Grass Grows*.
62. Whyte, "Indigenous Experience."

rhetorics that resist environmental injustices faced by Indigenous peoples and nations and that draw from Indigenous environmentalisms built from traditional knowledges.

This book amplifies Western Shoshones, Southern Paiutes, Skull Valley Goshutes, and Indigenous allies making arguments based in ecological knowledge, concerns for the environment, and spiritual connections to Lands. The opponents of these sites engage with nuclear waste as, in part, an environmental issue, ally with Indigenous environmental groups like the Indigenous Environmental Network and Honor the Earth, and work with non-Indigenous environmental activists and groups.[63] Some of the Western Shoshone, Southern Paiute, and Skull Valley Goshute agents in this story describe themselves as Indigenous environmentalists. Calling nuclear decolonization a form of Indigenous environmentalisms or Indigenous environmental justice advocacy is not meant to subsume it within mainstream environmentalisms, particularly enactments founded on settler colonialism that often come into conflict with Indigenous rights or rely on stereotypical and romanticized notions of Indigenous peoples' closeness to nature. While it would be wrong to characterize these struggles with a non-Indigenous definition of environmentalism, it is worth analyzing how those Western Shoshone, Southern Paiute, and Skull Valley Goshute peoples and nations who resisted these sites relate their work closely with environmental and ecological issues.[64] In the case of nuclear decolonization, what Zoltan Grossman has called "unlikely alliances" have developed between Western Shoshone, Southern Paiute, and Skull Valley Goshute peoples and nations with local environmental and antinuclear groups, state governments, and ranching groups also fighting high-level nuclear waste sites.[65] Contemporaneously, there are some similarities between nuclear decolonization efforts and the Indigenous Waters and Lands protectors fighting against oil and gas pipelines in the US and Canada, both with regard to environmental injustices and with regard to alliances with non-Indigenous environmental groups. These alliances are not without tensions. As Paul Nadasdy notes, "For every success story, for every productive alliance between environmental advocates and indigenous peoples, there is a matching horror story, a story of misunderstanding and conflict. Time and again, environmentalists and indigenous people have found themselves on opposing sides in particular

---

63. Groups such as the Indigenous Environmental Network and Honor the Earth are Indigenous-led organizations that focus specifically on intersections between environmental justice, Indigenous ecological knowledges, and Indigenous Lands.

64. Whyte, "Indigenous Environmental Movements"; and LaDuke, *All Our Relations*.

65. Grossman, *Unlikely Alliances*.

environmental struggles."[66] By situating this book as contributing to an understanding of Indigenous environmentalisms and Indigenizing environmental justice, it is crucial to attend not only to these tensions but also to challenging the ecological Indian stereotype that posits that Indigenous peoples are closer to nature.[67] Whether the rhetorical tactics presented in this book count as "environmental" or "environmentalism" is not the point. Rather, this book follows an imperative to center Indigenous environmentalisms and Indigenous forms of environmental justice more in environmental communication and environmental studies research.[68] More importantly, this book seeks to take seriously the ethic of care that Phaedra Pezzullo advocates for in her articulation of environmental communication as a crisis and care discipline.[69]

Finally, this book seeks to intervene in conversations around new materialisms, object-oriented ontologies, and posthumanisms in the field of rhetoric and beyond. The sorts of relations to and with nonhuman beings that animate new materialisms, posthumanisms, and object-oriented ontologies need not rely on continental theorists and settler scholars. Rather, Indigenous theories, practices, and knowledges are a way to understand materiality, relations with ecosystems and the more-than-human world, and nonhuman agency. While being cognizant to prevent harmful appropriations of Indigenous knowledges, turning to Indigenous knowledges as a source of theory that can expand beyond Indigenous contexts affords them the sort of respect and value that scholars have long given to continental theorists whose ideas are readily adopted and adapted into different cultures and contexts. In terms of rhetorical studies, one implication of this book is its contribution to articulating theories of the materiality of rhetoric and the rhetoricity of more-than-human beings that respectfully draw from Indigenous knowledges.[70]

---

66. Nadasdy, "Transcending the Debate," 292.

67. While there is a risk that readers will interpret these pieces of evidence into a stereotypical view of Indigenous peoples as the first, and still primitive, environmentalists, it is my hope that directly addressing this stereotype here will encourage readers to think critically about their own assumptions. Nadasdy, "Transcending the Debate."

68. Endres, "Environmental Criticism"; Pezzullo and de Onís, "Rethinking Rhetorical Field Methods"; Pezzullo and Sandler, "Introduction"; and T. Johnson et al., "Environmental Justice."

69. Pezzullo, "Environment."

70. It is important to note that there has been a move to integrate new materialisms, Indigenous knowledges, and decolonial approaches. See, for instance, Clary-Lemon and Grant, *Decolonial Conversations*.

WHAT FOLLOWS

Nuclear decolonization rhetorics, in the cases of Yucca Mountain and Skull Valley, engage two key topoi: Lands and sovereignty. Based in Indigenous knowledges, the book highlights Indigenous Lands rhetorics and Indigenous national interest rhetorics that animate nuclear decolonization. To build a foundation for demonstrating these rhetorical tactics, the first chapter delves more deeply into nuclear decolonization and nuclear colonization as significant material/rhetorical phenomena. It develops nuclear decolonization as a framework that guides the analysis in subsequent chapters; maps historical and contemporary manifestations of nuclear technological production in relationship to Native peoples, nations, and Lands; shows how the nuclear production process has had disproportionate effects within Indigenous populations; and documents the various modes of nuclear decolonization used by Indigenous peoples and nations.

Place is central to Indigeneity. Chapter 2 delves into the two specific places that Indigenous peoples and nations sought to protect from nuclear waste sites. The chapter begins with a focus on Indigenous relationships with the Great Basin, within which both the Yucca Mountain and Skull Valley PFS sites are located. Focusing on Western Shoshone, Southern Paiute, and Skull Valley Goshute histories, spiritualities, and cultures, the chapter demonstrates how Yucca Mountain and Skull Valley are Indigenous Lands, from time immemorial to present to future. After telling the stories of Western Shoshone, Southern Paiute, and Skull Valley Goshute relations with Lands in the Great Basin, I close the chapter with a specific focus on their relationships with Yucca Mountain and Skull Valley. As these specific places are integral to the tactics of nuclear decolonization in chapters 3 and 4, this chapter offers stories about Yucca Mountain and Skull Valley that undergird Indigenous Lands rhetorics and Indigenous national interest rhetorics.

Chapter 3 engages with Lands, a form of Indigenous theory, perspective, practice, and pedagogy based on the value of Lands for Indigenous peoples and nations, in this case, Western Shoshones, Southern Paiutes, and Skull Valley Goshutes. It presents Indigenous Lands rhetorics as tactics of nuclear decolonization. These Lands rhetorics are both modeled on past/present Lands protection efforts by Indigenous persons of various cultures and nations and provide models for present/future campaigns to protect Indigenous Lands. In this case, Lands are one center of the struggle over potential nuclear waste sites—exposing well-worn incommensurabilities between Indigenous and settler notions of the value and use of Lands/land. Lands-based decolonization tactics not only resist dominant settler perceptions of both Yucca Mountain and Skull Valley as wastelands but also enact other ways of knowing, being with, and engaging in relationality with Lands. With a particular focus on appeals to home Lands, sacred Lands, and Lands as relations, this chapter highlights how nuclear decolonization is fundamentally a struggle for the well-being of Indigenous Lands.

In addition to Lands protection, Western Shoshone, Southern Paiute, and Skull Valley Goshute peoples and nations also enacted sovereignty as a second tactic of nuclear decolonization. A focus on Indigenous national interests rhetorics not only centers Indigenous sovereignty but also represents a form of resistance to the settler government's decisions about nuclear waste siting framed in terms of US national interest. The fourth chapter unpacks the complex concepts of nationhood, sovereignty, and citizenship within Indigenous nations and highlights how nuclear decolonization activists tactically worked in what Kevin Bruyneel has called the "third space of sovereignty," selectively moving between Indigenous nationhood and US citizenship to resist settler decision-making.[71] Depending on the situation, Indigenous peoples and nations define themselves or are defined by others as within or outside the US national interest, meaning that the term can be both enabling and constraining. Appeals to national interest can be both a strategy and a tactic within nuclear de/colonialization. In particular, the tactics of Indigenous national interests that are analyzed in this chapter insist that Indigenous peoples and nations must be involved in any decision-making about their Lands.

The conclusion ties together the two tactics of nuclear decolonization at play in the Yucca Mountain and Skull Valley PFS nuclear waste siting controversies, revealing how these tactics work together to advance efforts toward survivance, radical resurgence, and decolonization. After reflecting on the implications of nuclear decolonization and areas for future research, I present some practical implications for the future of high-level nuclear waste siting in the US that can support continued nuclear decolonization while also finding a needed solution to nuclear waste.

CONCLUSION

Instead of showing how to solve nuclear colonialism, this book offers tangible examples of how Native peoples and nations used rhetorical tactics of nuclear decolonization to prevent two high-level nuclear waste sites within Western Shoshone, Southern Paiute, and Skull Valley Goshute Lands. This book is a

---

71. Bruyneel, *Third Space of Sovereignty.*

retelling from the lens of rhetoric and an appreciation of the rhetorical tactics that played a role in preventing these two waste sites. It is not the only story, it is not the final story, and it is not the story as it would be told by those immediately involved in the efforts. It is a story of survivance of Indigenous peoples that celebrates their successes.

CHAPTER 1

From Nuclear Colonization to Nuclear Decolonization

On one of my visits to Newe Sogobia for a multiday Mother's Day gathering to protest the Nevada Test Site (NTS)—now known as the Nevada National Security Site—I witnessed and participated in the use of Western Shoshone permits by non–Western Shoshone people as they walked into the NTS in defiance of the settler government's no trespassing mandate.[1] Western Shoshone National Council permits authorized bearers—both Indigenous and non-Indigenous—to travel within Western Shoshone territory under the 1863 Treaty of Ruby Valley (see figure 1). Western Shoshone peoples did not issue themselves permits to walk within these Lands because these Lands have been part of the Western Shoshone homeland since time immemorial.[2] The issuing of the permits, then, is a rejection of federal control over Western Shoshone Lands. In this case, Western Shoshone permits invite people to join Western Shoshone people in walking into the NTS as an act of civil disobedience that affirms and enacts Western Shoshone sovereignty in their homelands. The NTS is located on Lands stolen by the federal government and repurposed to host over one thousand nuclear weapons tests between 1950 and 1992. For this reason, the late Western Shoshone spiritual leader Corbin Harney called the

---

1. This gathering happened in May 2007.
2. Recall that I deliberately capitalize *Lands* in recognition of the many more-than-human beings and relationships that inform Indigenous ways of knowing and being in relation with Lands. I learned this from Liboiron, *Pollution Is Colonialism*.

FIGURE 1. Portion of a Western Shoshone permit issued to Danielle Endres May 12, 2007. Scanned by Danielle Endres with identifying information omitted.

Western Shoshone Nation "the most bombed nation on earth."[3] Following the previous day's lectures, workshops, and shared meals held in a large gathering tent in "Peace Camp," the event culminated with a Mother's Day action at the NTS. Participants, led by Harney and other Western Shoshone elders, walked from Peace Camp to the gates of the NTS in a peaceful march (see figure 2). Non–Western Shoshone people who had decided to peacefully trespass in the NTS showed their Western Shoshone National Council permits to the federal guards as they were arrested for trespassing on federal land.[4] Western Shoshone people who walked into the NTS were also arrested for trespassing. Western Shoshone people and allies embodied and emplaced Western Shoshone sovereignty and resistance to the US federal government's occupation of this particular place—a part of Newe Sogobia the settler government unilaterally restricted for nuclear testing and development. The use of Western Shoshone permits, an act of reoccupying Newe Sogobia with permission from the Western Shoshone Nation, not the federal government, is a potent embodied and emplaced tactic of nuclear decolonization that creates a crack in settler colonialism that is combined with the many hundreds of actions and arrests that have happened at the NTS since the 1980s.

---

3. Harney, "Yucca Mountain."

4. Although this gathering happened after the 1992 moratorium on nuclear testing, the Nevada Test Site was still involved in nuclear weapons research on stolen Western Shoshone Lands.

FIGURE 2. Participants in a 2007 Mother's Day demonstration walking toward the gates of the Nevada Test Site. Photo taken by M. Wayne Davis.

Nuclear decolonization is grounded in historical, contemporary, and future resistance to nuclearism within Indigenous homelands. Embodied and emplaced enactments of inherent Indigenous sovereignty and protection of Lands from nuclear technologies are at the core of this resistance to the US settler government's decisions to site parts of the nuclear production process on or adjacent to Indigenous Lands without the explicit consent of affected Indigenous peoples and nations. The rhetorical tactics of nuclear decolonization are practices of prefigurative politics that enact the changes, values, and knowledges Indigenous peoples and nations imagine for their futures. Nuclear decolonization, however, is not only praxis (a set of tactics) but also a theoretical framework built from Indigenous ways of knowing and being in relation with the earth. This chapter begins by focusing on nuclear decolonization as an Indigenous theoretical framework that interweaves Indigenous knowledges, decolonization, survivance, and radical resurgence. Next, it traces the origins of nuclear colonization in Indigenous communities' discourse and advocacy, reviews scholarly work on nuclear colonization, and argues for the importance of a shift from nuclear colonization to nuclear decolonization. The chapter ends with an accounting of both nuclear colonization and nuclear decolonization across the full life cycle of nuclear technologies.

NUCLEAR DECOLONIZATION

Nuclear decolonization is an Indigenous theory of social change. It is the hope for and imagining of nuclear decolonization that has animated the decades of embodied and emplaced actions by Indigenous peoples and nations to protect their Lands, sovereignty, lifeways, and futures from nuclearism. Nuclear decolonization as a framework is built from decades of specific place-based struggles by particular Indigenous peoples and nations to address the relationships between the nuclear production process and Indigenous Lands from the perspectives and goals of those Indigenous peoples and nations. It is simultaneously a form of resistance to domination and a positive assertion of Indigenous inherent sovereignties. As I will argue, nuclear decolonization is also a rhetorical phenomenon. This is not to say that nuclear decolonization is solely rhetorical, but it would be a mistake to overlook the role that forms of advocacy, persuasion, justification, and influence play in decolonization efforts. In this section, I write about nuclear decolonization as a theoretical framework based in Indigenous knowledges, decolonization, survivance, and radical resurgence.

Nuclear decolonization centers Indigenous ways of knowing. Kyle Whyte uses the term *Indigenous knowledges* as shorthand for Indigenous knowledge systems that "possess lessons, principles, and practices that can teach peoples of other heritages and nations about living sustainably—the seven generations philosophy."[5] As a set of movements and actions led by Indigenous peoples and nations, the rhetorical tactics used in struggles against high-level nuclear waste sites and other forms of nuclear technologies are informed by the lived experiences, cultural practices, spiritualities, and knowledges of Indigenous peoples and nations. These are not ways of knowing and being that are frozen in time, based in stereotypical historical and romanticized notions of noble savages or ecological Indians.[6] They are knowledges that are

---

5. Whyte, "What Do Indigenous Knowledges," 62.

6. It is particularly important to pause on the concept of the ecological Indian stereotype that paints Indigenous peoples as the "first environmentalists" who lived in balance with nature. Criticisms of the ecological Indian stereotype range from challenging historical and contemporary practices of Indigenous nations and peoples to explaining how positioning Indigenous people as closer to nature serves to reinforce racist and colonial perceptions of Indigenous people as subhuman and savage to discussions about the exoticization of Indigenous peoples and particularly Indigenous women. We must be aware of and wary of these stereotypes. As is the case with many stereotypes, while these tactics may reflect genuine appeals to Indigenous spiritual practices and ways of knowing as well as tactical invocations, they can also still have the consequence of perpetuating the stereotype with some audiences. For more on the ecological Indian stereotype, see Nadasdy, "Transcending the Debate"; Kretch, *Ecological Indian*; and Schmitt, "Invoking the Ecological Indian."

contemporary, diverse, and influenced but not determined by settler colonialism. In the case of the proposed Yucca Mountain and Skull Valley PFS high-level nuclear waste sites, Western Shoshone, Skull Valley Goshute, and Southern Paiute peoples' and nations' lived experiences, cultural perspectives, ecological knowledges, and forms of research often invoke the sacredness of Lands, communication between humans and the highly animate more-than-human world, and preservation of spiritual and traditional lifeways as core reasons to reject high-level nuclear waste sites. In an effort to center Indigenous knowledges, I rely primarily on the words and actions that Western Shoshone, Southern Paiute, and Skull Valley Goshute peoples and nations use in their rhetoric about nuclear waste siting but also on secondary academic sources that can provide additional insight into belief systems and knowledges of Western Shoshone, Southern Paiute, and Skull Valley Goshute cultures. In the case of nuclear decolonization, many of the actors and tactics rely on calls to protect the environment/ecology from the harms of radioactivity, invocations of Native spiritualities, and cultural practices that promote reverence for Lands and more-than-human beings. Some of these secondary sources come from fields of study—namely anthropology and ethnology—that have been criticized for complicity with colonization and presenting incorrect information about the Indigenous cultures being studied.[7] As a result, I am careful with my use of these secondary sources, drawing on them for support and not seeing them as definitive fact. I also rely on secondary research from Native American and Indigenous studies that identifies generalizations about Indigenous knowledges, including spiritualities, ecological sensibilities, and forms of government, while being careful to not essentialize all Indigenous peoples and nations into one.[8] Western Shoshone, Southern Paiute, and Skull Valley Goshute knowledges form the foundation of the nuclear decolonization efforts I amplify in this book.

As the name implies, nuclear decolonization is a type of decolonization effort. This book neither claims to be decolonizing in itself nor argues that there is only one way to work toward decolonization. My goal is to recount and celebrate how Western Shoshone, Southern Paiute, and Skull Valley Goshute peoples' and nations' resistance to nuclear waste sites on their Lands enacts a form of decolonization, even if sometimes ephemeral. As a result, nuclear decolonization is informed by decolonial, decolonization, and anticolonial practices and scholarship. I do not take one scholar's approach to decolonization as the foundation of nuclear decolonization but instead draw

---

7. A. Simpson, *Mohawk Interruptus*; and L. Smith, *Decolonizing Methodologies*.

8. Cajete, "'Look to the Mountain'"; Bruyneel, *Third Space of Sovereignty*; and A. Simpson, *Mohawk Interruptus*.

from a vibrant conversation—particularly scholarship that highlights Indigenous knowledges and Indigenous on-the-ground efforts—to help to tell this story of nuclear decolonization. By focusing specifically on those theorists accounting for the experience of Indigenous peoples and nations living within and resisting settler colonialism in the North American context, I root nuclear decolonization in the protection of Indigenous Lands and sovereignties in what settlers named the US.[9] My choice does not deny that structures and events of colonization also affect peoples within or outside of the North American continent; indeed, colonization is a multifaceted ongoing project of imperialism throughout the world with pasts, presents, and futures. Yet, given the specificity of settler colonialism as it plays out in the context of North America—and struggles over nuclear waste in the Great Basin region of this continent—my account is necessarily specific in terms of Indigenous decolonization on this continent.

Decolonization can mean many different things. In general, it is a form of anticolonial theory and practice that is geared toward overturning colonial structures, overturning colonizer rule, and securing political and economic independence. It can involve colonized peoples restoring Indigenous political control over territory and nation, as Frantz Fanon discusses in the Algerian context.[10] It can also refer to the ways that colonized peoples reject non-Indigenous structures, epistemologies, and definitions in their everyday lives, such as acts of refusal by Indigenous peoples and nations.[11] It can also refer to a freeing of one's mind from colonial epistemologies[12] or a historical time period when European colonial empires in Africa and Asia collapsed and new nation-states were created after World War II.[13] While Eve Tuck and K. Wayne Yang's catalytic article "Decolonization Is Not a Metaphor" has brought much attention to theories of decolonization coming from Native American and Indigenous studies,[14] decolonization has been a long-standing part of scholarly conversations and the rhetoric of Indigenous peoples, governments, and activists.

As a starting place, decolonization assumes that colonization is not over and still needs to be dismantled. In the case of Indigenous peoples and nations bordering and living within the US, settler colonialism is a political, eco-

---

9. Byrd, *Transit of Empire*; A. Simpson, *Mohawk Interruptus*; L. Simpson, *As We Have Always Done*; and Bruyneel, *Third Space of Sovereignty*.
10. Fanon, *Wretched of the Earth*.
11. A. Simpson, *Mohawk Interruptus*.
12. Brayboy, "Toward a Tribal Critical Race Theory."
13. D. Kennedy, *Decolonization*.
14. Tuck and Yang, "Decolonization."

nomic, cultural, and epistemological set of structures that continue to constrain Indigenous self-determination over Lands and life. It justifies the settler government's oppressive and violent actions toward Indigenous peoples and nations. Decolonization is a practice of deconstruction, resistance, and enactment that centers Indigenous self-determination, epistemologies, and futurities. Kristina Sailiata writes, "Decolonization makes the positive intervention of 'unsettling' settler colonialism. It suggests that we do not have to accept the current colonial conditions and can transform them."[15] More specifically, as Tuck and Yang argue, decolonization involves the repatriation of Lands and lifeways to Indigenous peoples.[16] Because senses of place and relationality with Lands is foundational to many Indigenous knowledges and practices, decolonization is an effort to get back Lands that were stolen by the settler nation through removal projects, treaties that were later invalidated, and what has been euphemistically called "gradual encroachment."[17] Return of Lands, or at least return of decision-making about Lands, is crucial to decolonization efforts. In addition to Lands, decolonization is also about the resurgence and enactment of Indigenous lifeways, knowledges, and self-determination. Though perhaps more nebulous than giving back stolen Lands, this aspect of decolonization is also crucial. I understand it to include a variety of actions that support inherent sovereignties and the right to live free from oppression, such as making decisions as governments, educating future generations in Indigenous languages and epistemologies, enacting traditional and spiritual ways of being, and creating space for Indigenous-led futures. Decolonization is a bottom-up project that starts with Ingenuous communities and cannot be dictated by the settler nation. This is not to say that decolonization can only be supported by Indigenous peoples and nations; indeed, decolonization efforts may rely on settler allies to support the work. In this case, Western Shoshone, Southern Paiute, and Skull Valley Goshute peoples and nations pursued strategic alliances with non-Indigenous antinuclear and environmental groups. Alliances aside, decolonization is a project by and for Indigenous peoples. As a result, this book is not decolonization. Rather, as a non-Indigenous author who has been involved in struggles over nuclear waste for over twenty years, I have written this book in an attempt to retell the stories of Western Shoshone, Southern Paiute, and Skull Valley Goshute peoples' and nations' decoloniza-

---

15. Sailiata, "Decolonization," 301.
16. Tuck and Yang, "Decolonization."
17. See, for example, the discussion of how the US settler government claims that the Western Shoshone Treaty of Ruby Valley is no longer valid because of the "gradual encroachment" of settlers who stole their land. UN Inter-American Commission on Humans Rights, *Report No. 75/02*.

tion efforts. This book is a narrative of what Audra Simpson calls "colonialism's ongoing life and simultaneous failure,"[18] which means that any discussion of decolonization has to reference the ongoing violence and trauma of colonialization while also showing how nuclear decolonization ultimately means that settler colonialism has failed its mission to completely eliminate Indigenous peoples, nations, and Lands from this continent.

Decolonization relies on rhetoric. As I have written elsewhere with Taylor Johnson, while decolonization should not be carelessly used as a metaphor for all forms of resistance to oppression, it is important to recognize the importance of rhetoric as a crucial tool in the decolonization project.[19] While I remain skeptical of discourse that simply signals decolonization but is not aligned with meaningful and sustained actions to make change, rhetoric is a crucial mechanism with which to engage in decolonization. Speaking in Indigenous languages, for example, is a powerful act of restoring Indigenous cultures and lifeways. Scott Lyons highlights rhetorical sovereignty as the ability of Indigenous peoples and nations to self-determine how they will be represented.[20] Just as the ongoing perpetuation of nuclear colonization relies on vast justification systems rooted in white supremacy, colonization, and national security, nuclear decolonization has an equally robust set of inventional topoi, justification systems, and rhetorical choices that are rooted in Indigenous knowledges, sovereignties, and Lands protection. These enactments take Lands back and affirm sovereignty in strategic moments, such as in the example that opened this chapter. They make possible continued embodied and emplaced enactments of Indigenous Lands and lifeways.

This book is only somewhat related to scholarship and theories of postcolonialism, neocolonialism, and decoloniality, all of which are related to but not the same thing as decolonization. Postcolonialism attends to the legacies of colonial systems, particularly the identities of colonized peoples in relation to race, gender, ethnicity, and nationality.[21] Within communication, Raka Shome and Radha Hegde have promoted a postcolonial approach in critical and cultural studies research.[22] In line with Jodi Byrd's approach to Indigenous critical theory, there are times that concepts from postcolonialism are useful when adapted to consideration of Indigenous issues.[23] Yet, on the whole, I

---

18. A. Simpson, *Mohawk Interruptus*, 33.
19. T. Johnson and Endres, "Decolonizing Settler Public Address."
20. Lyons, "Rhetorical Sovereignty."
21. Spivak, "Can the Subaltern Speak?"
22. Shome, "Postcolonial Interventions"; Shome, "Postcolonial Approaches to Communication"; Shome, *Diana and Beyond*; and Shome and Hegde, "Culture, Communication."
23. Byrd, *Transit of Empire*.

tend to align with those who caution that the *post* in *postcolonial* can imply that colonization is over or with those who argue that postcolonialism is more appropriate for studying the machinations of colonialism in different lands and places.[24] In some contexts, colonizers no longer rule, leaving postcolonial peoples to grapple with the legacies of colonialism. However, as stated by Linda Tuhiwai Smith, "Naming the world as 'post-colonial' is, from indigenous perspectives, to name colonialism as finished business.... Post-colonial can mean only one thing: the colonizers have left. There is rather compelling evidence that in fact this has not happened."[25] Likewise, I tend to avoid the term *neocolonialism*, which implies continued economic, rhetorical, or political control over former colonies.[26] This does not mean that settler colonialism does not take on new forms as contexts change—an aspect of neocolonial theory that is useful. Rather, neocolonialism deemphasizes Lands struggles in favor of economic and resource studies and is, therefore, less relevant to this study of nuclear decolonization. Decoloniality encourages a split or delinking from Western epistemologies.[27] Decoloniality is certainly relevant to nuclear decolonization. What Bryan Brayboy has referred to as "decolonizing the mind" is a form of delinking that is an essential step in decolonization.[28] While decoloniality falls within the realm of epistemic structures, decolonization refers to on-the-ground struggles to regain sovereignty and Lands. All of these approaches, including decolonization, fall under the mantel of anticolonialisms.[29] Following Max Liboiron, I see my own work on this project as anticolonial, reporting and amplifying the decolonization efforts of Western Shoshone, Southern Paiute, and Skull Valley Goshute peoples and nations.

Nuclear decolonization is also connected to survivance. Settler colonialism, though still ongoing, is not complete in large part due to the ongoing survivance of Indigenous peoples, who have engaged in active and persistent protection of their Lands, cultures, spiritualities, and societies. Gerald Vizenor coined the term *survivance* as a way to emphasize the presence and continuance of Indigenous peoples and nations.[30] He writes, "Native survivance is an active sense of presence over absence, deracination, and oblivion; surviv-

---

24. Byrd, *Transit of Empire*; G. Morris, "International Law and Politics"; Valaskakis, *Indian Country*; and L. Smith, *Decolonizing Methodologies*.
25. L. Smith, *Decolonizing Methodologies*, 98.
26. Buescher and Ono, "Civilized Colonialism"; and Black, *American Indians*.
27. Mignolo, "Delinking"; Mignolo, "Epistemic Disobedience"; and Wanzer, "Delinking Rhetoric."
28. Brayboy, "Toward a Tribal Critical Race Theory."
29. Lechuga, "Anticolonial Future"; and Liboiron, *Pollution Is Colonialism*.
30. Vizenor, "Aesthetics of Survivance."

ance is the continuance of stories, not a mere reaction, however pertinent."[31] Survivance is a practice that combines survival, endurance, and resistance. Vizenor continues, "Native survivance stories are renunciations of dominance, tragedy, and victimry."[32] Western Shoshone, Southern Paiute, and Skull Valley Goshute struggles against nuclear waste sites within Yucca Mountain and Skull Valley are examples of survivance, in line with the multiple uses of the term. Their enactments of Lands protection and sovereignties not only address a particular struggle over a nuclear technology but also are in and of themselves embodied and emplaced moments of survivance. Survivance is an essential element of decolonization efforts because an essential assumption of settler colonialism is to take over the Lands and extinguish Indigenous peoples and nations through assimilation or elimination. Survivance pushes for decolonization and asserts the ongoing presence and power of Indigenous peoples and nations.

Nuclear decolonization is also a form of radical resurgence, which Leanne Simpson defines this way: "Radical resurgence has come to me to represent a radical practice in Indigenous theorizing, writing, organizing, and thinking, one that I believe is entirely consistent with and inherently from Indigenous thought."[33] Related to Indigenous knowledges, radical resurgence signals active movements led by Indigenous peoples based in Indigenous ways of knowing and being that move toward Indigenous futures. Simpson offered the Idle No More movement among First Nations peoples as an example of radical resurgence. Western Shoshone, Southern Paiute, and Skull Valley Goshute peoples' and nations' work toward nuclear decolonization is likewise a form of radical resurgence—an unapologetic assertion of Indigenous sovereignty and Lands protection that builds from Indigenous worldviews.

Nuclear decolonization is not a concept or set of practices I have created, nor is it a new theoretical framework. It is a long-standing embodied and emplaced theory that describes on-the-ground actions Indigenous activists engage in to survive and thrive. As Michael Lechuga puts it, "Activism is a source of knowledge,"[34] and activists are akin to theorists. My contribution is to recount stories of nuclear decolonization through the lens of rhetoric in an effort to encourage more awareness in the communication discipline about what these knowledges and theories can bring to communication areas of study. Embodied and emplaced rhetorical tactics are a primary means through which Indigenous peoples and nations have enacted Indigenous knowledges,

---

31. Vizenor, 1.
32. Vizenor, *Manifest Manners*, vii.
33. L. Simpson, *As We Have Always Done*, 48.
34. Lechuga, "Anticolonial Future."

decolonization, survivance, and radical resurgence. Nuclear decolonization not only supports Indigenous imaginations and futures but also creates fissures in settler colonialism, in this case, by contributing to the prevention of two high-level nuclear waste storage sites within Western Shoshone, Southern Paiute, and Skull Valley Goshute Lands.

NUCLEAR COLONIZATION

Nuclear decolonization is inherently intertwined with nuclear colonization. Yet, *nuclear colonialization*—and the related terms *nuclear colonialism* and *radioactive colonization*—refers to the disproportionate siting of uranium mining, nuclear testing, nuclear weapons production, and nuclear waste within Indigenous Lands, both reservation and nonreservation Lands. The nuclear production process has also negatively affected settlers, and in following with the preponderance of environmental injustices in the US, particularly settlers that are marginalized or underrepresented through intersecting structures of oppression including racism, heteropatriarchy, and classism. These environmental injustices are important and need to be addressed. However, the terms *radioactive colonization, nuclear colonialism,* and *nuclear colonization* are used by Indigenous scholars and activists to explain the unique position of Indigenous peoples as sovereign nations navigating within a system of settler colonialism.[35] It means that Indigenous peoples and nations disproportionately experience burdens of the nuclear production process, not just in terms of health and Lands but also in terms of sovereignty and self-determination.

An interdisciplinary corpus of literature related to nuclear colonization has documented the disproportionate relationship between nuclear production and Indigenous peoples and nations through mapping the locations of nuclear sites in relation to Indigenous Lands, interviews with Indigenous peoples, and calculations of the percentage of nuclear production sites on or near Indigenous Lands.[36] At the 2002 "People's Summit on High-Level Radioactive Waste," the Indigenous Environmental Network released a statement opposed to the Yucca Mountain and Skull Valley PFS sites that defines *nuclear colonialism*:

---

35. I address my use of Ward Churchill's writing in footnote 2 in the preface. LaDuke and Churchill, "Native America," *Critical Sociology.*
36. For example, Hooks and Smith, "Treadmill of Destruction"; LaDuke, *All Our Relations*; and Kuletz, *Tainted Desert.*

> The nuclear industry has waged an undeclared war against our Indigenous peoples and Pacific Islanders that has poisoned our communities worldwide. For more than 50-years, the legacy of the nuclear chain, from exploration to the dumping of radioactive waste has been proven, through documentation, to be genocide and ethnocide and a deadly enemy of Indigenous peoples. The ancestral lands of the Indigenous peoples in the United States has been used for testing nuclear weapons, experimenting with biological and chemical warfare agents, incinerating and burying hazardous wastes, and mining uranium. United States federal law and nuclear policy has not protected Indigenous peoples, and in fact has been created to allow the nuclear industry to continue operations at the expense of our land, territory, health and traditional ways of life. This system of genocide and ethnocide policies and practices has brought our people to the brink of extinction. This disproportionate toxic burden—called environmental racism—has culminated in the current attempts to dump much of the nation's nuclear waste in the homelands of the Indigenous peoples of the Great Basin region of the United States. This action does not provide homeland security to our Indigenous peoples. Indigenous peoples have already made countless sacrifices for this country's nuclear programs.[37]

The Indigenous Environmental Network highlights the important interconnections between nuclearism and settler colonialism as practiced in the US. Later in the statement, the network lays out a series of recommendations, such as stopping the Yucca Mountain and Skull Valley PFS sites, instituting a moratorium on building new nuclear power plants until nuclear waste can be safely stored, demanding that industry and the federal government clean up the radioactive contamination already within Indigenous Lands, calling on those who have benefitted from nuclear colonialism to "pay up, in the form of developing tribal 'just transition' programs for sustainable economic development and education and training for the Indigenous tribal nations that have been the target of these nuclear waste programs and the legacy of nuclear colonialism," and calling "upon the United States to honor all treaty rights, agreements and executive orders entered into with the Indigenous peoples of this country."[38] The Indigenous Environmental Network's statement, therefore, offers not only a concise and insightful analysis of nuclear colonization but also a set of tactics that can support nuclear decolonization for Native peoples and nations. Although just one of many articulations of nuclear coloniza-

---

37. Indigenous Environmental Network, "Indigenous Anti-Nuclear Statement."
38. Indigenous Environmental Network, "Indigenous Anti-Nuclear Statement."

tion, I return over and over again to the Indigenous Environmental Network's statement because of how it intertwines nuclear colonization and nuclear decolonization.

This section traces *nuclear colonization* and related terms through scholarly and Indigenous activist and protector discourses. While many different phrases have been used—such as *radioactive colonization* and *nuclear colonialism*—I primarily use the term *nuclear colonization* to emphasize an active and ongoing process. *Nuclear colonization* continues to be more widely used, particularly in academic scholarship, than *nuclear decolonization*. Only recently have activists and scholars begun to use the term *nuclear decolonization,* though scholarship and activism has consistently focused on forms of resistance to nuclear colonialism.[39]

I first encountered the term *radioactive colonization* when I read the book *Struggle for the Land* as an undergraduate student.[40] Yet, the term was first used by Winona LaDuke—Indigenous environmentalism activist and leader of Honor the Earth—in 1983 in an article about uranium mining within Navajo and Laguna Pueblo Lands.[41] In a series of articles and book chapters, Winona LaDuke and a collaborator[42] use *radioactive colonization* or *radioactive colonialism* as a way to talk about the disproportionate harms experienced by Indigenous peoples and nations as a result of the nuclear production process, expanding from LaDuke's original focus on uranium mining to other aspects of the nuclear production process.[43] As LaDuke wrote in 1999, "Much of the world's nuclear industry has been sited on or near Native lands."[44] In response, "American Indians, those who have been selected by the dynamics of radioactive colonization to be the first 20th century national sacrifice peoples, must stand alone, or with their immediate allies, for a common survival. It is a gamble, no doubt, but a gamble that is clearly warranted."[45] From the

---

39. An example of the use of *nuclear decolonization* is found in Barker, Lucero, and Pritikin, "Loom of the Future."

40. Churchill, "Radioactive Colonization."

41. It is unclear why the author is listed as "Winona La Duque" when the author note lists "Winona LaDuke." La Duque, "Native America."

42. See footnote 2 in the preface for my explanation of why I am not using the name of LaDuke's collaborator.

43. Churchill and LaDuke, "Radioactive Colonization"; Churchill and LaDuke, "Native America," *Insurgent Sociologist*; Churchill and LaDuke, "Native America," *IWGIA Yearbook*; Churchill and LaDuke, "Native North America"; Churchill, "Radioactive Colonization"; Churchill, "Cold War Impacts"; Churchill, "Nuclear Trust"; Churchill, "Breach of Trust"; Churchill, "Geographic of Sacrifice"; La Duque, "Native America"; and LaDuke, *All Our Relations*.

44. LaDuke, *All Our Relations,* 97.

45. Churchill and LaDuke, "Native North America," 262.

very beginning, the concept represents a blend of scholarship and activism, as is often the case for environmental justice topics.

Indigenous activists, protectors, and organizations, such as Grace Thorpe of the National Environmental Coalition of Native Americans (NECONA), the Indigenous Environmental Network, Margene Bullcreek of Ohngo Gaudadeh Devia, Western Shoshone elder Corbin Harney, and Winona LaDuke, often address nuclear colonization in their writings and campaigns. For example, the major goals of NECONA are:

- to educate Indians and Non-Indians about the health dangers of radioactivity and the transportation of nuclear waste on America's rails and roads.
- to network with Indian and Non-Indian environmentalists to develop grassroots counter-movement to the well-funded efforts of the nuclear industry.
- to declare Tribal NUCLEAR FREE ZONES across the nation.[46]

Across these groups, there is a focus on resistance to nuclear colonization across the life cycle of nuclear technologies, particularly uranium mining, nuclear weapons production and testing, and nuclear waste. Although not always the most visible of issues facing Indigenous peoples and nations on this continent, there has been sustained engagement, albeit at times stronger than others, with challenging nuclear colonization.

Nuclear colonization has been extended and further theorized in a small but robust body of scholarship. Valerie Kuletz, for example, offers a nuanced mapping of the relationship between the Southwest and nuclear technologies in her book *The Tainted Desert*. She argues that the "nuclear landscape is a contemporary form of colonialism that won the West."[47] Other research has approached the concept in relation to nuclear waste siting in the US and Taiwan, nuclear testing in the US and the Marshall Islands, and uranium mining in the US and African nations, illustrating that nuclear colonization is a global phenomenon that spans the life cycle of nuclear technologies.[48] Furthermore,

---

46. NECONA, "National Environmental Coalition."
47. Kuletz, *Tainted Desert*, 115.
48. Barad, "After the End"; Boyd, "Black Rainbow, Blood-Earth"; Butrim et al., "Ippen Dron,"; Chamberlain, "Nuclear Colonialism"; Danielsson and Danielsson, *Poisoned Reign*; Edwards, "Nuclear Colonialism"; Endres, "Rhetoric of Nuclear Colonialism"; Endres, "From Wasteland to Waste Site"; Endres, "Sacred Land"; Endres, "Animist Intersubjectivity as Argumentation"; Gard, "Looking for Light"; Hamel-Green, "Networking Against Nuclear Colonialism"; R. Jacobs, "Nuclear Conquistadors"; R. Jacobs and Broderick, "United Nations Report"; Runyan, "Disposable Waste"; Schwartz, "Matters of Empathy"; and Richter, "Energopolitics and Nuclear Waste."

not all research explicitly uses the terms *radioactive* or *nuclear colonialism/ colonization* while engaging with the nexus of nuclear technologies and Indigenous peoples. For example, in her research on environmental justice, Kristin Schrader-Frechette states that Native peoples have been subjected to "nuclear related environmental justice" issues because of the "continuing problem of colonialism and the ability of wealthy developed nations (and their corporations) to exploit indigenous people."[49] Nuclear colonization describes the development of nuclear technologies with an insistence on linking it with structures of settler colonialism and nuclearism.

Settler Colonialism

Centering the tactics of nuclear decolonization as a form of resistance to the rhetorical/material conditions of nuclear colonization requires grounding in research on settler colonialism.[50] Decolonization is resistance to colonization, in this case, colonization by settlers. Colonialism can be defined in many ways but generally refers to a system in which marginal populations (as perceived by imperial powers) are put in the service of a core center of power through violence, direct political control, and rhetorical justification systems. Settler colonialism is a form of colonization that describes the conditions of places where settlers arrived and decided to stay. This necessitates elimination of the Indigenous peoples and nations so that their Lands can be stolen and owned by settlers. Patrick Wolfe describes settler colonialism as "premised on a cultural logic of elimination that insistently seeks the removal of indigenous humans from the land in question."[51] In the US context, the first immigrants to North America were colonists from the United Kingdom, France, Spain, Russia, and other monarchies in Europe. While the original plan of these monarchies was to set up colonies to support those nations, the American Revolution changed that plan. The new settler state was founded

---

49. Shrader-Frechette, *Environmental Justice*, 118.
50. Although Winona LaDuke and Ward Churchill—in their first conceptualizations of radioactive colonization in the 1980s—use the term *internal colonialism*, this book's discussion of Indigenous nuclear decolonization relies on advances that identify settler colonialism as the form of colonialism that best describes the experience of Indigenous people in what is known as the North American continent. Jodi Byrd argues that *settler colonialism* does a better job of highlighting the unique situation of Indigenous people in North America than *internal colonialism*, which usually refers to a marginalized racial or ethnic group within a nation-state. Byrd, *Transit of Empire*; Wolfe, "Settler Colonialism"; A. Simpson, *Mohawk Interruptus*; Morgensen, "Destabilizing the Settler Academy"; Bruyneel, *Third Space of Sovereignty*; Mackey, *Unsettled Expectations*; and L. Simpson, *As We Have Always Done*.
51. Wolfe, "Corpus Nullius," 147.

on stealing from Indigenous peoples and nations in the eastern region of the continent, setting in motion a massive migration of newly identified Americans across the continent concomitant with land grabs, violence, and genocide. This book is not a history of settler colonialism in the North American, particularly US context. Yet, I do assume that my readers are aware of this history (if not, I recommend a deep dive into US-Indigenous history).[52] This history of settler colonization is foundational to nuclear colonization; it is half of what enables nuclear colonization, with nuclearism being the other half. Importantly, though, it is not just a history. Settler colonization is ongoing, and nuclear decolonization tactics are more than resistance to nuclear technologies; they are resistance to stolen Lands and affronts to Indigenous sovereignties. Despite the common settler belief that colonization of Indigenous peoples and nations is a thing of the past, settler colonialism in the US (and beyond) is ongoing and matters to Indigenous peoples and nations.

Settler colonialism, through its attempts to steal Lands and eliminate Indigenous peoples, is an environmental injustice because it severs Indigenous relationships with their Lands and the entirety of more-than-human beings that make up Lands.[53] As Dina Gilio-Whitaker argues, "The origin of environmental justice for Indigenous peoples is dispossession of land in all its forms; injustice is continually reproduced in what is inherently a culturally genocidal structure that systematically erases Indigenous peoples' relationships and responsibilities to their ancestral places."[54] Nuclear colonization's harms to Indigenous Lands are, therefore, an environmental injustice. As I will argue in chapter 3, Indigenous Lands protection is an essential element of nuclear decolonization that simultaneously resists settler colonial structures while also seeking to continue and restore relationality with Lands.

Colonialism, in all of its forms, is dependent on rhetoric. Mary Stuckey and John Murphy point out that rhetorical colonialism is a key way that colonial projects are justified.[55] In order to create these justification systems, rhetoric acts as a form of violence, which serves either as a justification for physical violence or to deny the rights and lived experiences of peoples.[56] The relationship between violence and settler colonialism is cyclical. A threat of violence is always present. If the threat turns into physical violence, the colonizer justifies

---

52. Here are a couple of resources: Dunbar-Ortiz, *Indigenous Peoples' History*; and Blackhawk, *Rediscovery of America*.
53. Whyte, "Indigenous Experience"; Tuck and Yang, "Decolonization"; and Gilio-Whitaker, *As Long as Grass Grows*.
54. Gilio-Whitaker, *As Long as Grass Grows*, 36.
55. Stuckey and Murphy, "By Any Other Name."
56. Stuckey and Murphy, "By Any Other Name"; and Russell, "Language, Violence."

the use of violence in a way that blames the colonized. This, in turn, reinforces the threat of violence. This cycle has played out throughout the history of contact between the US and Indigenous peoples and nations. It is precisely these justification systems, or the rhetoric of colonialism, that must be critiqued in a variety of contemporary settings. My previous research has made these connections between rhetoric, settler colonialism, and nuclear technologies, revealing the rhetorical strategies of nuclear colonialism.

Nuclearism

Nuclear decolonization considers the state of Indigenous Lands, peoples, and governments starting in 1939, when the US first began to develop nuclear weapons technologies, although the official start of the nuclear age is often marked as 1945, when the US used atomic weapons to devastate Hiroshima and Nagasaki. In 1939 the vast majority of Indigenous Lands had been settled and stolen by the US through treaties and executive orders that removed and relocated Indigenous peoples and nations to reservation Lands representing only a small portion of their ancestral territories. A lot has happened in Indigenous-US relations between 1492 and 1939, which, though outside the scope of this book, is nonetheless necessary for a deep understanding of settler colonialism and decolonization in the US.[57] This book takes as a starting point the sociopolitical status of Indigenous peoples and nations from 1939 to the present. This is as a key moment for the rhetorical/material development of nuclear colonization and nuclear decolonization (although these specific terms may not have been used by rhetors at the time).

Nuclearism, an ideology that emerged in the nuclear age, seeks to promote the value of nuclear technology as a crucial component of contemporary society, tying in notions of patriotism, national security, and faith in technology.[58] There is an assumption that nuclear weapons and nuclear power are crucial to the US national interests and national security, which then normalizes and justifies all aspects of the nuclear production process. As an ideology and a discursive system, nuclearism is "intertextually configured by present discourses such as militarism, nationalism, bureaucracy, and technical-rationality."[59] Nuclearism is omnipresent in contemporary US policy, such as calls to license new nuclear reactors as a response to climate change, the

---

57. See, for example, Dunbar-Ortiz, *Indigenous Peoples' History*; Black, *American Indians*.
58. Mathur, "Nuclearism"; Taylor, "Nuclear Weapons"; and Taylor, Kinsella, and Depoe, *Nuclear Legacies*.
59. Taylor, "Nuclear Weapons," 301.

development of new nuclear weapons technologies, and research into new nuclear power technologies. Everyone is affected by nuclearism's presence. As Joseph Masco writes,

> How individuals engage with the nuclear complex puts them in a tactile experience not only with the technology of the bomb but also with the nation-state that controls it, making the interrelationship between the human body and nuclear technologies a powerful site of intersection in which to explore questions of national belonging, justice, and everyday life.[60]

While Masco refers to the bomb, nuclearism exceeds the bomb to include uranium mining, nuclear power, and nuclear waste. The US federal government justifies nuclear production as serving the US national interest and national security. This justification works with the structure of settler colonialism that defines Indigenous peoples and nations as part of the US nation, not as separate, inherently sovereign entities whose national interests may not be to store nuclear waste on their Lands.[61]

Nuclear communication criticism recognizes the rhetoricity of nuclearism. Bryan Taylor and William Kinsella call for more research into the "nuclear legacies" of the nuclear production process.[62] The material legacies of the nuclear production process include illness and deaths among Diné uranium miners, the Church Rock uranium mill disaster, Western Shoshone and Southern Paiute downwinders, and, of course, high-level nuclear waste. Yet, there are also discursive legacies of nuclearism that must be addressed, such as nuclear colonialism.[63] Nuclear waste needs more examination as both a material and rhetorical legacy of nuclearism. Taylor wrote, "Nuclear waste represents one of the most complex and highly charged controversies created by the postwar society."[64] One of the reasons why nuclear waste is such a complex controversy is its connection with nuclear colonialism.

---

60. Masco, *Nuclear Borderlands*, 12.

61. Nuclearism is, in one sense, related to what Gabriel Hecht calls *nuclearity*, or the contested nature of defining what counts as being nuclear and what does not. Her analysis of uranium mining in African nations demonstrates how nuclearity "is a technopolitical phenomenon that emerges from political and cultural configurations of technical and scientific things, from the social relations where knowledge is produced." While nuclearism and nuclearity are not the same thing, the important point is that nuclearism is an ideology that relies, in part, on nuclearities. Hecht, *Being Nuclear*, 15.

62. Taylor and Kinsella, "Introduction," 1.

63. Kinsella, "One Hundred Years"; and Kinsella, Andreas, and Endres, "Communicating Nuclear Power."

64. Taylor, "Nuclear Waste," 288.

Nuclear colonization, a convergence of the structures of nuclearism and settler colonialism, is a pervasive material/rhetorical phenomenon. It is the structure nuclear decolonization seeks to dismantle. In the next section, I describe specific place-based instances of nuclear colonization and nuclear decolonization across the life cycle of nuclear technologies, showing that high-level nuclear waste siting is not the only node.

NUCLEAR DE/COLONIZATION ACROSS THE LIFE CYCLE

Both globally and nationally, key processes in the nuclear production complex occur on or near Indigenous Lands with significant implications for the ecological and human health of these regions and communities.[65] All aspects of the nuclear production process are implicated in the system of nuclear colonization, such as uranium mining and milling within Lands in the Black Hills and Four Corners regions, nuclear testing on Lands claimed under the 1863 Treaty of Ruby Valley by the Western Shoshone peoples and nations, nuclear reactors sited close to Prairie Island Lands, and nuclear waste facilities considered within Skull Valley Goshute, Western Shoshone, Southern Paiute, Mescalero Apache, and other Indigenous Lands. Yet, a focus on nuclear decolonization highlights how Indigenous peoples and nations are not and were never passive victims of the violence of nuclear colonization. On the contrary, nuclear decolonization affirms the agency of Indigenous peoples and nations in defending their sovereignties and Lands from the twin assaults of nuclearism and settler colonialism.

Uranium (the Cradle)

All nuclear power reactors and some nuclear weapons begin with uranium mining and milling. Uranium is mined and then milled into yellowcake, which is enriched to increase the concentration of uranium 235. Enrichment makes the product capable of a fission reaction and able to be used to fabricate

---

65. Endres, "From Wasteland to Waste Site"; Grinde and Johansen, *Ecocide of Native America*; Kuletz, *Tainted Desert*; Gallagher, *American Ground Zero*; Edwards, "Nuclear Colonialism"; Gowda and Easterling, "Voluntary Siting and Equity"; Fan, "Environmental Justice"; Ishiyama, "Environmental Justice"; and Makhijani, Hu, and Yih, *Nuclear Wastelands*.

fuel for nuclear power reactors.[66] There are severe environmental and health hazards associated with mining, milling, and enrichment.[67]

Across the globe, uranium mining is inextricably linked with "indigenous, colonized, and other dominated peoples."[68] As LaDuke notes, "Some 70 percent of the world's uranium originates from Native Communities."[69] Of course, given that the entirety of the US is within stolen Indigenous Lands, 100 percent of uranium reserves, mining, and milling in the US are occurring within Indigenous Lands. Because nuclear weapons and nuclear power production are within the stated US national interest, the Bureau of Indian Affairs (BIA) worked with the Atomic Energy Commission to negotiate leases between corporations and Indigenous nations for uranium mining and milling on their Lands, particularly during the uranium boom between the 1950s and early 1980s.[70] These leases heavily favored the corporations, and Indigenous nations received only a small percentage of the market value of the uranium, low-paid jobs, and illnesses.[71] Although domestic uranium mining decreased in the 1980s, throughout the 2000s interest in expanding nuclear power production via a purported nuclear renaissance has sparked industrial interest in reopening shuttered mines or opening new mines.[72] I recently read a headline in the *Salt Lake Tribune* about plans to reopen a uranium mine in southern Utah. Beyond inequitable compensation, uranium mining within Indigenous Lands had devastating effects on the health and well-being of Indigenous peoples and Lands.[73]

Uranium mining and milling also resulted in severe health and environmental legacies for affected Native people and their lands. From uranium mining on Diné Lands, there have been at least 450 reported cancer deaths among Diné mining employees.[74] A book of oral histories called *Memories Come to Us in the Rain and Wind* tells the stories of Diné miners and family members who experienced unsafe and, in some cases, deadly exposure to radiation.[75] The devastation extended beyond employees to the larger communities sur-

66. US Energy Information Administration, "Nuclear Fuel Cycle."
67. Makhijani et al., "Health Hazards."
68. Yih et al., "Uranium Mining," 105.
69. LaDuke, *All Our Relations*, 97.
70. Grinde and Johansen, *Ecocide of Native America*; and LaDuke and Churchill, "Native America," *Journal of Ethnic Studies*.
71. Voyles, *Wastelanding*; and Fox, *Downwind*.
72. McCombs and Knickmeyer, "Trump Proposal"; Thompson, "Green Metal Mining Boom"; Barringer, "Uranium Exploration"; and Yurth, "Uranium Mining Claims."
73. Fox, *Downwind*; and Voyles, *Wastelanding*.
74. Grinde and Johansen, *Ecocide of Native America*, 217.
75. Benally, Stillwell, and Harrison, *Memories Come to Us*.

rounding the mines and mills. The United Nuclear Uranium mill at Church Rock surrounded by the Navajo Reservation is the site of the largest nuclear accident in the US. On July 16, 1978, over 100 million gallons of irradiated water contaminated the Rio Puerco River, plant and animal life, and Diné peoples.[76] Even now, the legacy of over one thousand abandoned mines and uranium tailing piles is radioactive dust that continues to put beings living near tailing piles at high risk for cancers, birth defects, and other health problems. As LaDuke puts it, "Once uranium is removed from the earth, radiation is released in great quantities. The land, in turn, becomes dangerous to continue living upon. To Indian people, this is the final act of genocide, we are in no position to 'evacuate' our land base."[77] The system of uranium extraction operates at the expense of the health of Indigenous peoples, their cultural survival, and their self-determination.

Indigenous nations have resisted and are currently resisting uranium mining and milling on their Lands. In the wake of early 2000s discussions of renewed uranium mining in the Four Corners to support new nuclear power in the purported nuclear renaissance, the Navajo Nation banned uranium mining on their Lands in an act of sovereignty.[78] Similarly, Lakota peoples fought the Canadian company Cameco Resources from expanding the Crow Butte Uranium mine near Crawford, Nebraska.[79] Further, the Ute Mountain Ute nation is currently fighting against a uranium mill site in White Mesa, a sacred site within view of Bears Ears.[80] Beyond these specific examples, the Indigenous Environmental Network explicitly calls for a cessation of uranium mining within Indigenous Lands, asking "governments, including tribal, state, national and international, to do whatever possible to stop all uranium exploration, mining, milling, conversion, testing, research, weapons and other military production, use, and waste disposals onto and into Mother Earth."[81] These examples are not only fissures in nuclear colonization—efforts that prevent nuclear colonization from becoming complete—but more importantly, they highlight the ongoing survivance, resilience, and strength of Indigenous peoples and nations.

76. Grinde and Johansen, *Ecocide of Native America*; and Yih et al., "Uranium Mining." In 2007 the Navajo nation succeeded in persuading the federal government to clean up the Church Rock site, which contaminated the water and soil near Navajo homes with radiation for twenty-four years. Hardeen, "Shirley Acknowledges Navajo."
77. It is unclear why the author is listed as "Winona La Duque" when the author note lists "Winona LaDuke." La Duque, "Native America," 19.
78. Southwest Research and Information Center, "Navajo Nation President."
79. "Uranium Mine Hearing"; and "Henry Red Cloud."
80. Woods, "U.S. Uranium Mill."
81. Indigenous Environmental Network, "Indigenous Anti-Nuclear Statement."

Weapons Production and Testing

Nuclear weapons production involves a variety of processes that are dangerous for humans and more-than-human beings, produce various forms of radioactive waste, and have left a legacy of highly toxic sites, such as the Hanford Site (now an Environmental Protection Agency Super Fund site), the Nevada Test Site (now called the Nevada National Security Site), and Rocky Flats (now a National Wildlife Refuge[82]). The edited volume *Nuclear Wastelands* provides a detailed analysis of the environmental and health effects from global nuclear weapons production efforts. According to Arjun Makhijani, "It is evident that nuclear weapons have profoundly damaged the very people and lands they were supposed to protect through the adverse environmental and health consequences of production and testing."[83] While nuclear weapons production has negatively affected more than only Native peoples and nations, one aspect of the nuclear weapons production process that has disproportionately harmed Indigenous peoples and nations is nuclear testing.

Nuclear testing programs involve the detonation of nuclear bombs both above and below ground. Nuclear testing serves as a symbol of power for nations in the nuclear club. The majority of nuclear testing occurred during the Cold War between the US and the former Soviet Union, but it continues in some countries on smaller scales. Reflecting on the legacy of global nuclear testing, Makhijani argued, "The main sites for testing nuclear weapons for every declared nuclear power are on tribal or minority lands."[84] In the case of the US, nuclear testing occurred within Indigenous Lands in the atolls of the South Pacific and in desert regions of the Great Basin and Southwest. The US tested its first nuclear weapon on July 16, 1945, at the White Sands Proving Ground in New Mexico, homelands of the Mescalero Apache peoples and nation. The Trinity test, as it was called, ushered in the so-called nuclear age. Three weeks after the Trinity test, the US detonated nuclear bombs in Hiroshima and Nagasaki, the only nuclear weapons to be deployed in war. From 1946 to 1948, the US tested nuclear weapons in the Marshall Islands, homelands of Marshallese Indigenous peoples, under Operations Crossroads and Sandstone.[85] Following these tests within Marshallese territories, the US sought a continental testing site due to "logistics, weather, and security and safety concerns" with the Marshall Island tests.[86] In 1950 President Tru-

---

82. The irony is not lost on me.
83. Makhijani, "Readiness to Harm," 1.
84. Makhijani, 8.
85. US Department of Energy, *Battlefield*.
86. US Department of Energy, 35.

man approved the Atomic Energy Commission's recommendation to convert the Las Vegas Bombing and Gunnery Range to a national test site called the Nevada Test Site. Between 1951 and 1992, the US conducted 1,021 nuclear detonations within the NTS, homelands of Western Shoshone and Southern Paiute peoples and nations. Nuclear testing continued until 1992, when former president George W. Bush enacted a moratorium on nuclear testing. Yet, because the Comprehensive Test Ban Treaty has not yet been ratified by the US, the possibility remains open for further testing.

Recall from the opening vignette that Corbin Harney proclaimed the Western Shoshone to be the most nuclear-bombed nation in the world. Western Shoshone, Southern Paiute, and other Native peoples have suffered more radiation exposure than non-Indigenous peoples because of their lifestyle of, as Western Shoshone Virginia Sanchez put it, "picking berries, hunting and gathering our traditional foods," resulting in "major doses of radiation."[87] While the US government maintained for years that nuclear testing was within safe levels of radiation, the National Cancer Institute proved otherwise, estimating at least seventy-five thousand cases of thyroid cancer associated with testing.[88] Yet, the settler state has made only small gestures toward compensating victims of nuclear testing—Indigenous and non-Indigenous. The Radiation Exposure Compensation Act has strict qualification guidelines that have excluded many downwinders from receiving compensation for the effects of nuclear testing. In addition to the effects on human health from nuclear testing, there is also an environmental toll through contaminated soil and water, which could harm animal and plant life.[89] As I have argued elsewhere, nuclear colonization is a form of domination not just over humans but also over all of the more-than-human beings that compose Indigenous Lands; the NTS, as a result, is a "colonized place wherein the entire ecological community—humans, animals, plants, soil, water—is disproportionately affected by its interaction with nuclear weapons tests."[90] This became painfully apparent to me when I took a tour of the Nevada Test Site with students and experienced the enormity of the testing program while moving through the pockmarked landscape in person. As Harney puts it,

> The Nevada Test Site was set aside for use as a military testing ground by President Truman in 1951. But the United States government never looked at the fact that this is Shoshone land under the Ruby Valley Treaty of 1863. We

---

87. As cited in LaDuke, *All Our Relations*, 99.
88. LaDuke.
89. Kuletz, *Tainted Desert*; and Endres, "Most Nuclear-Bombed Place."
90. Endres, "Most Nuclear-Bombed Place," 255–56.

were told a lie. They said under the treaty that they were going to protect the land, not explode thousands of nuclear bombs on it. My people used to camp on that land before it was a test site. I didn't appreciate what the nuclear bombs were doing to the land, the animals, the birds, and the plants. They were put there by Nature to survive off the land, but now they're all gone. The medicine roots of all different kinds that were put there by Nature. Those things I have seen disappear from the Nevada Test Site.[91]

The consequences of the US nuclear testing program are unconscionable and cannot be reduced to a national sacrifice, especially for Western Shoshone and Southern Paiute peoples and nations with different national interests.

Western Shoshone and Southern Paiute peoples and nations actively resisted nuclear testing from the 1980s to 1992 and continue to challenge proposals that emerge periodically to renew testing at the NTS.[92] For many years, antinuclear advocates, including Indigenous peoples and nations, participated in Mother's Day events at the Nevada test site, such as the one described in the opening vignette. Furthermore, resistance from Western Shoshone and Southern Paiute peoples and nations, in a strategic alliance with Utah downwinders, resulted in the cancellation of a nonnuclear subcritical test (Divine Strake) proposed for the NTS in June 2006.[93] These actions are forms of nuclear decolonization. They are not just about stopping nuclear tests. More importantly, they are rooted in inherent sovereignty and responsibilities to be in good relations with Lands.

Nuclear Power

Nuclear power is not as directly related to nuclear de/colonization as uranium mining, nuclear weapons production, and proposed nuclear waste sites. The stories of nuclear colonization and nuclear decolonization are most often focused on how the cradle and grave of nuclear power—uranium mining and nuclear waste—disproportionately harm Indigenous peoples and nations.[94] Yet, there is still a story to tell about how some Indigenous peoples and nations living near nuclear power plants resist these sites. Decades of research in environmental justice shows that marginalized communities are more likely to live and work in or near polluting and toxic industries, including power plants,

---

91. Harney, *Nature Way*, 26.
92. T. Johnson, "'Most Bombed Nation.'"
93. Dickson, "People Speak."
94. Endres, "From Wasteland to Waste Site."

than nonmarginalized communities.[95] While every nuclear power plant in the US is on stolen Indigenous ancestral and traditional territories, there has not been extensive research about the locations of nuclear power plants in relation to reservation Lands. One example, though, is the Prairie Island Nuclear Generating Plant (Xcel Energy) that is adjacent to the Prairie Island Indian Community reservation, descendants of the Mdewakanton Band of Eastern Dakota. In addition to worries about a possible accident at the plant, the Prairie Island Indian Community calls for spent fuel rods (a form of high-level nuclear waste) to be removed from the aging power plant.[96] Fuel rods are used in a reactor core of a nuclear power plant to produce a fission reaction that heats water to create steam power. When nuclear fuel rods are spent, they are moved to on-site interim storage either in storage pools or aboveground dry cask storage. Currently, spent fuel rods from US nuclear power plants are stored on-site at operating nuclear power plants. Because the US has yet to find a site for permanent storage of this form of high-level nuclear waste (which was slated for both the failed Yucca Mountain and Skull Valley PFS sites), on-site storage pools and dry cask storage sites are increasingly becoming overcrowded, compounding the safety concerns of those living or working near a nuclear power plant. The Fukushima Daiichi nuclear disaster's near-miss in terms of a catastrophic leak from the spent fuel rod pools has raised alarm about the additional risks of on-site high-level nuclear waste storage that could release radiation via flooding, earthquakes, or other natural disasters, some of which will be more likely as a result of climate change.[97] While the Prairie Island Indian Community is concerned about spent fuel rods stored on-site, they still opposed the Yucca Mountain permanent storage site because of its location on Western Shoshone and Southern Paiute Lands. This represents an additional layer of complexity in the politics of nuclear waste siting. One answer is to stop producing more high-level nuclear waste until an equitable solution can be found, as the Indigenous Environmental Network argues:

> United States citizens must oppose the generation of more nuclear waste by demanding a moratorium on the building of new nuclear power plants, a moratorium against re-commissioning old nuclear power plants and demanding the phase-out of current nuclear power plants. The continued production of all levels of radioactive waste and transportation to either an

---

95. United Church of Christ Commission for Racial Justice, *Toxic Wastes*; Bullard, *Quest for Environmental Justice*; and Bullard and Johnson, "Environmentalism and Public Policy."
96. M. Walker, "Flooding and Nuclear Waste."
97. Stone, "Near Miss at Fukushima."

interim or permanent repository does nothing to solve the nuclear waste problem in our country.[98]

Although nuclear power may not have as direct a relationship to nuclear colonization and nuclear decolonization as other parts of the cycle, it still plays an important role.

Nuclear Waste (the Grave)

It is no accident that most proposals for nuclear waste sites are within Native Lands. In the cradle-to-grave of nuclear technologies, nuclear waste—also called radioactive waste—is the sometimes forgotten but always present by-product of nuclear production and consumption. Not all nuclear waste is the same, with differing radionuclides, half-lives, forms, and levels of danger to our more-than-human (including humans) ecology.[99] What is true of all nuclear waste, however, is that it contains radioactive nuclides that need to be contained until there is no longer a threat to ecological systems. Containment times and methods depend on the specific radionuclides, their half-lives (or the amount of time it takes for a radioactivity of a radioactive isotope to decrease by half), and their decay cycle. All nuclear waste will eventually decay into stable nuclides that are no longer radioactive, but in some cases, this occurs on a geologic timescale far longer than modern human society has existed. It is for this reason that some scholars have identified the beginning of the Anthropocene—a new planetary era that expresses the impact human technology has had on global ecological/geological systems—as the uranium enrichment that led to the creation of the first atomic bombs and later to nuclear energy.[100] The radioactive by-products from global nuclear technology production and use have left a geographic mark that will be detectable for millennia. This mark reflects the introduction of new radioactive elements

---

98. Indigenous Environmental Network, "Indigenous Anti-Nuclear Statement."
99. Conventionally, the impacts of high-level nuclear waste are described in terms of impacts to humans and to the environment. In an effort to see humans as not separate from the environment, I use the terms *ecology* or *ecological system* to describe the impacts on both humans and more-than-human beings, both of whom are part of an ecological system. My intent here is not to erase the human by using ecology—that is, I am not replacing *environment* with *ecology* and dropping the *human*. Rather, the limits of anthropocentric symbol systems don't provide an easy term to convey the interconnection of humans within ecosystems, so I am making do with *ecology*. Future uses of the term *ecology* will not specify human inclusion in the ecological system but will imply this connection.
100. Biello, "Nuclear Blasts"; and Zalasiewicz et al., "When Did the Anthropocene Begin?"

such as cesium 137 (no known natural sources) and a substantial increase in plutonium 239 and 240 (only exist in trace amounts naturally) that leave an indelible mark within the earth's ecosystem.

The classification and regulation of radioactive waste in the US involves a byzantine and bureaucratic set of actors, regulations, and forms of waste. The Nuclear Regulatory Commission classifies and regulates low-level waste, waste incidental to reprocessing, high-level nuclear waste, transuranic waste, and uranium mill tailings.[101] The focus of this book is on high-level nuclear waste, including waste from reprocessed nuclear fuel (such as surplus plutonium) and spent nuclear fuel, which is the most highly radioactive by-product of the reactions that occur inside nuclear power reactors.[102] There are two main sources of high-level nuclear waste in the US: the commercial nuclear power industry produces spent nuclear fuel, and the federal government (including the Department of Energy and the Department of Defense) produces both reprocessed waste and spent nuclear fuel. The Yucca Mountain and Skull Valley PFS nuclear waste sites were intended to primarily store high-level nuclear waste from nuclear power production.

The world faces a high-level nuclear waste crisis, with harmful nuclear wastes accumulating each year that people consume nuclear power and governments continue to test and build nuclear weapons.[103] The United States is no exception. The crisis in the US worsens with each year nuclear energy is used to produce electricity, with approximately two thousand metric tons of spent nuclear fuel—the by-product of nuclear power operations—produced

---

101. Additionally, the US Department of Energy's Waste Isolation Pilot Plant in New Mexico (a repository for defense-generated transuranic waste) is regulated primarily through the Environmental Protection Agency and the New Mexico Environment Department. US Nuclear Regulatory Commission, "NRC: Radioactive Waste"; and US Department of Energy, Waste Isolation Pilot Plant, "Regulatory Background."

102. Nuclear energy production and consumption also produces other forms of low-level waste. Reprocessing separates uranium and plutonium from used nuclear fuel. The by-products from reprocessing can be used in the development of nuclear weapons. The reprocessed high-level nuclear waste that will be stored in a national repository was reprocessed from reactors for the purpose of nuclear weapons development. High-level nuclear waste is highly radioactive and must be solidified before permanent storage. Spent nuclear fuel is removed from commercial, naval, or research reactors because it is no longer energy efficient. Commercial spent nuclear fuel is not reprocessed because federal law prohibits commercial reprocessing. Spent nuclear fuel is highly radioactive and must be cooled in on-site dry cask storage pools before permanent storage. Most spent nuclear fuel in the country is being stored in on-site pools and some is in dry cask storage.

103. The International Atomic Energy Agency tells us that although thirty countries in the world use nuclear energy, no country has yet opened a permanent deep geologic disposal facility for high-level nuclear waste storage. International Atomic Energy Agency, "Managing Spent Nuclear Fuel."

each year.[104] This is not a new crisis, though it may not be widely recognized by governments, publics, and industries. In 1975 members of the Energy Research and Development Administration "warned that the 'nation's nuclear power program is now approaching a point of crisis' because of the 'problems that have developed in the 'back end' of the fuel cycle.'"[105] Fast-forward twenty-seven years to a 2002 report by former secretary of energy Spencer Abraham that states, "We have a staggering amount of radioactive waste in this country—nearly 100,000,000 gallons of high-level nuclear waste [reprocessed waste] and more than 40,000 metric tons of spent nuclear fuel [primarily from commercial reactors] with more created every day."[106] Fast-forward another nineteen years to September 2021, when a Government Accountability Office report indicates there are eighty-six thousand metric tons of spent nuclear fuel, with a projection of increasing to a total of over 140,000 metric tons considering the lifetime of current nuclear reactors.[107]

Although the volume of high-level nuclear waste in the US is relatively small—a point the nuclear power industry often points to by explaining that all of the country's high-level nuclear waste can be stored in a single football field[108]—what is most concerning is its content, including the level of radioactivity, the long half-lives of the radionuclides, and the potential harm to ecological systems, including human and more-than-human beings. According to the NRC, "Since the only way radioactive waste finally becomes harmless is through decay, which for high-level wastes can take hundreds of thousands of years, the wastes must be stored and finally disposed of in a way that provides adequate protection of the public for a very long time."[109] The timeframe for decay of nuclear isotopes in high-level nuclear waste can range from approximately twenty-eight years (half-life of strontium 90) to twenty-four thousand years (half-life of plutonium 239) to millions of years (iodine 129 has a half-life of 15.7 million years). The NRC continues,

> High-level wastes are hazardous because they produce fatal radiation doses during short periods of direct exposure. For example, 10 years after removal from a reactor, the surface dose rate for a typical spent fuel assembly exceeds 10,000 rem/hour—far greater than the fatal whole-body dose for humans of about 500 rem received all at once. If isotopes from these high-level wastes get into groundwater or rivers, they may enter food chains. The dose pro-

---

104. US Department of Energy, Office of Nuclear Energy, "5 Fast Facts."
105. J. Walker, *Road to Yucca Mountain*, 111.
106. Abraham, "Recommendation," 1.
107. US Government Accountability Office, "Commercial Spent Nuclear Fuel."
108. US Department of Energy, Office of Nuclear Energy, "5 Fast Facts."
109. US Nuclear Regulatory Commission, "NRC: High-Level Waste."

duced through this indirect exposure would be much smaller than a direct-exposure dose, but a much larger population could be exposed.[110]

In the case of the proposed Yucca Mountain site, Environmental Protection Agency standards set radiation dose limits and require the DOE to assess the possible effects of climate change and natural disasters on the waste storage canisters stored in Yucca Mountain for 1 million years.[111] To put this into perspective, modern humans (Homo sapiens) have been on the planet for only approximately two hundred thousand to three hundred thousand years, meaning that high-level nuclear waste storage facilities need to be designed to contain nuclear waste and prevent radioactive exposure for longer than modern humans have existed.

The United States' plan for high-level nuclear waste is primarily governed by Congress through the Nuclear Waste Policy Act.[112] The act specifies the nation's high-level nuclear waste will be stored in a centralized deep underground geologic storage facility run by the Department of Energy, reflecting the international scientific consensus supporting deep geologic storage as the best storage option.[113] An amendment to the Nuclear Waste Policy Act in 1987 specified that instead of a comparative analysis of two sites, only one site would be analyzed: Yucca Mountain. Opponents of the Yucca Mountain site often call the 1987 amendment the "screw Nevada Bill," because it unilaterally chose Nevada, a state with no nuclear power reactors and a relatively small congressional delegation, to be the host of the national repository. In 2002, after a twenty-year process of researching the Yucca Mountain site, the secretary of energy, President George W. Bush, and both houses of Congress authorized the Yucca Mountain repository as the future home to seventy thousand metric tons of high-level nuclear waste.[114] Authorization triggered a process for the DOE to prepare a site license for review by the NRC, which was

110. US Nuclear Regulatory Commission, "NRC: Backgrounder on Radioactive Waste."
111. US Environmental Protection Agency, "40 CFR Part 197."
112. There are some mechanisms the executive branch can use to influence funding and regulation of high-level nuclear waste, and nuclear waste policy has been litigated in the federal court system. For a useful review of the history and politics of high-level nuclear waste before the passage of the act, see J. Walker, *Road to Yucca Mountain*.
113. The act also allows for interim MRS facilities that would allow for temporary storage at one or more repositories before the centralized facility opens. Easterling and Kunreuther, *Dilemma of Siting*; J. Walker, *Road to Yucca Mountain*; and Vandenbosch and Vandenbosch, *Nuclear Waste Stalemate*.
114. Vandenbosch and Vandenbosch report that the Nuclear Waste Policy Act designated seventy thousand metric tons as the capacity for Yucca Mountain to ensure that one site would not take all of the waste for the whole country. The current amount of high-level nuclear waste already exceeds seventy thousand metric tons. Vandenbosch and Vandenbosch, *Nuclear Waste Stalemate*.

submitted in 2008. In 2010 President Obama terminated the licensing process and announced a Blue Ribbon Commission that would make recommendations for future nuclear waste. The commission released a report in 2012 recommending a consent-based process for selecting a new site.[115] The DOE followed suit in 2013 by announcing a plan for both temporary storage sites and a centralized site other than Yucca Mountain. In 2013, as the result of a lawsuit filed against the NRC, a federal appeals court ordered the NRC to continue to evaluate the Yucca Mountain license. The NRC reported in 2015 that while the Yucca site would adhere to most NRC regulations, additional review was needed. Although this additional review was projected to take several years and cost an additional $330 million, Congress has not yet provided budgetary funding to support it.[116] For example, in 2018 and 2019 fiscal requests, President Trump included funding to revive the Yucca Mountain site's licensing process, but Congress choose not to fund it. President Biden has not given any indication of seeking to revive the Yucca Mountain site, and the DOE is continuing to focus its energy on possible interim storage facilities in Texas and New Mexico. As the federal government has not yet opened a high-level nuclear waste repository, spent fuel rods from nuclear reactors are stored on-site at eighty facilities in thirty-five states in the US, mainly at storage pools or in dry casks at running or decommissioned nuclear reactor sites.[117] This reality led to some private corporations seeking out licenses from the NRC for private interim storage facilities, which is the case for the Private Fuel Storage proposal for an interim waste site within Skull Valley Goshute Lands.

The permanent or temporary high-level nuclear waste storage sites that were or are being given serious consideration are disproportionately located within Indigenous Lands. This includes not only the Yucca Mountain and Skull Valley PFS sites but also the MRS program and current efforts to open interim storage sites. Because of anticipated delays in authorizing a permanent storage site by the original 1998 completion date stipulated in the Nuclear Waste Policy Act, Congress created the Office of the Nuclear Waste Negotiator in early 1987 with the goal of finding a site for voluntary temporary MRS. Although both state and local governments and Indigenous nations were approached by the office, "when the siting process was implemented, however, the only parties who ultimately remained in serious consideration turned out to be Native American tribes."[118] At least sixteen Native nations were involved in studies for MRS sites, including the Skull Valley Goshutes,

---

115. Blue Ribbon Commission on America's Nuclear Future, *Report to the Secretary*.
116. US Government Accountability Office, "Disposal."
117. Congressional Research Service, "Nuclear Waste Storage Sites."
118. Gowda and Easterling, "Voluntary Siting and Equity," 917.

who later worked independently with Private Fuel Storage on the temporary high-level nuclear waste facility that is a focus of this book. The incentive for becoming involved in an MRS proposal was an initial $100,000 grant and the possibility of 5 million dollars if the site was selected. LaDuke states, "A good deal of money and influence was intended to persuade tribes to accept the waste."[119] After learning of the Sac and Fox Nation of Oklahoma's participation in the MRS program, Grace Thorpe started the National Environmental Coalition of Native Americans that succeeded in encouraging seventy-five Indigenous nations bordering the US and Canada to establish nuclear-free zones, an enactment of sovereignty and nuclear decolonization.[120] Until a US permanent facility opens, the focus on interim storage continues. As I reviewed edits of this book, the NRC approved a license for a privately owned interim high-level nuclear waste storage facility on Pueblo Lands in New Mexico, which allows for interim storage of five hundred canisters containing 8,680 metric tons for forty years.[121] The Holtec site, although not located within Indigenous reservation Lands, is opposed by a resolution of the All Pueblo Council of Governors.[122]

Furthermore, although current locations of defense-related nuclear waste are not the primary focus of this book, the locations with the largest amounts of high-level nuclear waste are also located on or near Indigenous Lands. The highest levels of nuclear waste are located at Hanford, Idaho National Engineering and Environmental Lab (INEEL), Savannah River, Argonne National Lab West (located within the INEEL site), and the West Valley Demonstration Project. The Hanford site is located on Yakima and Walla Walla traditional Lands, stolen by the US through 1855 treaties with the Yakima and Walla Walla nations. The Confederated Tribes of the Yakama Nation's reservation is due west of the Hanford site. The DOE has a special program to interact with Umatilla, Nez Perce, Wanapum, and Yakama peoples and nations, which all have historical, present, and future connections to the Lands.[123] The Idaho National Engineering and Environmental Lab is located just west of the Fort Hall Indian Reservation (Shoshone-Bannock Lands). The DOE has an agreement with the Shoshone-Bannock Tribes that encourages government-to-

---

119. LaDuke, *All Our Relations*, 103.
120. Thorpe, "Our Homes."
121. NRC licensing does not guarantee that the site will open. The PFS site also had an approved NRC license, and a site in Texas received an NRC license in 2021, but construction has not yet begun. Chamberlain, "Nuclear Colonialism"; Rott, "New Mexico Is Divided"; Feldblum, "New Mexico on Track"; and US Nuclear Regulatory Commission, "NRC Issues License."
122. Chamberlain, "Nuclear Colonialism."
123. US Department of Energy, "Department of Energy's Tribal Program."

government relations.¹²⁴ Savannah River is on the traditional territories of the Yuchi Tribal Organization, the National Council of Muskogee Creek, and the Muskogee Tribal Town Confederacy. In preparing the Savannah River site, the environmental impact statement considered the impact of the site on tribal artifacts subject to the National Historic Preservation Act, the American Indian Religious Freedom Act, and the Native American Graves Protection and Resources Act.¹²⁵ Finally, the West Valley Demonstration Project is located on Seneca Lands.¹²⁶ Low-level nuclear waste sites as well as the Waste Isolation Pilot Plant site are beyond the scope of this chapter and book but follow similar patterns to high-level nuclear waste in terms of locations on or near Indigenous Lands. In all of these cases of high-level nuclear waste sites, Indigenous peoples and nations have advocated for their roles in decision-making. In some cases, there are cooperative agreements in place. In other cases, such as the Yucca Mountain and PFS sites, Indigenous peoples and nations have prevented nuclear waste from coming to their lands.

Later chapters demonstrate how resistance to high-level nuclear waste siting on Native Lands is a form of nuclear decolonization. Here, I will focus on the creation of nuclear-free zones as a form of nuclear decolonization that began with resistance to the MRS program. Grace Thorpe, a member of the Sac and Fox Nation, is credited with starting the push for Indigenous peoples and nations to declare their reservation and trust Lands nuclear-free zones. After participating in a successful campaign to convince her own nation's government to withdraw from an application for a nuclear waste repository in Oklahoma during the MRS process, Thorpe continued to be active in promoting nuclear-free zones for many years. Under the National Environmental Coalition of Native Americans (NECONA), which was founded by Thorpe in 1993, seventy-five Indigenous nations bordering the US and Canada declared their land to be nuclear-free zones by 1997.¹²⁷ LaDuke argues that NECONA effectively contributed to the discontinuation of the MRS program through the nuclear-free zone campaign. In 1998, there were only two Indigenous nations still participating in the MRS program: the Skull Valley Goshutes and Paiutes.¹²⁸ Thorpe saw nuclear-free zones as a key way to assert Indigenous sovereignty and protect Indigenous Lands from nuclear colonization. An appeal to join NECONA reads: "I would like to invite you to consider expressing your sovereign national rights in a different way by joining a grow-

---

124. "Agreement-in-Principle."
125. *Final Environmental Impact Statement.*
126. "Memorandum of Understanding between the Seneca Nation."
127. NECONA, "Nuclear Free Zones."
128. LaDuke, *All Our Relations.*

ing number of tribal governments that are choosing to declare their lands *Nuclear Free Zones.*"[129]

This section has provided a brief overview of how nuclear decolonization and nuclear colonization have affected the entire life cycle of nuclear technologies. I have provided this information to make the point that nuclear decolonization far exceeds the cases I focus on in this book: the Yucca Mountain and Skull Valley PFS sites. Enacting Indigenous sovereignty to protect Indigenous Lands is a core focus of nuclear decolonization, regardless of the specific case.

CONCLUSION

Nuclear decolonization is not only a theoretical lens through which to see Indigenous resistance to nuclear technologies; it is also a set of practices based in Indigenous knowledges. Thus far, there has been limited scholarly engagement with the term *nuclear decolonization* and far more engagement with *nuclear colonization*. This book, then, represents an important turn in the scholarship on these phenomena, a shift from the important work of detailing the strategies of colonization to the equally important work of detailing the tactics of decolonization from the perspective of the Indigenous peoples and nations doing the work. More broadly, it is a framework that, although specific to the relations between Indigenous people and nuclear technologies, might be expanded, challenged, and refined in relation to broader decolonization rhetorics. The next three chapters focus on nuclear decolonization in the cases of Western Shoshone, Southern Paiute, and Skull Valley Goshute efforts to prevent the Yucca Mountain and Skull Valley PFS high-level nuclear waste sites.

---

129. Thorpe, "Statement of Grace Thorpe."

CHAPTER 2

The Indigenous Lands of Yucca Mountain and Skull Valley

When I moved to Utah, one of the first things I did was to drive out to see Skull Valley. I had read about it through my research on high-level nuclear waste siting and, with my relocation to Utah, had decided to expand my past research on the Yucca Mountain site to also include the Skull Valley PFS site. In 2005 the PFS site was still awaiting the NRC's decision on whether to grant a license for the interim high-level nuclear site within the Skull Valley Goshute Reservation (see figure 3). Skull Valley is located about seventy miles southwest from where I live and work in Salt Lake City. Driving west on the 80 gave me an expansive view of the Great Salt Lake to my right and a keen sense of the basin and range geography on my left as I passed the Oquirrh range, Tooele valley, and the Stansbury range, reaching what would soon become the familiar exit 77. Advertised as having no services, the exit gives drivers only one option: to drive south on Highway 196 into Skull Valley. The arid desert ecology of the Skull Valley—part of the larger Great Salt Lake desert—was, to my untrained eye, populated mostly with sage and other shrubs and grasses, some birds visible in the sky, and a distinct absence of water. In the Cedar and Stansbury ranges that flanked the valley, I could see the flora transition into pine trees. Though I would later visit some of the natural springs and learn more about the flora and fauna of the valley and surrounding mountains, my first reaction to the place was that it felt desolate, hot, dusty, and brown—not unlike the reactions of some of the first settlers to visit Skull Valley. While I

THE INDIGENOUS LANDS OF YUCCA MOUNTAIN AND SKULL VALLEY · 61

FIGURE 3. Skull Valley with the Cedar Mountains in the background. Photo taken by Danielle Endres.

knew better than to call it "one of the most rocky, wintry, repulsive wastes that our country or any other can exhibit," as Mark Twain did in *Roughing It*, as a person who had grown up and primarily lived with ocean, redwoods, golden grassy hills, and lush green trees up until moving to Utah, it felt quintessentially desertlike and, to be honest, unappealing. Skull Valley, however, was strikingly similar to several places I had visited in the previous few years within Western Shoshone and Southern Paiute Lands. In the early days of my time spent in the Great Basin, I could not see the beauty, ecological diversity, and sacredness of this place. Over time, and through my deep study of this place and conversations with their first Indigenous inhabitants, my perspective began to shift. Now, when I drive out to Skull Valley, I relish a visit to Horseshoe Springs, a chance to feel the stillness, a sighting of a red-tailed hawk, or the view of the blue sky against the peaks of the Cedar and Stansbury ranges. I can feel, not just understand, why Margene Bullcreek and others worked so hard to protect it.

There are many ways one might define or characterize the Great Basin as Lands—a rich and complex ecology of relationships between plants, humans, animals, water, climate, mountains, valleys, and more.[1] The Great Basin is a

---

1. Recall that I use *Lands* to reference the entire ecological system of relations in a place. Liboiron, *Pollution Is Colonialism*.

large desert bordered by the Sierra Nevada to the west, the Wasatch range to the east, the Columbia Plateau to the north, and the Mojave Desert to the south. It spans nearly all of what settlers named Nevada, as well as portions of what settlers named Utah, Oregon, and California. The name Great Basin may belie the basin and range topography, a series of mountains and valleys that create more of a rolling feel to the landscape than, as those who have not been there might imagine, a smooth bowl. The Great Basin is so named because of its internal drainage system in which water never reaches the sea—the Great Salt Lake is one of the larger catchment basins within the region, which is spotted with freshwater rivers, springs, and lakes. While arid deserts are often seen by settlers, especially those from different bioregions of the continent, as lifeless wastelands, the Great Basin actually hosts an incredibly complex array of biodiversity and endemic species. Moreover, the Great Basin, due in part to its geological qualities, includes abundant minerals, metals, and rocks, including uranium, coal, silver, and copper.

Yucca Mountain and Skull Valley are both part of the Great Basin. The deep connections Western Shoshone, Southern Paiute, and Skull Valley Goshute peoples and nations have with this region form a key foundation for their efforts to protect it from high-level nuclear waste sites. Understanding the Great Basin, and more specifically Yucca Mountain and Skull Valley, from the perspective of Indigenous peoples and nations is essential for understanding the rhetorical tactics of nuclear decolonization I will amplify in the following chapters. This chapter offers a narrative of Indigenous peoples' and nations' relations to the Great Basin region and Yucca Mountain and Skull Valley. I begin broadly with Great Basin and then narrow to retell the stories of Western Shoshone, Southern Paiute, and Skull Valley Goshute relationality with Lands in this region. The chapter ends with specific discussions of the importance of Yucca Mountain and Skull Valley to Western Shoshone, Southern Paiute, and Skull Valley Goshute peoples and nations.

INDIGENOUS LANDS OF THE GREAT BASIN

Humans have lived in the Great Basin since time immemorial. Origin stories and cosmologies say Indigenous peoples were placed here by the Creator. While there are a variety of Indigenous peoples and nations with homelands in the Great Basin, I focus here on Western Shoshone, Southern Paiute, and Skull Valley Goshute peoples and nations. Western Shoshone, Skull Valley Goshute, and Southern Paiute are not the names that the peoples themselves use; they refer to themselves as "the people"—*Newe* in Western Shoshone and

Skull Valley Goshute, and *Nuwuvi* in Southern Paiute.[2] Though varied, creation stories of Shoshone (including Western Shoshone and Skull Valley Goshute) and Paiute peoples often feature coyote and sometimes his brother wolf.[3] Most versions of the story feature coyote carrying a basket or jug of humans across the Great Basin.[4] Coyote lets people out or people jump out at various places, resulting in the people being scattered throughout the Great Basin, representing the traditional territories of different Shoshone, Paiute, and Goshute peoples. In one version of the creation story,

> the Newe were placed in their homeland by the Creator (Uteen Taikwahn).... Once placed on the land, two native women instructed coyote to carry a large, pitched water-basket with him on his journey into the Basin area. Coyote was specifically told not to open the lid. Moved by irrepressible curiosity, he periodically opened the basket during his trip. The beings concealed inside jumped out here and there.[5]

A Skull Valley Goshute version of the story features Sinav, who encountered a mother and daughter living in the middle of the Great Salt Lake. As they bore children, they were placed in a jug.

> Finally the older woman told Sinav to go south and take the jug with him. ... At first as he walked along, the jug was light and easy to carry. It became heavier. After a while, he had to set it down. He went on again and set it down again.... Sinav heard a buzzing noise like a bee inside the jug. He wanted to look. When he began to open it, men jumped out and made a lot of dust. They knocked him over and ran away. Three times he removed the stopper and people come out. He watched them. They ran in all directions. They were Shoshoni, Ute, Paiute, and other tribes. The last man to come out was all covered with dust. He was a Goshute [*Gosip,* meaning "dust"]. He is tougher than other people; he is bullet proof.[6]

---

2. Smoak, "Great Basin"; Stoffle, Arnold, and Bulletts, "Talking with Nature"; Harney, *Way It Is*; and Harney, *Nature Way*.

3. Steward, "Some Western Shoshoni Myths"; Smoak, "Great Basin"; Crum, *Road on Which We Came*; Fowler, *Native Americans and Yucca Mountain*.

4. Variations include Wolf and Sinav as the ones carrying the basket or jug. Steward, "Some Western Shoshoni Myths." Historian Greg Smoak has challenged some of anthropologist Julian H. Steward's analysis and explanation of Great Basin peoples as environmentally determined. The Steward book cited here, though flawed, is a collection of Shoshone stories that are presented without analysis. Smoak, "Great Basin."

5. Crum, *Road on Which We Came*, 1.

6. Steward, "Some Western Shoshoni Myths," 267–68.

A Nuwuvi version of the story goes like this:

> The Paiutes trace their origin to the story of Tabuts, the wise wolf who decided to carve many different people out of sticks. His plan was to scatter them evenly around the earth so that everyone would have a good place to live, but Tabuts had a mischievous younger brother, Shinangwav the coyote. Shinangwav cut open the sack and people fell out in bunches all over the world. The people were angry at this treatment, and that is why other people always fight. The people left in the sack were the Southern Paiutes. Tabuts blessed them and put them in the very best place.[7]

These stories explain the dispersal of the original inhabitants in the Great Basin—relatives of present-day Newe and Nuwuvi peoples.

In much settler-conducted historical and ethnographic research, Great Basin Indigenous peoples were often grouped together and conveyed as unsophisticated, nomadic, weak, lacking political structure, and overly determined by the harsh desert landscape.[8] Yet, Great Basin Indigenous peoples and nations paint a different picture of precontact Great Basin societies that were diverse; had nuanced social, kinship, and political organization; comprised both nomadic and farming communities; and were sophisticated in their relationships with the more-than-human world. Racist portrayals of Great Basin Indigenous peoples as simplistic "Digger Indians" stem from early encounters with travelers and settlers who encountered unfamiliar peoples and landscapes and mistook different lifeways for a lack of civilization.[9] Yet, there were some early positive accounts, particularly of first contact with the Southern Paiute peoples by Spanish missionaries that, not surprisingly, get lost in the dominant settler narrative.[10] Early studies by settler anthropologist Julian Steward and his students in the 1940s and '50s are some of the few written records of Great Basin peoples. While widely cited, this research is deeply flawed and often criticized for perpetuating the widespread stereotype of Great Basin Indigenous peoples as simple, solely nomadic, savage, and uncivilized.[11]

Western Shoshone, Skull Valley Goshute, and Southern Paiute peoples generally organize themselves in kinship groups. Prior to settler encroach-

---

7. Utah American Indian Digital Archive, "The Paiutes."

8. Stoffle and Zedeno, "Historical Memory and Ethnographic Perspectives," 232.

9. It is important to note that some colonizer accounts did convey Southern Paiute peoples as farmers, but this often gets lost in descriptions of Great Basin Indians as nomadic. Stoffle and Zedeno, 230–32.

10. Stoffle and Zedeno.

11. Smoak, "Great Basin"; Stoffle and Zedeno, "Historical Memory and Ethnographic Perspectives," 232; and Hebner and Plyler, *Southern Paiute*, 3–4.

ment, each kinship group had a home range not governed by a system of exclusive property rights but rather shared with other kinship groups through protocols of permission and relationship.[12] Western Shoshone, Skull Valley Goshute, and Southern Paiute peoples hunted, harvested, and, in some cases, grew crops, resulting in extensive knowledge of and relationships with a wide array of plants and animals that they engaged with for food, shelter, tools, medicine, and ceremony.[13] While there was Native movement throughout the Great Basin region, this movement was not random. As Western Shoshone elder Corbin Harney puts it: "The seasons are the reason they [Newe] kept moving from one place to another all the time."[14] Newe and Nuwuvi kinship groups had both territories with semipermanent settlements as well as temporary camps that would be returned to over and over again for harvesting, hunting, and ceremony. Oral histories indicate that when kinship groups visited another group's territory, they needed permission to use the local group's resources.[15] In the case of Southern Paiute peoples, there is also evidence of precontact farming practices, including the story that Southern Paiute farmers held corn in the air to greet Escalante and Dominguez in 1776, the first known contact between Paiutes and European colonists.[16] Farming, however, did not preclude Southern Paiute peoples from moving and traveling to camps for hunting, harvesting, and ceremonies. Kinship groups throughout the Great Basin were connected regionally and nationally through trade, political relations, marriages, and information flows.[17] While there are enough similarities between Great Basin Indigenous peoples to warrant some generalizations, it is also important to emphasize their diversity. Indigenous peoples in the Great Basin maintain different spiritual, political, cultural, and kinship relations; the similar but also varied origin stories noted above are one example.

Great Basin Indigenous peoples and nations have strong connections to their homelands, hold on to cultural practices, and continue to resist settler colonial attempts to control their Lands (see figure 4). The 1848 Treaty of Guadalupe Hidalgo at the close of the Mexican-American War transferred, without the consent or participation of Native peoples and nations, the Great Basin region to the US and represented the start of concerted efforts to colonize and remove Indigenous peoples from the Great Basin in the second half

---

12. Smoak, "Great Basin."
13. Pritzker, "Great Basin"; Smoak, "Great Basin"; and Stoffle et al., *Native American Cultural Resource Studies*.
14. Harney, *Way It Is*, 73.
15. Fowler, *Native Americans and Yucca Mountain*, 13.
16. Stoffle and Zedeno, "Historical Memory and Ethnographic Perspectives," 230.
17. Stoffle et al., *Native American Cultural Resource Studies*, 34.

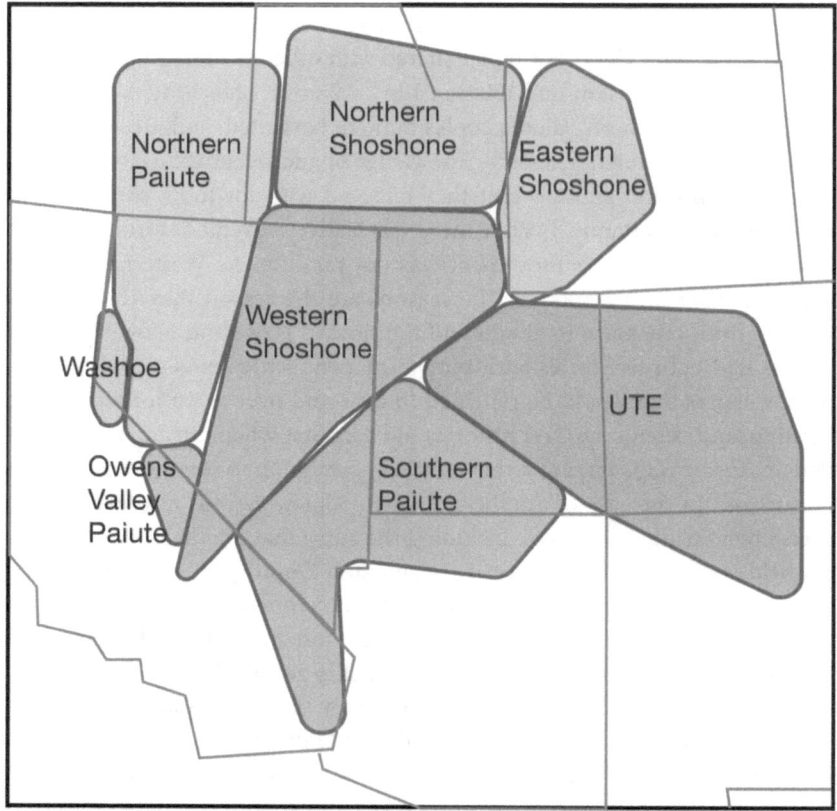

FIGURE 4. Traditional territories of Great Basin and Colorado Plateau Indigenous peoples. Skull Valley Goshutes are included in Western Shoshone territories. Map drawn by M. Wayne Davis.

of the century. Yet, Great Basin peoples had already experienced the "shockwaves" from Spanish occupations in the Rio Grande Valley, introducing guns, diseases, horses, and different economic systems that transformed life in the Great Basin.[18] Despite these "advance agents" of colonialism,[19] British and American fur traders were the first to travel through the Great Basin region, followed by the creation of migration trails for settlers traveling west. As Barry Pritzker notes, "Because of the isolation and relatively harsh environment of the Great Basin, it was the last region in the contiguous United States to be taken over by non-natives. However, the change, when it did come, was rapid, largely because the ecology of the region was so fragile."[20] Settlers from

---

18. Smoak, "Great Basin," 382.
19. Smoak, 382.
20. Pritzker, "Great Basin," 222.

the Church of Jesus Christ of Latter-day Saints (LDS) and miners were some of the most aggressive settlers seeking to occupy and settle land in the Great Basin for spiritual and economic motivations. US settlement of the Great Basin resulted in a massive decline in Indigenous populations; the first studies of Great Basin Indigenous peoples were based on already depleted population numbers.[21] Eventually, through settler treaties, executive orders, and policies, Great Basin Newe and Nuwuvi peoples and nations were violently pushed into a series of Western Shoshone, Goshute, and Paiute governments with reservation boundaries representing a fraction of the size of their traditional and ancestral territories. Contact with settlers resulted in big changes to social and political ties, and, in some cases, changed the composition and definition of sociopolitical groups. In the region where Yucca Mountain is, contact with American settlers, for example, resulted not only in decimated populations but also in more intermarriage between Shoshone and Paiute peoples who shared the region.[22] American settler colonists imposed designations of Western Shoshone, Southern Paiute, and Skull Valley Goshute—including multiple reservations and colonies, tribal governments, and ethnic categories—in ways that are muddied by practices and policies of removal, placing different Indigenous peoples onto the same reservations, and misrepresentations, including the use of the terms *Northern Paiutes* and *Southern Paiutes* for groups that are not branches of the same peoples.[23] Western Shoshone, Skull Valley Goshute, and Southern Paiute peoples and nations never stopped resisting settler violence, in many cases insisting on remaining in their traditional Lands instead of relocating. The remaining sections of this chapter first engage Western Shoshone, Southern Paiute, and Skull Valley Goshute relations with Great Basin Lands and then focus specifically on the Yucca Mountain and Skull Valley regions.

WESTERN SHOSHONES

As Western Shoshone historian Steven Crum details in *The Road on Which We Came*, Western Shoshone peoples lived within the Great Basin region since time immemorial. Crum narrates how Western Shoshone bands that lived in the many valleys throughout what settlers named Nevada reacted to and resisted settler attempts to claim their Lands. American settler encroachment on Newe Lands ramped up in the mid- to late 1800s, in part because the

---

21. Stoffle et al., *Native American Cultural Resource Studies.*
22. Stoffle et al., 54.
23. Smoak, "Great Basin."

Treaty of Guadalupe Hidalgo in 1848 declared the Great Basin region a territory of the US without the consent of Great Basin Indigenous peoples and nations. For the Western Shoshones, the 1863 Treaty of Ruby Valley recognized 60 million acres within what settlers named Southern California, Nevada, and Idaho as Western Shoshone Lands.[24] The treaty did not grant ownership of the Lands to the federal government but allowed right of way passage, mining rights, and rights to build towns to support mining. The treaty also gave the US president the authority to create reservations for Western Shoshone peoples and nations.

Following the 1863 Treaty of Ruby Valley, the federal government tried many times to relocate Western Shoshone families to reservations, allotment lands, and colonies. As Crum tells it, a reservation was created at Duck Valley (in northwestern Nevada) in 1880, but only a small portion of Western Shoshone peoples moved there, mainly those who had traditionally lived in that region. For many years, a large population of what the US government called nonreservation Western Shoshones continued to live in their traditional homelands and refused to relocate to Duck Valley. After the Indian Reorganization Act of 1934, the federal government created four new Western Shoshone reservations, set aside additional allotment acreage, and ultimately increased the land base with twenty-four thousand new acres. These efforts were more successful than previous attempts because the Indian Bureau (the present-day Bureau of Indian Affairs) "accepted the Shoshones' cultural trait of deep attachment to the land and took the initiative in creating reservations in some native Shoshone valleys."[25] Regardless, due to both size constraints on reservations and attachment to Lands, many Western Shoshone families continued to live outside of the reservations within traditional homelands.

Understanding the contemporary political structure of Western Shoshone peoples and its relationship to pretreaty kinship, cultural, and political organization is complicated. The moniker *Western Shoshones* is a colonialist construct, created to demarcate those Great Basin Shoshones generally living in what is now colonially called Nevada, southeastern California bordering Nevada, and the border of Nevada and Oregon. There are also Eastern Shoshone, Northern Shoshone, Northwestern Shoshone, and Shoshone-Bannock peoples spanning what settlers call Utah, Idaho, and Wyoming. In the words of Corbin Harney:

---

24. The treaty was ratified by US Senate in 1866, confirmed by President Grant in 1869.
25. Crum, *Road on Which We Came*, 97.

One time the Shoshone roamed this country before the Europeans came into this country and divided it. According to the Shoshone people we roamed in seven different states, California, Nevada, Utah, Idaho, Montana, Wyoming, and Colorado. This was Shoshone territory, where they roamed and hunted for different things like buffalo in the east, salmon in the north, and they even went down to the coast of California near where San Diego is today. The 1863 treaty restricted the land on which the Shoshone roamed and told us we were a different tribe from each other, Western, Eastern, Northern, and Southern, but we were all one Shoshone tribe at the time. They wanted to divide and conquer us, they're still trying to divide us today.[26]

Just as there are many divisions, bands, kinship relations, and political structures among Shoshone peoples and nations, there is no one Western Shoshone nation or kinship group but rather a series of Western Shoshone nations that self-govern within their reservations and colonies. Some of these reservations, such as Duck Valley, are integrated with Northern Paiute peoples. Some Western Shoshone communities resisted moving to reservation locations outside their ancestral lands and are not represented in the political structure of contemporary Western Shoshone governments. For many years, an entity called the Western Shoshone National Council worked to create policy and govern across the dispersed reservations and governments. The council collaborated on Lands protection and other issues of shared concern for the Western Shoshone governments at each reservation. The Yucca Mountain site was one such issue of shared concern.

SOUTHERN PAIUTES

Southern Paiute is a contemporary designation for about sixteen Great Basin Indigenous peoples.[27] Traditional and ancestral Southern Paiute territories span almost eighty thousand square feet of what settlers named southwest Utah, southern Nevada, northwest Arizona, and southeast California.[28] Some Southern Paiute peoples and nations resided in or interacted with the Col-

---

26. Harney, *Nature Way*, 37.
27. Southern Paiute nations include the Las Vegas Paiute Tribe, Kaibab Band of Paiute Indians, Moapa Band of Paiute Indians, Paiute Indian Tribe of Utah, Cedar City Band of Paiutes, Kanosh Band of Paiutes, Koosharem Band of Paiutes, Indian Peaks Band of Paiutes, Shivwits Band of Paiutes, Chemehuevi Indian Tribe, Pahrump Band of Paiutes, and San Juan Southern Paiute Tribe of Arizona.
28. Stoffle, Arnold, and Bulletts, "Talking with Nature."

orado Plateau region in addition to the Great Basin. While some Southern Paiute peoples and kinship groups, including those in the region near Yucca Mountain, practiced agriculture prior to the 1800s, Southern Paiute peoples primarily moved around their territories seasonally in small autonomous groups to harvest different foods and visit hot springs.[29] Anthropologist Martha Knack writes, "The people's movements were far from random. . . . Their movements were based on extensive knowledge of the growth preferences of specific plants and solid familiarity with the seasonal blooming and ripening of each species."[30] Southern Paiute peoples had deep respect for and knowledge about their Lands, seeing them not as barren wastelands but as a source of life and relations.[31]

First contact with Europeans is assumed to be in 1776 via a Spanish expedition through the region. Historical and archeological evidence, flawed as it is, indicates that contact with the Spanish did not result in Southern Paiute peoples adopting Spanish practices, including horse riding, meaning that Southern Paiute peoples mainly carried on with traditional practices for many years after first contact.[32] Yet, by 1830, settlers began to heavily use a trail that had been established by the Spanish, which started impacting Southern Paiute communities. In addition to Spanish slavery practices, Diné and Ute people who adopted the horse also often raided Southern Paiute communities to secure slaves for trading.[33] LDS settlers arrived in the Great Basin in 1847, representing a wave of aggressive settlement, displacement, and violence toward Southern Paiutes. Like other Great Basin Native nations, settler attempts at domination were "historically late, unofficial, local, and instantaneous."[34] Southern Paiute peoples did not seek to address settler encroachment with war but rather engaged with newly formed settler communities.[35]

In the late 1800s, the settler state entered into political relations with Southern Paiute peoples and nations, well after non-Native settlers had already become rooted in the region. Southern Paiutes, prior to colonization, lived in kinship groups and districts across their vast territory.[36] This system

---

29. Southern Paiute farming included cultivation of corn, squash, sunflowers, beans, and other native plants, particularly in the Muddy River, Virgin River, and Santa Clara Creek regions. Even those who cultivated crops still moved around the region. Fowler and Fowler, "Notes"; and Knack, *Boundaries Between*.
30. Knack, *Boundaries Between*, 14.
31. Knack, *Boundaries Between*; and Stoffle, Arnold, and Bulletts, "Talking with Nature."
32. Fowler and Fowler, "Notes."
33. Fowler and Fowler.
34. Knack, *Boundaries Between*, 3.
35. Knack.
36. Stoffle, Arnold, and Bulletts, "Talking with Nature."

of organization was disrupted via settler American encroachment, resulting in many different nations, governments, and reservations created for Southern Paiute peoples that did not always align with Southern Paiute kinship and political organization structures. There is no one Southern Paiute nation or government entity but rather Southern Paiute peoples and nations aligned with the various reservations that were created. Although "the Southern Paiute had no treaties with the U.S. government," a series of reservations and associated Indigenous governments were established, including the Moapa Reservation (1872), Shivwits Reservation (1891), Chemehuevi (1907), Kaibab (1907) Las Vegas Colony (1911), and others.[37] These reservations reduced Southern Paiute Lands to about 1 percent of their original territories, often displacing Southern Paiutes and moving them to less desirable areas that could not sustain Southern Paiute lifestyle and practices.[38] As a result, many Southern Paiutes lived off reservation and integrated, but did not assimilate, into settler towns.[39]

> Southern Paiute reservations are a series of postage stamps scattered throughout their homelands. This points to another Southern Paiute trait: they simply would not leave their lands. They rejected efforts to move them north to Fort Duchesne, Utah, with the Ute, who were traditional enemies and considered to be powerful sorcerers. After that failure, J. W. Powell, a special commissioner of Indian affairs as of the spring of 1873, tried to move them all to Moapa, Nevada, which had potential. But that reservation was crushed down from three thousand and nine hundred square miles to less than two square miles by pressure from mining companies. Initial willingness to move by some Southern Paiute vanished. By 1879, the Moapa subagent declared with a straight face, "As for the Indians, they are doing well. None of them live on the reservation now."[40]

Southern Paiutes hold a deep attachment to their Lands despite the many settler colonial attempts to take control of those Lands. Southern Paiute peoples and nations were and are resilient in defending their Lands.

---

37. Hebner and Plyler, *Southern Paiute*, 18.
38. Stoffle, Arnold, and Bulletts, "Talking with Nature."
39. Knack, *Boundaries Between*.
40. Hebner and Plyler, *Southern Paiute*, 12.

SKULL VALLEY GOSHUTES

Skull Valley Goshute peoples have always lived in the Skull Valley, just southwest of the Great Salt Lake. Recall the creation story above that tells of the tough but dusty Goshutes emerging last from Sinav's jug. As historian Dennis Defa notes, "At the time of the first contacts with whites, the Goshute people lived in the desert regions southwest of the Great Salt Lake."[41] He continues, "Before the white invasion of the Goshute homeland, the [Goshutes] were largely concentrated in small camps in a crescent area around the southern half of the Great Salt Lake Desert."[42] Goshute peoples are ethnically Shoshone, closely related to Western Shoshone and other Shoshone peoples and nations. The Skull Valley Goshutes are one of two contemporary bands of Goshute peoples and nations, the other being the Confederated Tribes of the Goshute Reservation located on ancestral Lands in Ibapah (also known as Deep Creek) straddling the border of what settlers named Utah and Nevada. Deep Creek hosts the large majority of Goshute peoples. Yet, the small band of Skull Valley Goshutes have contiguously occupied the Skull Valley since time immemorial.[43]

Prior to 1850, Goshute peoples and nations had sporadic contact with European and American settlers including slave traders, fur traders, settlers taking the Oregon and California trails, and eventually LDS settlers who stayed, stealing Indigenous Lands. Similar to Western Shoshone and Southern Paiute peoples and nations, Skull Valley Goshute peoples and nations are deeply attached to traditional and ancestral Lands and have successfully resisted numerous settler relocation and assimilation efforts. As a result, the Skull Valley Goshute Reservation is within traditional homelands, although it is just a fraction of the size (see figure 5). As historian Steven Crum wrote:

> So strongly were the Skull Valley and other Goshute bands tied to their native homeland that they delineated their tribal territory in a treaty negotiated with federal officials in 1863. Although this treaty was primarily a pact of "peace and friendship," it had provisions relating to the Goshute land base. In Article 5 the Goshute bands "described" and "defined" the territory they

---

41. Defa, "Goshute Indians of Utah," 73.
42. Defa, 75.
43. I call this a small band because over the years I have been involved, the Skull Valley Goshute nation's membership has ebbed and flowed in the 100 to 140 range, with a smaller portion living on the reservation.

FIGURE 5. Entrance to the Skull Valley Goshute Reservation. Photo taken by Danielle Endres.

had "occupied" and "claimed" as their birthright. This area consisted of a sizable portion of western Utah, including Skull Valley.[44]

Importantly, this treaty was not a land cession but an agreement of peace in which Goshute peoples did not give up sovereignty.[45] The treaty also included a provision that reservations would be created, which was later used by Goshute people to push against an 1864 US settler government plan to move them to the Uintah and Ouray Reservation in northeastern Utah, populated by Ute peoples. In 1869 Utah's Indian agent J. E. Tourtellotte (Seneca) recommended two small reservation areas for the Goshutes, one in Deep Creek and one in Skull Valley. Although his recommendation was not acted on immediately, the resilience and insistence of Skull Valley Goshute peoples eventually led to the creation of the Skull Valley Goshute Reservation in 1912, which was expanded in 1917 and 1918 (see figure 6). As Crum puts it, "This action was important because it established the first permanent Goshute reservation, created forty-nine years after the signing of the 1863 treaty."[46]

---

44. Crum, "Skull Valley Band," 253.
45. Defa, "Goshute Indians of Utah."
46. Crum, "Skull Valley Band," 260.

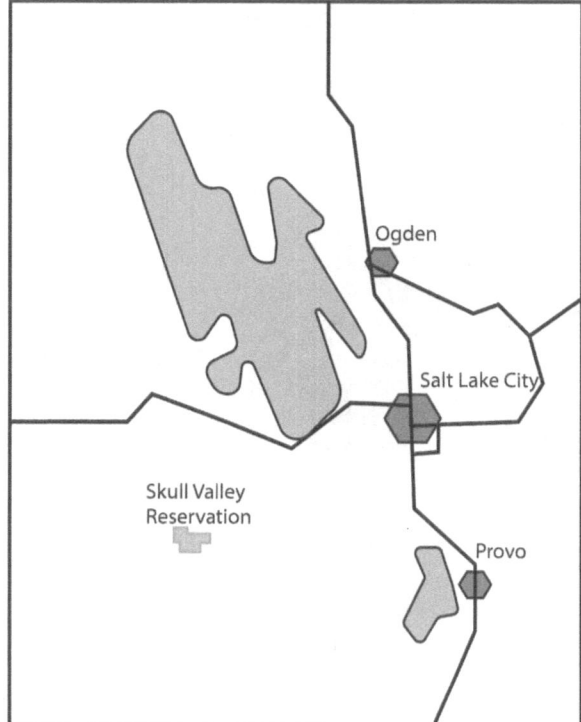

FIGURE 6. Map of Skull Valley Goshute Reservation. Map drawn by M. Wayne Davis.

Even after the treaty and establishment of their reservation, Skull Valley Goshutes continued to resist pressure from the US settler government to relocate to the larger Goshute community at the Ibapah reservation. Little Moon and Sam Moon wrote in a letter to the BIA: "The same fellows named above have been trying to move us away to Ibapah, Utah. We told them we are not going to move. We want to stay here on Skull Valley Reservation. They want us to join the self government [Indian Reorganization Act]. We don't want to take it. They are forcing us to sign the self government papers."[47] Moreover, the Skull Valley Goshute nation successfully resisted efforts during the Termination era. As told by Crum, Skull Valley Goshute peoples "refused to consent to federal termination, and five of the leaders, Ennis Moon, Tom Wash, Iby Bear, Richard Bear, and Lisa Moon Neck, state specifically: 'We don't want to sell our reservation land. . . . This is our territory and our reservation land for our use [as] long as we Indians [are] living on it.' Their opposition proved to be effective, and the Skull Valley Reservation was not abolished as a result of

---

47. As cited in Crum, 265.

the termination drive of the 1950s."[48] The Skull Valley Goshute Reservation is currently 17,920 acres of land in the middle of Skull Valley. Among the small population of Skull Valley Goshute peoples (hovering around a little over one hundred enrolled members), only a small number of families—including the late Margene Bullcreek and her family—live on the reservation. While the reservation is within a portion of traditional territories, the reservation does not include the Cedar and Stansbury foothills and mountains, which were important places for gathering food and spirituality. This, along with the numerous toxic facilities surrounding the reservation, puts the Skull Valley Goshute nation in a difficult position with limited options for economic development. Deep rifts have developed within the Skull Valley Goshute nation over how to enact sovereignty, preserve culture, and survive within a settler colonial system that severely limits their livelihood.

Western Shoshone, Southern Paiute, and Skull Valley Goshute peoples and nations, as presented in the brief information here, are all indigenous to the Great Basin region. They are deeply connected to their ancestral territories throughout what settlers named Utah, Nevada, and California. A small fraction of these traditional territories are contemporary sovereign reservation Lands, but these arbitrary boundaries belie the long-standing relationships that Western Shoshone, Southern Paiute, and Skull Valley Goshute peoples and nations continue to have with their traditional homelands, even those set aside by the US as federal land, as is the case for Yucca Mountain. Due to settler perceptions of the deserts of the Great Basin as wastelands, it is not surprising that the settler government and nuclear industry saw these areas as suitable for nuclear waste.[49] Yet, for Indigenous peoples and nations from the Great Basin, these Lands are part of them. They have always been Indigenous Lands. The next two sections of this chapter focus on Western Shoshone, Southern Paiute, and Skull Valley Goshute relationships with the two proposed locations for high-level nuclear waste.

THE YUCCA MOUNTAIN SITE

Mountains are important spiritually to both Western Shoshone and Southern Paiute peoples and nations. Mountains can be places where puha (Southern Paiute for *power*) circulates, sources of creation, sites for ceremony, and pathways to the afterlife. Moreover, within the basin and range, mountains sup-

---

48. Crum, 267.
49. Endres, "From Wasteland to Waste Site."

ported different forms of life, such as plants, animals, and rocks that Western Shoshone and Southern Paiute peoples used for sustenance, medicine, and ceremony.⁵⁰ Western Shoshone and Southern Paiute concerns over Yucca Mountain are not limited to Yucca Mountain itself but also include other nearby mountains in the region. Speaking about a visit she had with Western Shoshone and Southern Paiute elders and spiritual leaders at Yucca Mountain, anthropologist Catherine Fowler notes, "All participants at the site visit [to Yucca Mountain hosted by the DOE] felt particularly angry that a repository ('dump') of such dangerous material should even be considered so close to these sacred mountains [Mt. Charleston, Telescope Peak, Bare Mountain, and Timber Mountain]."⁵¹ Yucca Mountain, then, is not only a sacred mountain itself, but it is also situated in a place where there are other sacred mountains.

Yucca Mountain is in the southwest region of Newe Sogobia and the western region of Nuwuvi Lands, just east of the Armargosa Desert. It is a mountain made by volcanic activity over 12 million years ago. Yucca Mountain, and the larger area that it lies within, is a border region between Western Shoshone and Southern Paiute territories and has therefore been related with and occupied by Indigenous peoples since time immemorial.⁵² Western Shoshone and Southern Paiute origin stories begin in the Great Basin, not telling of movement from other places. While removal, migration, and reservation establishment in the late 1800s and early 1900s altered where people lived and worked, current Western Shoshone and Southern Paiute reservations, colonies, and allotments are all within the larger boundaries of traditional homelands. The same is true for Yucca Mountain. Although not located within Indigenous reservation Lands, there is no doubt that Yucca Mountain is a cultural, spiritual, and treaty-bound site for Western Shoshone and Southern Paiute peoples and nations.⁵³ I will engage with anthropological studies of Yucca Mountain, and the broader Nevada Test Site, that were conducted as a part of the site characterization process for the proposed nuclear waste repository. These are important because they specifically consider Western Shoshone and Southern Paiute peoples' and nations' connections with Yucca Mountain and the surrounding region. The studies, though conducted by non-Indigenous anthropologists, facilitated official physical access to Yucca Mountain—a restricted

---

50. Fowler, *Native Americans and Yucca Mountain*; and Stoffle et al., *Native American Cultural Resource Studies*.
51. Fowler, *Native Americans and Yucca Mountain*, 29.
52. Stoffle et al., *Native American Cultural Resource Studies*, 29.
53. Crum, *Road on Which We Came*; Fowler, *Native Americans and Yucca Mountain*; Harney, *Way It Is*; Harney, *Nature Way*; Kuletz, *Tainted Desert*; and Stoffle et al., *Native American Cultural Resource Studies*.

federal site—for Western Shoshone and Southern Paiute peoples and nations for the first time in years.

The Nuclear Waste Policy Act specified that whatever site would be chosen for a national nuclear waste repository required consultation with affected Indigenous nations (i.e., affected tribal governments) and, if relevant, attention to laws such as the Native American Graves Protection and Repatriation Act and the American Indian Religious Freedom Act. To do so, the federal government called for anthropological studies that would survey Indigenous cultural resources in the Yucca Mountain region. Studies led by Richard Stoffle and another set by Catherine Fowler confirm ongoing Western Shoshone and Southern Paiute relationships with Yucca Mountain and the surrounding area up until but also after the area was restricted by the federal government for military use through the Tonopah Bombing Range, Nellis Airforce Range, and later the Nevada Test Site (now called the Nevada National Security Site) between 1940 and 1951. Richard Stoffle and Michael Evans wrote: "The Western Shoshone and Southern Paiutes are the American Indian ethnic groups having the most direct affiliation with cultural resources that may be located in the Yucca Mountain area."[54] Although anthropological studies can be flawed accounts of Native history and at odds with oral histories and Indigenous goals, these studies included some collaboration with Western Shoshone and Southern Paiute communities, interviews with elders and political leaders, outreach to descendants of communities, and site visits to Yucca Mountain and surrounding areas in which participants engaged with the land, plants, and animals (in some cases, for the first time since the land was restricted in the 1940s and 1950s). Regardless, some Western Shoshone peoples have been critical of these studies because the US government limited their focus to identifying historic cultural resources over considering the contemporary needs of the nations.[55] According to Urban Environmental Research and Ian Zabarte, "The focus on cultural resources or spiritual belief leaves little room for other existing rights and interests of the tribe to be considered, and this myopia manifests itself in the Yucca Mountain controversy and claims made by Native Americans."[56] They are not perfect. For the purposes of this chapter,

---

54. Stoffle and Evans, "American Indians."
55. Zabarte, "View of the Western Shoshone."
56. This is not to say that culture and spiritual connections to Yucca Mountain are not important to Western Shoshone and Southern Paiute peoples and nations. Rather, the criticism is about the focus on identifying resources toward compliance with federal laws such as the Native American Historic Preservation Act as opposed to engagement in government-to-government relations. Urban Environmental Research and Zabarte, *Tribal Concerns*, 14.

they stand alongside what Western Shoshone and Southern Paiute peoples already know: Yucca Mountain is part of their homelands.

Western Shoshone and Southern Paiute origin stories narrate how they were placed or distributed in their territories, which include Yucca Mountain and its surroundings, by the creator. Anthropological studies report Indigenous peoples "have lived on and around Yucca Mountain for thousands of years," with clovis points for hunting game, tools, sandals, baskets, cans, shovels, and burial sites all serving as evidence of continuous use of Yucca Mountain and the broader Nevada Test Site prior to, during, and after contact with colonizers.[57] Many of the anthropological studies are not solely focused on Yucca Mountain but also on the broader range of the Nevada Test Site. Stoffle and colleagues' studies identify three districts within the NTS—Ogwe'pi (Oasis Valley-Western Shoshone), Eso (White Rock Spring-Western Shoshone), and Ash Meadows-Southern Paiute—that used Yucca Mountain. Each district included a cluster of permanent settlements linked by kinship within a territory where food and medicinal plants were hunted and harvested and, in the case of Southern Paiute, crops were cultivated. In addition to these districts, there were also temporary camps throughout the Yucca Mountain and NTS region that were used annually for water springs, harvesting pinyon pine nuts and wild seeds, collecting plants, and hunting game, not only by members of the districts but also by other kinship groups of Western Shoshone and Southern Paiute peoples.[58]

As late as the 1900s, there were few American settlers in the Yucca Mountain region, such that Indigenous residents outnumbered non-Indigenous residents. Up until then, little changed in terms of access to and usage of this region. Yet, the 1900s brought massive change to the Yucca Mountain region. From the early 1900s through 1910, a mining boom in the region precipitated much more American conquest, with settlers eventually outnumbering Native peoples and creating dramatic negative effects on the environment. Once the mining boom was over, the number of settlers declined, although Indigenous inhabitants remained a minority in the region. Within the Yucca Mountain and NTS region, because settler mining and ranching were limited, Western Shoshone and Southern Paiute peoples continued to practice traditional lifeways, including hunting, gathering, and ceremony. Some continued to live in the region while others traveled there periodically, living and working in settler towns.[59] Stoffle and colleagues note, "Native American people were still harvesting wild food resources and medicinal plants in the area that is now

---

57. Stoffle et al., *Native American Cultural Resource Studies*, 80.
58. Stoffle et al., *Native American Cultural Resource Studies*.
59. Stoffle et al.

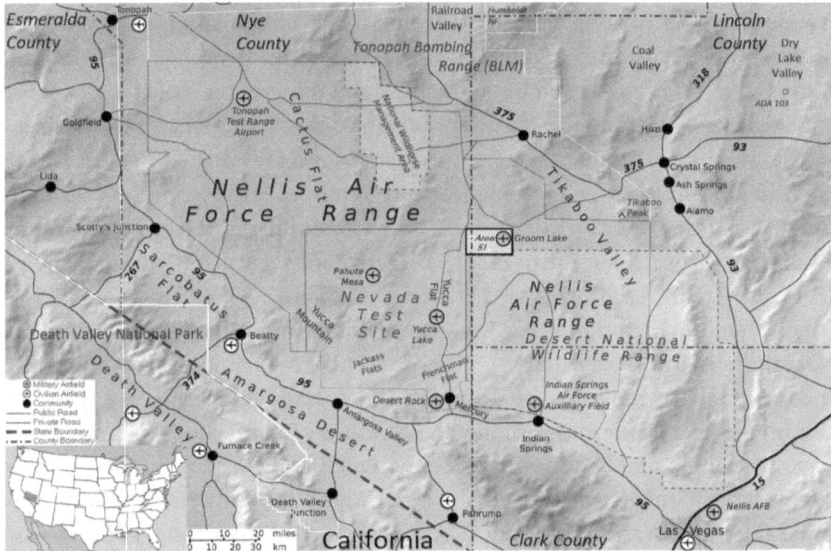

FIGURE 7. Federal Lands in Southern Nevada. Map created by Finlay McWalter, CC BY-SA 3.0, http://creativecommons.org/licenses/by-sa/3.0/, via Wikimedia Commons. Available here: https://commons.wikimedia.org/wiki/File:Wfm_area51_map_en.png.

known as the Nevada Test Site, at the time this area began to be withdrawn from public usage during the 1940s."[60] When the federal government created a series of reservations for Western Shoshone and Southern Paiute peoples in the 1940s that were all a distance from the NTS, there was less Western Shoshone and Southern Paiute interaction with the region because of both relocation and restricted access. Catherine Fowler wrote, "Although Native American people have been denied access to this area since the 1940's and 1950's, it is clearly still within their cultural traditions. They have been cognizant of this loss of access to the Nevada Test Site and the bombing and gunnery range for some time, and the Yucca Mountain site visits reminded them of this loss."[61]

From the time when the Yucca Mountain site first came under consideration to the present, the US federal government has claimed that Yucca Mountain is located on federally controlled land. Indeed, a large portion of Western Shoshone and Southern Paiute Lands are now designated by the settler government as federal lands (see figure 7). Western Shoshone and Southern Pai-

---

60. Stoffle et al., 29.
61. Fowler, *Native Americans and Yucca Mountain*, 32.

ute peoples and nations, on the other hand, cite treaty-based, ancestral, and spiritual connections to argue that Yucca Mountain continues to be Indigenous Lands.[62] Due to flawed treaty-making and reservation-making processes, the Western Shoshones are the only Native peoples with a treaty that includes Yucca Mountain, though there are no current reservations on or near Yucca Mountain. Southern Paiute peoples were removed to reservations through executive orders. A DOE fact sheet about cultural resources in the Yucca Mountain region identifies seventeen Indigenous governments or equivalent organizations with ties to the Yucca Mountain region.[63] Stoffle and colleagues' studies identify twenty Indigenous communities with relationships to Yucca Mountain (see figure 8).[64] While I did not track down the source of the inconsistency in numbers between these two sources, there is a consensus that numerous Western Shoshone and Southern Paiute peoples and nations have ongoing connections with Yucca Mountain and its surroundings. As a report from Urban Environmental Research and Ian Zabarte notes, "Southern Paiute and Western Shoshone lands pre-historically overlapped. No distinct border existed and today people of both tribes recognize approximately 2 million acres of joint use area that includes the Yucca Mountain Region."[65] Of particular focus within Western Shoshone governments are the Yomba Shoshone Tribe, the Duckwater Shoshone Tribe, and the Timbisha Shoshone Tribe, which range from 30 to 150 miles from the Yucca Mountain site and include groups with ancestors who used Yucca Mountain.[66] Within Southern Paiutes, the three most affected are the Moapa Band of Paiutes (Moapa Reservation), the Las Vegas Paiute Tribe (Las Vegas Indian Colony), and the Pahrump Paiute Tribe (Pahrump and Lower Armargosa Valley), ranging from

---

62. Harney, *Way It Is*; and Kuletz, *Tainted Desert*.
63. The seventeen tribes are the Benton Paiute Tribe, Bishop Paiute Tribe, Big Pine Paiute Tribe of the Owens Valley, Fort Independence Paiute Tribe, Lone Pine Paiute/Shoshone Tribe, Timbisha Shoshone Tribe, Yomba Shoshone Tribe, Duckwater Shoshone Tribe, Ely Shoshone Tribe, Pahrump Paiute Tribe, Las Vegas Paiute Indian Colony, Las Vegas Indian Center, Moapa Paiute Tribe, Chemehuevi Indian Tribe, Colorado River Indian Tribes, Kaibab Paiute Tribe, and the Paiute Indian Tribe of Utah (Shivwits Paiute Tribe, Cedar City Paiute Tribe, Indian Peaks Paiute Tribe, Kanosh Paiute Tribe, Koosharem Paiute Tribe). US Department of Energy, Office of Civilian Radioactive Waste Management, "Preservation through Cooperation."
64. Stoffle et al., *Native American Cultural Resource Studies*. In an email conversation with Dr. Stoffle in January 2023, he indicated that the map shown in figure 8 does not represent more recent data about the boundaries of the Southern Paiutes. He suggested the following publication, which includes a more recent map of Southern Paiute homelands territories. I chose to use this older map here because it is the only one I know of that maps the locations of Native nations in relation to the Yucca Mountain site. Please see the following for a newer map of Southern Paiute boundaries: Stoffle et al., "Incised Stones."
65. Urban Environmental Research and Zabarte, *Tribal Concerns*, 10.
66. Fowler, *Native Americans and Yucca Mountain*.

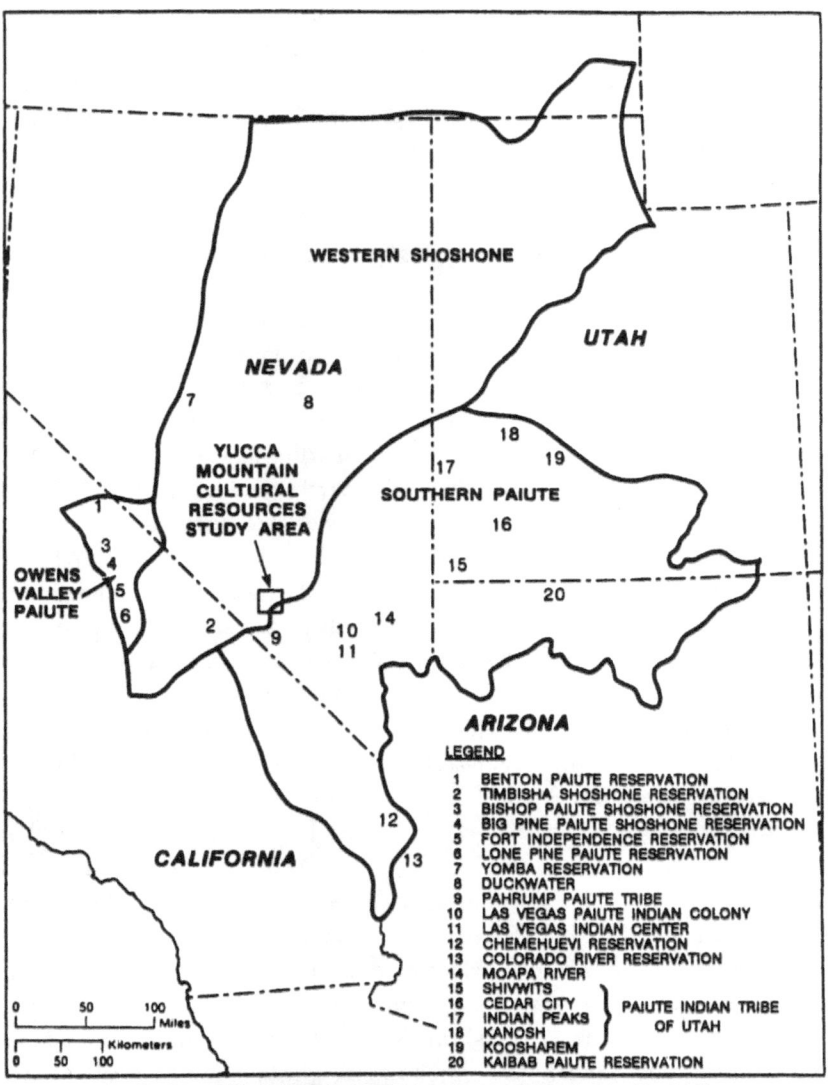

Map 2. Traditional Ethnic Boundaries and Locations of Tribes Involved in the Yucca Mountain Project (adapted from D'Azevedo, 1986).

FIGURE 8. Contemporary Indigenous governments in relationship with Yucca Mountain. Map created by Richard Stoffle, David Halmo, John Olmsted, and Michael Evans.

59 to 106 miles from Yucca Mountain.[67] Yet, the impacts from a potential high-level nuclear waste site within Yucca Mountain would not be limited to these groups in closer proximity to the mountain. Due to the dynamism and interconnections within broader Western Shoshone and Southern Paiute communities and the fact that Yucca Mountain is part of broader territories, the waste site also matters to Western Shoshone and Southern Paiute peoples and nations currently located further afield.

Western Shoshone Relations with Yucca Mountain

Within Western Shoshone knowledges, Yucca Mountain is a snake. Ian Zabarte, principal man for Western Bands of the Shoshone Nation and representative of the Native Community Action Council, stated, "Yucca Mountain is a serpent, we know how to live and if you don't do the things you're supposed to do the snake will release its poison. We're part of this, we're part of it. You don't just destroy it. This is our place of communion with the land."[68] Likewise, Corbin Harney wrote, "Someday when we wake that snake up, we will have to sit down and talk to that snake. It will get mad and rip open. When it awakens, we will all go to sleep. With his tail, that snake will move the mountain, rip it open, and the poison will come out on the surface."[69] Preventing the snake from ripping open the mountain and releasing radioactive pollution is a key motivation for resistance to the proposed Yucca Mountain facility.

Throughout the siting decision-making, Western Shoshone peoples and nations claimed Yucca Mountain as ancestral homelands under the Ruby Valley Treaty of Peace and Friendship of 1863 and expressed opposition to the site. Western Shoshone spiritual leader Corbin Harney states, "The land that you guys are talking about, the DOE, we still haven't heard from the federal government or the state that they own the land. Under the Treaty of 1863, we still own it under your federal law."[70] Moreover, the Western Shoshone National Council—made up of representatives of most of the specific Western Shoshone governments—spoke out against the Yucca Mountain site, arguing that the Lands were never ceded, nuclear waste would damage the Lands, and the site would inhibit Western Shoshone spiritual and cultural practices.[71] Western Shoshones see the Yucca Mountain waste site as connected to

---

67. Fowler, *Native Americans and Yucca Mountain*.
68. "Yucca Mountain: Serpent Swimming Westward."
69. Harney, *Way It Is*, 154.
70. "US Department of Energy Public Hearing," December 5, 2001, 7.
71. Harney, *Way It Is*; and Urban Environmental Research and Zabarte, *Tribal Concerns*.

their struggles for Lands protection throughout their ancestral territory.[72] For example, Western Shoshone sisters Carrie Dann and Mary Dann worked tirelessly against mining on sacred Lands in Crescent Valley. In a conversation with Pauline Estevez at a gathering by the Nevada Test Site, she indicates she was working with a coalition of Southern Paiutes and Western Shoshones to protect aquifers from being diverted to feed the insatiable thirst of Las Vegas. The UN Committee for the Elimination of Racial Discrimination called for the US government to "desist from all activities planned/or conducted on the ancestral lands of Western Shoshone or in relation to their natural resources, which are being carried out without consultation with and despite protests of the Western Shoshone peoples."[73] Yucca Mountain is not only an important site for Western Shoshone peoples and nations, but it is also one of many threatened places.

Southern Paiute Relations with Yucca Mountain

Yucca Mountain is also part of Southern Paiute ancestral homelands since time immemorial. Although Southern Paiute reservations cover only about 1 percent of their original territories, Southern Paiute peoples maintain relationships with traditional homelands and spiritual sites.[74] Southern Paiute elder Vivienne Caron-Jake wrote: "We have continuously made our home here on the Colorado Plateau, in the Great Basin, and on the Mojave Desert—in the most beautiful, scenic, and sacred of lands."[75] Southern Paiute peoples and nations are somewhat less well-known in their opposition to the Yucca Mountain site than Western Shoshone peoples and nations.[76] Yet, there was strong engagement from Southern Paiute peoples and governments throughout the various stages of decision-making about the Yucca Mountain site. For example, Edward Smith, member of the Chemehuevi Indian Tribe's Tribal Council, states in a public hearing about the proposed Yucca Mountain site: "We have been telling the government about the importance of Yucca Mountain area to our people since 1987. During every study, at every meeting, we tell the

---

72. This includes the fight with the Indian Claims Commission over whether the treaty still stands or was abrogated such that the Western Shoshones lost claim to land in the treaty area but outside of reservations.
73. UN Committee for the Elimination of Racial Discrimination, "Early Warning," 3.
74. Stoffle, Arnold, and Bulletts, "Talking with Nature."
75. Hebner and Plyler, *Southern Paiute*, xi.
76. Fowler, *Native Americans and Yucca Mountain*.

government the same thing. Today I tell you the same thing yet again. Yucca Mountain is sacred to our people."[77]

THE SKULL VALLEY PFS SITE

Skull Valley is a forty-mile valley between the Stansbury and Cedar mountain ranges, typical of the basin and range topography. It is a beautiful desert valley, with natural springs, sagebrush that transitions into alpine landscape in the mountains, and a diversity of plant and animal species. According to Western Shoshone historian Steven Crum, the Skull Valley Goshutes are deeply connected to their ancestral territory and resisted numerous relocation efforts from 1864 to the mid-1950s. This resistance is a testament to Skull Valley Goshute relationships with Lands and their survivance. Crum writes: "Adhering to its policy of 'Indian removal,' the federal government made numerous attempts to remove the Skull Valley Indians from their native valley. These efforts failed because the band remains bonded to its indigenous homeland."[78]

The proposed Skull Valley PFS nuclear waste site was to be located within a part of the Skull Valley Goshute Reservation. Unlike Yucca Mountain, this nuclear waste site involves only one Indigenous nation. In this case, the controversy over a proposed nuclear waste site was not between them and the federal government but instead centered on a disagreement within the Skull Valley Goshute nation's members over whether to pursue leasing some of their Lands for a high-level nuclear waste facility. During the time the Skull Valley Goshutes were considering the proposed nuclear waste site, the Skull Valley Goshute government supported bringing the nuclear waste facility to the reservation and a small organization of Skull Valley Goshute citizens opposed the site under the name of Ohngo Gaudadeh Devia.

A key point brought up by both proponents and opponents to the proposed nuclear waste site was centered on options for the survival of the small rural reservation, located in a desert region turned into a wasteland by settlers. The areas surrounding the Skull Valley Goshute Reservation to the east, north, and south have been used for chemical and biological weapons development and testing, a nerve gas storage facility, a coal-fired electrical power plant that causes air pollution, a low-level radioactive disposal site, two hazardous waste incinerators, one hazardous waste landfill, and a magnesium plant. Speaking specifically about the surrounding Tooele County,

---

77. "Yucca Mountain Project Comments," 24–25.
78. Crum, "Skull Valley Band," 251.

Mike Davis called it "the nation's greatest concentration of hyper-hazardous and ultra-deadly materials."[79] Further, Rupert Steele, former vice-chair of the Consolidated Tribes of the Goshute Reservation, notes, "We all know that land [surrounding the Skull Valley Goshute Reservation] has been a dumping area for a long time, a wasteland."[80] For members of the Skull Valley Goshute government, this toxicity supported their argument for the proposed nuclear waste site; they reasoned that being surrounded by other toxic sites outside of their control constrained opportunities for economic development. Storing nuclear waste, they concluded, would be one of few opportunities for economic development on Lands perceived by outsiders as wastelands. An old and now discontinued Skull Valley Goshute website home page included this narrative of the toxic waste surrounding the reservation:

> At one time the Goshute homeland extended from the Wasatch front westward past Wells, Nevada and occupied several hundred square miles. Today, the Skull Valley Goshute Reservation is comprised of approximately 18,000 acres. South of Skull Valley on traditional Goshute territory there was wild game which roamed the country freely and served as a vital food supply. The area is now the location of Dugway Proving Grounds where the United States government developed and tested chemical and biological weapons. In 1968 chemical agents escaped from Dugway and approximately 6,000 sheep and other animals died. At least 1600 of those contaminated sheep were buried on the Reservation by the Government. The Band fully investigated this incident. A model program for the nation has been developed by the Department of Defense Office of Environmental Security in concert with Indian Tribes to cleanup the contamination and impacts of defense activities on Native American lands.
>
> East of Skull Valley in the area known as Rush Valley there was native sagebrush, pine trees, food plants, and also wild game. Today, this area serves as a nerve gas storage facility for the United States government. The world's largest nerve gas incinerator has recently been built to destroy thousands of tons of these deadly chemicals.
>
> South of Skull Valley lies the Intermountain Power Project which provides coal-fired electrical power primarily for California. Air pollution fills the skies of the Western Desert and impacts the Skull Valley Reservation.
>
> Northwest of Skull Valley, is the Envirocare Low-Level Radioactive Disposal Site which buries radioactive waste for the entire country. Within this

---

79. Davis, "Utah's Toxic Heaven," 35.
80. Mims, "Different Views."

immediate area there are also two hazardous waste incinerators and one hazardous waste landfill.

Finally, north of the Reservation is the Magnesium Corporation plant, a large magnesium production plant which has been identified by the US EPA as the most polluting plant of its kind in the United States. Chlorine gas releases from MagCorp also impact the Skull Valley Reservation. In the citing [sic] of these facilities on the aboriginal territory of the Goshutes, the Skull Valley Tribal Government and people were never once consulted.

In view of the current hazardous waste facilities and nerve gas incinerators surrounding the Skull Valley Reservation, the Band has carefully considered a variety of economic ventures, including the storage of spent nuclear fuel. After careful consideration, the Skull Valley Band of Goshutes have leased land to a private group of electrical utilities for the temporary storage of 40,000 metric tons of spent nuclear fuel. This web site examines these deliberations, tours of nuclear facilities, consultation with renowned scientists, and corporate and government officials worldwide.[81]

I quoted this in full to let the Skull Valley Goshute nation speak in its own words about its homeland and reasons for supporting a nuclear waste site. Ohngo Gaudadeh Devia, on the other hand, reasoned that even though the areas surrounding the reservation are filled with toxicity, the Skull Valley Goshute nation still has the sovereignty to protect their Lands from nuclear waste. They argued that the risks of bringing nuclear waste to the reservation for their cultural practices and Lands are too great, despite the potential for economic development. Though differing, both perspectives highlight the bind faced by the Skull Valley Goshute nation due to the way Skull Valley was treated by settlers who saw it as nothing more than wasteland.

CONCLUSION

This chapter offers an admittedly limited narrative of Western Shoshone, Southern Paiute, and Skull Valley Goshute relationships with the Great Basin, and more specifically Yucca Mountain and Skull Valley. Readers interested in more detail in these histories would benefit from reading Indigenous and scholarly histories to learn more.[82] The material provided in this chapter affirms that Yucca Mountain and Skull Valley are traditional, ancestral, and

---

81. Skull Valley Band of Goshutes, "Skull Valley Goshutes."
82. Crum, "Skull Valley Band"; Crum, *Road on Which We Came*; Fowler and Fowler, "Notes"; and Hebner and Plyler, *Southern Paiute*.

contemporary homelands of sovereign Western Shoshone, Southern Paiute, and Skull Valley Goshute nations and peoples. The details of these relationships do not always make it into specific Indigenous nuclear decolonization rhetorical tactics, but they are nonetheless foundational to the tactics I amplify in the following chapters. Indigenous Lands rhetorics and Indigenous national interest rhetorics, which will be the subject of the next two chapters, are grounded in these deep connections to the Great Basin.

CHAPTER 3

Indigenous Lands Rhetorics

> We the Native people, the caretakers, have got a right here on this land, but we're the ones that are suffering. Maybe this is the reason they keep telling us Native people, "we're going to put nuclear waste on your land." Is that protecting the land like they said they were going to do under the treaty? I really don't think so. I think they are trying to destroy our spiritual grounds, our burial sites.
> —Corbin Harney, Western Shoshone spiritual leader[1]

My first formal introduction to Newe Sogobia (Western Shoshone territory) was in May 2004 when I attended the Western Shoshone National Council annual spring gathering at Crescent Valley (see figure 9) to learn more about Western Shoshone opposition to the Yucca Mountain nuclear waste site.[2] I remember participating in the daily sunrise ceremonies led by late Western Shoshone spiritual leader Corbin Harney. This was the first time I had been invited to participate in an Indigenous spiritual practice, though I had been reading and writing about Indigenous Lands protection for years. With the sun just rising and in the chill of a desert morning, we stood bundled in jackets and sweatshirts forming a circle around a fire while Harney prayed to the bah (water), dabeh (sun), dewe sungup (plant life), Bunn Narumnichee (rocks), neyipe (wind), and more.[3] The gathering was a mix of mainly white and Native people, and at these morning circles, Indigenous participants led non-Native newcomers like myself through example, demonstrating how to approach and engage with the fire, the burning cedar, and the water. At times,

---

1. Harney, *Nature Way,* 39.
2. Crescent Valley was home to Western Shoshone sisters Mary and Carrie Dann, within whose Lands the gathering took place. The gathering was not solely focused on Yucca Mountain but on a series of related efforts to protect Western Shoshone Lands.
3. The Western Shoshone language terms cited here come from Corbin Harney's biography, *The Nature Way.*

we held hands and circled the fire while Harney sang in Shoshone. Although I do not specifically remember which songs he sang, he likely sang a variant of this morning prayer:

> I pray this morning, Sun, that as you come out,
> you will warm our bodies and cause all living things
> to grow on this Earth; for without you
> coming out everyday, Sun, nothing will survive.
> I pray that you will keep us healthy, keep us pure.[4]

Harney described the importance of a morning circle in his book:

> When we form a circle for the morning ceremony, I ask people to stand straight up and down, standing up on Mother Earth. We make as perfect a circle as we can. The circle is important, because ceremony ties in with the fire. Fire ties in with the land. I use some cedar, some herbs that I get off my own land in that part of the world. And, when I gather them, I pray for them, I bless them, and I have to give something when I take it out of the ground. None of us can just go over there and grab something and take it out of the ground. We have to talk to it first. There's a song for everything. There's a song for the cedar. The fire has a song. The smoke has a song, you name it.[5]

Corbin Harney was one of many traditionalists who worked to keep the knowledges, epistemologies, ontologies, and spiritualities about Lands—including the animal life, plant life, water, air, and humans who relate to it—centered in the practices of Western Shoshone, Southern Paiute, and Skull Valley Goshute peoples. I later learned that Harney made a strong effort not only to revive Indigenous spiritual practices among Western Shoshone and other Native peoples but also to explicitly bring non-Indigenous people into the movement to protect Lands and Waters from pollution, radiation, and toxicity. He wrote: "Everybody, I don't care who they are, what they look like, or what color they are—we're all going to have to start working together to save our planet here."[6] Harney, like many other Native peoples working to protect Lands, actively sought coalitions with non-Indigenous, and mostly white, environmentalists like myself as a way to both amplify the cause and display what it looks like to protect the Earth. Participating in these morning circles was the first time I experienced in an embodied and emplaced way what I had

---

4. Harney, *Way It Is,* 48.
5. This is a prayer presented and translated by Harney in *Way It Is,* 50.
6. Harney, 10.

FIGURE 9. Western Shoshone Lands in Crescent Valley. Photo taken by Danielle Endres at the 2006 Western Shoshone Defense Project Gathering.

read, thought, and written about for years: Indigenous perspectives on relationality with Lands.

This chapter engages with *Lands* as not only physical places but also sites of Indigenous theory, practice, pedagogy, advocacy, decolonization, survivance, and radical resurgence. As noted earlier in the book, I capitalize *Lands* following Max Liboiron's reference to Land as a "unique entity that is the combined living spirit of plants, animals, air, water, humans, histories, and events recognized by many Indigenous communities."[7] Land, they argue, is not a noun but a verb that never settles: "It is about relations between the material aspects some people might think of as landscapes—water, soil, air, plants, stars—and histories, spirits, events, kinships, accountabilities, and other people that are not human."[8] I use *Lands,* plural, to celebrate the multiplicity of relationships that Indigenous peoples, nations, and communities

---

7. Liboiron, *Pollution Is Colonialism,* 7. Liboiron draws from Styres and Zinga's Community-First Land-Centered Theoretical Framework. Styres and Zinga, "Community-First Land-Centred Theoretical Framework."

8. Liboiron, *Pollution Is Colonialism,* 43.

value in their own diverse and specific ways.⁹ In other words, there is no one generalizable understanding of Land but a multiplicity of Indigenous Lands that may overlap or diverge in a series of complex relations. Lands are akin to what some refer to as the more-than-human world. The value of Lands for Indigenous peoples and nations throughout this continent (and beyond) is well documented in Native American and Indigenous studies scholarship and through Indigenous knowledges. In the case of nuclear waste siting, Lands protection is a significant point of conflict over potential sites—demonstrating how Indigenous approaches to the value and agency of Lands differ radically from non-Indigenous Western approaches to land as resource, property, or object (indeed, as Liboiron notes, a settler notion of land is better characterized without the capital *L*).¹⁰ In this chapter, I weave together stories about the Lands proposed for high-level nuclear waste sites from the perspective of Western Shoshone, Southern Paiute, and Skull Valley Goshute peoples and nations, illustrating how protecting these Lands from radioactive contamination and settler encroachment enacts both nuclear decolonization and radical resurgence of Indigenous ways of relating to Lands.¹¹ I recount how Lands is an essential topos for resistance to nuclear waste sites on Western Shoshone, Southern Paiute, and Skull Valley Goshute Lands.

The central argument is that Indigenous Lands protectors use embodied and emplaced arguments about Lands—what I am calling *Indigenous Lands rhetorics*—to ground their resistance to high-level nuclear waste sites and posit other futures through resurgence of relationality with Lands. By thematizing rhetorical appeals to and for Lands, this chapter contributes to an understanding of Indigenous Lands rhetorics, both a theory and form of rhetorical practice invented by Indigenous peoples. Grounded in analysis of archives, Indigenous stories-as-theory, participant observation, and oral history interviews, I focus on home Lands, sacred Lands, and Lands as relations as three intersecting rhetorical tactics, in this case, grounded in Western Shoshone, Southern Paiute, and Skull Valley Goshute knowledges and spiritualties. Nuclear decolonization is fundamentally a struggle for both the return of Indigenous Lands (decolonization) and the ability to be in good relations with those Lands (resurgence). Western Shoshone, Southern Paiute, and Skull Valley Goshute rhetorical tactics centered in this chapter are both in relationship with past/present Lands protection efforts by Indigenous peoples of various

---

9. Tuck, McKenzie, and McCoy, "Land Education"; Lowan, "Exploring Place"; and Cajete, "'Look to the Mountain.'"

10. Liboiron, *Pollution Is Colonialism*, 7.

11. I will talk more about Simpson's concept of radical resurgence in the coming pages. L. Simpson, *As We Have Always Done*.

nations and provide models for present/future campaigns to protect Lands from settler violence and destruction. Indigenous Lands rhetorics stand in direct contrast to settler imaginaries and descriptions of proposed nuclear waste sites as wastelands and sacrifice zones in an already corrupted Atomic West (these efforts are also known as strategies of nuclear colonialism).[12]

I begin by describing Indigenous Lands rhetorics as a theory of Indigenous rhetoric that is strongly rooted within particular places. Then, I amplify Indigenous Lands rhetorics used by Indigenous antinuclear-waste advocates, focusing on appeals to home Lands, sacred Lands, and Lands as relations. I conclude with a reflection on how Indigenous Lands rhetorics are central to both decolonization and resurgence.

INDIGENOUS LANDS RHETORICS

As a genre, Indigenous Lands rhetorics use Lands as their primary topos. They are simultaneously specific to particular places—such as Yucca Mountain or Skull Valley—and also characterizations based in similarities across different Indigenous peoples' relationalities with Lands. Indigenous Lands rhetorics reflect Lands as animate, talking, listening, acting, sacred, and relational beings. Lands are worthy of protection because they are centers of relationality, spirituality, and communication that are fundamental to Indigenous ways of knowing. Lands-based and Lands-as rhetorics provide a vocabulary for thinking of Lands as both grounding for or the subject of rhetorical appeals and as having rhetorical agency themselves.[13] Lands-based and Lands-as rhetorics not only resist dominant settler perceptions of Yucca Mountain and Skull Valley as wastelands and national sacrifice zones but also enact other ways of knowing, being with, and engaging in relationality with Lands as living beings. Indigenous Lands rhetorics are, then, embodied and emplaced Indigenous ways of knowing and being. In the remainder of this section, I work through the concept of Indigenous Lands rhetorics by further defining Lands, place, decolonization, and radical resurgence.

---

12. For more on strategies of nuclear colonialism, see Endres, "Sacred Land"; Endres, "From Wasteland to Waste Site"; and Voyles, *Wastelanding*.

13. These two ways of thinking about Indigenous Lands rhetorics draw from a conceptualization of the relationship between place-based and place-as rhetorics in Endres and Senda-Cook, "Location Matters."

Lands

Indigenous peoples living in what settler colonists named the US are anything but monolithic.[14] What Anishinaabe peoples call Turtle Island is a space of many different overlapping Lands with relationships to hundreds of different Indigenous nations. Yet, the value of Lands is a central tenet of the past, present, and future for many Indigenous peoples on the continent.[15] As Andrea Riley-Mukavetz puts it, "Indigenous survival and self-determination is deeply tied to the land."[16] An entire book could be written about the importance of Lands to Indigenous peoples and nations—indeed, this work has been done. My purpose is not to provide an extensive review of this voluminous scholarship but to set a foundation for the importance of Lands to and for Indigenous peoples, cultures, spiritualities, and lifeways. Before moving on, it is important to note that the way I use *Lands* is intended to be inclusive of water, air, and sky, yet for some Indigenous peoples, particularly those in relationship with oceans, *Waters* might be a more appropriate term that sheds a Lands-based bias among Indigenous peoples of Turtle Island.[17] I use *Lands* because the Western Shoshone, Southern Paiute, and Skull Valley Goshute peoples opposing nuclear waste regularly used variations of the word in their rhetoric.

Rhetorical appeals to/about/from Lands can be characterized by three intersecting themes: home Lands, sacred Lands, and Lands as relations. Home Lands are those relations that connect with having lived in and called a place home for many generations, if not since time immemorial.[18] Sacred Lands are those relations that connect with the spirituality of particular places (including all of the beings and spirits that reside in those places) for Indigenous

---

14. Within the US settler state, there are over 574 federally recognized Indigenous nations (including tribes, bands, organized communities, pueblos, and Alaska Native villages or corporations) and more nonfederally recognized or state-recognized peoples; Kānaka 'Ōiwi, Kānaka Maoli, and Lāhui (Native Hawaiians) peoples' Native Hawaiian Organizations; and Indigenous peoples of the territories (e.g., Puerto Rico and Guahan).

15. Na'puti, "Archipelagic Rhetoric"; Na'puti, "Oceanic Possibilities"; Liboiron, *Pollution Is Colonialism*; Kimmerer, *Braiding Sweetgrass*; Cajete, "'Look to the Mountain'"; L. Simpson, *As We Have Always Done*; LaDuke, *Recovering the Sacred*; LaDuke, *All Our Relations*; and Deloria, *God Is Red*.

16. Riley-Mukavetz, "Developing a Relational Scholarly Practice," 550.

17. Tiara Na'puti, for example, has written about both Oceanic and Archipelagic rhetoric as ways of amplifying Pacific Islander ways of knowing based in relations to Waters. Na'puti, "Speaking of Indigeneity"; and Na'puti, "Oceanic Possibilities."

18. Forced relocations, the most well-known of which is the Trail of Tears, mean that some Indigenous peoples and nations have land bases outside of their ancestral homelands from time immemorial. In the case of Western Shoshone, Southern Paiute, and Skull Valley Goshute peoples, many are able to continue to live in ancestral homelands, whether in urban areas or reservations that lie within their ancestral territories.

peoples and religions. Lands as relations highlights how relationality is central to Indigenous perspectives about Lands—they are neither static locations nor unliving landscapes but a living set of relations with the entire ecology of a location. Because relationality extends across and within home Lands and sacred Lands as well, I use *Land as relations* to more specifically home in on appeals based in communication with and responsibility to Lands.

As Leanne Simpson argues, "Indigenous bodies don't relate to the land by possessing or owning it or having control over it. We relate to land through connection—generative, affirmative, complex, overlapping, and nonlinear *relationship*."[19] This is not a one-way connection in which humans seek to commune with, or worse consume, Lands; it is a two-way mutually constitutive relationship that recognizes Lands as animate, feeling, and able to communicate with humans. This relationality is not a new materialism, but a deeply rooted way of living that is at once very old, contemporary, and future-oriented, reflective of Indigenous understandings of place and time as cyclical. Robin Kimmerer homes in on relationality with Lands as something that is core to the ongoing survivance of Indigenous peoples:

> In the face of such loss [removal, assimilation, boarding schools], one thing our people could not surrender was the meaning of land. In the settler mind, land was property, real estate, capital, or natural resources. But to our people, it was everything: identity, the connection to our ancestors, the home of our nonhuman kinfolk, our pharmacy, our library, the source of all that sustained us. Our lands were where our responsibility to the world was enacted, sacred ground. It belonged to itself; it was a gift, not a commodity, so it could never be bought or sold.[20]

Lands, then, are constellations of past, ongoing, and future relations that are always in process.

Places

Lands are intricately connected to places. In the words of Gregory Cajete, the word *Indigenous* "means being so completely identified with a place that you reflect its very entrails, its insides, its soul."[21] While settlers—immigrants

---

19. L. Simpson, *As We Have Always Done*, 43.
20. Kimmerer, *Braiding Sweetgrass*, 17.
21. Cajete, "'Look to the Mountain,'" 6.

and arrivants[22] alike—have come to develop senses of place and connections with the stolen lands they occupy, original Native peoples of this continent are the only peoples who are indigenous to these Lands. Whether they live in their original territories, on reservation Lands, in cities, or some combination of these, Indigenous peoples know that they are always within Indigenous Lands—their own territories, the territories of other Indigenous peoples and nations, or borderlands shared by Indigenous peoples of different nations or cultures. Settler senses of place are often unaware of or deliberately deny the Indigenous Lands they occupy.[23] Regardless of the settler legal system's recognition that Indigenous nations have sovereignty over only about 2 percent of original ancestral territories, Indigenous peoples in this part of the continent maintain strong emplaced relationships with Lands both within and outside their legal territories. Yucca Mountain and Skull Valley are part of the original territories of Western Shoshone, Southern Paiute, and Skull Valley Goshute peoples and nations. A deep connection to these particular places is inherent in the rhetorical tactics used to defend them from high-level nuclear waste.

The deep attachment to and reciprocal relationship with Lands is, in part, an emplaced way of knowing that is situated in particular places for particular Indigenous peoples. Vanessa Watts uses *Place-Thought* to describe "a theoretical understanding of the world via physical embodiment."[24] While Indigenous lifeways tend to enact a reciprocal relationship with the entire ecology of beings that live on this earth, it is through particular places that each Indigenous culture develops reciprocity and relationality with specific emplaced Lands, be they traditional territory or new territory as a result of forced relocation. According to Cajete, "The land has become an extension of Indian thought and being because, in the words of a Pueblo elder, 'It is this place that holds our memories and the bones of our people . . . This is the place that made us.'"[25] Likewise, Sheridan and Longboat argue, "When things happen only in traditional landscapes, they are understood as needing to happen there. Because those places possess mind and orchestrate psychological and spiritual ecologies wherein ideas live simultaneously visible and invisible lives."[26] Sometimes, as in the case of Yucca Mountain or Bears Ears, a

---

22. For more on the term *arrivants,* see Byrd, *Transit of Empire.*
23. Of course, the rise in Indigenous land acknowledgment statements has changed this to some extent. Regardless, I think it is fair to say that it is not yet common practice among most settlers to recognize on whose land they live, work, and gather in a consistent way. Less common is moving beyond a land acknowledgment to engage in tangible actions to support and ally with Indigenous peoples and nations in decolonization efforts.
24. Watts, "Indigenous Place-Thought," 21.
25. Cajete, "'Look to the Mountain,'" 3. Ellipsis in original.
26. Sheridan and Longboat, "Haudenosaunee Imagination," 371.

place has profound significance for more than one Indigenous nation. In other cases, such as Skull Valley, the place is deeply tied to one Indigenous nation. These relations with particular places are typical of many Indigenous cultures that "hold their land—places—as having the highest possible meaning, and all their statements are made with this reference point in mind," according to Vine Deloria Jr.[27] Cajete adds that places are spiritual: "Although Native peoples' cultures were quite diverse, there was also adherence to a common set of life principles. . . . They expressed a 'theology of place,' which, while focused specifically on their place, extended to include all nature."[28] I see Watt's concept of Place-Thought as inclusive of many relations Indigenous peoples and nations have to Lands. She further defines Place-Thought as "the non-distinctive space where place and thought were never separated because they never could or can be separated. Place-Thought is based upon the premise that land is alive and thinking and that humans and non-humans derive agency through the extensions of these thoughts."[29] Place, therefore, is part of the conception of Lands.

Decolonization and Radical Resurgence

Given the necessity of relationships with Lands for Indigenous peoples, protecting Lands is linked with both decolonization and radical resurgence. Indigenous Lands, Waters, Skies, and Airs protectors mobilize to protect soil, air, water, mountains, animals, plants, and the whole ecology of relations in particular places.[30] While sometimes called Indigenous environmentalists[31]—

---

27. Deloria, *God Is Red*, 61.
28. Cajete, "'Look to the Mountain,'" 6.
29. Watts, "Indigenous Place-Thought," 21.
30. While presented here as separate ways of protecting, many would include water and air within the concept of Land.
31. While Lands are central to Indigenous ways of knowing, relationality with Lands does not map directly onto environmentalism—particularly white, settler, and mainstream environmentalisms—or claims that Natives are the first environmentalists. Indigenous perspectives on Lands are not the embodiment of the ideals of the modern Western environmental movement. Scholars argue over whether Indigenous peoples really do have stronger environmental ethics than Western peoples, whether linking Indigenous peoples to the environment perpetuates stereotypes such as the "noble savage," and whether Indigenous peoples (pre- and post-Columbus) lived in sustainable relationships with their environments. It is important to note that settler scholars must be cautious of essentializing Native peoples and nations as fundamentally ecological or environmentalist. As is true with any culture, there are differences between ideal cultural beliefs and actual practices. D. Johnson, "Reflections"; Kretch, *Ecological Indian*; Nelson and Shilling, *Traditional Ecological Knowledge*; Weaver, "Introduction"; and Nadasdy, "Transcending the Debate."

by themselves and by others—Lands protectors are deeply rooted in Indigenous epistemologies, even when settlers are invited in as allies or coalitions are built with non-Indigenous groups. Winona LaDuke distinguishes Indigenous environmentalisms as always related to Lands: "Grassroots and land-based struggles characterize most of Native environmentalism. We are nations of people with distinct land areas, and our leadership and direction emerge from the land up. Our connection and tenacity spring from our deep connection to land. This relationship to land and water is continuously reaffirmed through prayer, deed, and our way of being."[32] Indigenous cultures have, of course, changed over time. In some cases, Indigenous peoples and nations have adopted and adapted settler practices and perspectives toward land as resource or land as economic opportunity. As a result, in addition to seeking return of Lands to Indigenous peoples and nations in an act of decolonization, Lands protection can be an act of decolonization of the mind and a radical resurgence of Indigenous ways of being in relationship with Lands.[33] Relationship with and reverence toward Lands is a grounding assumption of Lands protection and Land Back movements.

As Frantz Fanon wrote from the perspective of Caribbean and African colonization, "For a colonized people, the most essential value, because it is the most meaningful, is first and foremost the land: the land, which must provide bread and, naturally, dignity."[34] While there are many decolonizations and decolonialisms depending on places, situations, and theories—as discussed in chapter 1—for Indigenous peoples living with settler colonial structures, decolonization is, according to Eve Tuck and K. Wayne Yang, "the repatriation of Indigenous land and life."[35] In other words, decolonization is the literal recovery of Lands and lifeways. It is not a metaphorical challenge to oppression. When decolonization is used metaphorically to add Indigenous perspectives to settler institutions (decolonizing rhetoric) or used as a metonym for addressing all forms of oppression (e.g., decolonize the body; decolonize the syllabus), "colonial land relations remain firmly in place."[36] Western Shoshone, Southern Paiute, and Skull Valley Goshute opponents of high-level nuclear waste sites within Yucca Mountain and Skull Valley seek literal decolonization in terms of exercising sovereignty over ancestral Lands and a resurgence of

---

32. LaDuke, *All Our Relations*, 4.
33. Brayboy, "Toward a Tribal Critical Race Theory"; and L. Simpson, *As We Have Always Done*.
34. Fanon, *Wretched of the Earth*, 9.
35. Tuck and Yang, "Decolonization." Note that some have criticized the use of *repatriation* as a gendered term rooted in patriarchy and propose the use of *rematriation* instead. See, for example, Newcomb, "Perspectives"; and Gray, "Rematriation."
36. Liboiron, *Pollution Is Colonialism*, 26.

Indigenous relationality with Lands. As Simpson argues, "Indigenous people require a land base and therefore require a central and hard critique of forces that propel dispossession."[37] Indigenous Lands protection is about restoring Indigenous relationality with Lands and rejection of settler understandings of land as a resource. In this way, antinuclear Lands protection mobilizations not only critique colonial land relations but also seek the return of Lands to Indigenous peoples and nations.

Decolonization is a goal of Indigenous Lands protection movements precisely because land acquisition is central to all forms of colonialism. Colonialism is "an assumed entitlement to Indigenous land,"[38] and it assumes a "system of land relations where the land is a Resource."[39] Settler colonialism, in particular, is premised on dispossession of Indigenous Lands so that settlers can occupy it permanently and make it their own.[40] Yet, the settler colonial project has never been fully realized because of the persistence of Indigenous peoples and nations in protecting their Lands, pushing for decolonization, and resisting tenacious settler encroachment. As Audra Simpson puts it, "But this ongoing and structural project to acquire and maintain land [settler colonialism], and to eliminate those on it, did not work completely. There are still Indians, some still know this, and some will defend what they have left. They will persist, robustly."[41] Western Shoshone, Southern Paiute, and Skull Valley Goshute antinuclear-waste advocates are one such example.

As much as Western Shoshone, Southern Paiute, and Skull Valley Goshute efforts to protect Lands from high-level nuclear waste seek literal decolonization of Lands, they also represent a form of what Leanne Simpson calls radical resurgence. She writes: "Radical resurgence means an extensive, rigorous, and profound reorganizing of things. To me resurgence has always been about this. It has always been a rebellion and a revolution from within. It has always been about bringing forth a new reality."[42] Protecting Lands from nuclear waste based in Indigenous relationships with Lands is a form of radical resurgence. It is an attempt to let Indigenous knowledges guide a set of relations with Lands that don't accept nuclear waste. It is an attempt to, as Corbin Harney does, train both Indigenous and non-Indigenous people to embrace Indigenous ways of relating with Lands. Simpson notes that "everyday acts of resurgence are taking place as they always have, on both individual and collective

---

37. L. Simpson, *As We Have Always Done*, 50.
38. Liboiron, *Pollution Is Colonialism*, 9.
39. Liboiron, 39.
40. Wolfe, "Corpus Nullius," 147.
41. A. Simpson, *Mohawk Interruptus*, 12.
42. L. Simpson, *As We Have Always Done*, 49.

scales on Indigenous lands irrespective of whether those lands are urban, rural, or reserve."[43] Western Shoshone, Southern Paiute, and Skull Valley Goshute peoples' and nations' resistance to nuclear waste on their Lands is a form of radical resurgent mobilization toward the coupled goals of decolonization (Land Back) and Indigenous futurity (resurgence). These forms of mobilization are embodied and emplaced in relation with particular, situated Lands.

Decolonization and radical resurgence cannot happen without rhetoric, from arguments made in decision-making spaces, to embodied and emplaced protests on Lands, to enactments of Indigenous relationality with Lands, to paying attention to the rhetoric of Lands themselves. These ways of engaging with Lands in all of their rich complexity and agency are "unapologetic place-based nationhoods using Indigenous practices and operating in an ethical and principled way from an in-tact land base."[44] Coupling decolonization with radical resurgence emphasizes place-based Indigenous relationality with Lands toward building Indigenous futures.

PROTECTING YUCCA MOUNTAIN AND SKULL VALLEY

A key tactic of nuclear decolonization is an embodied and emplaced defense of Indigenous Lands from nuclear technologies—in this case, nuclear waste storage—based in relationships with those Lands. Yucca Mountain and Skull Valley are both located in the Great Basin region of this continent, which I described in chapter 2. Yucca Mountain and Skull Valley are places within the Great Basin, but they are also Lands that are valued by Western Shoshone, Southern Paiute, and Skull Valley Goshute peoples. Appeals to home Lands, sacred Lands, and Lands as relations represent three interconnected rhetorical tactics of Lands protection enacted by Western Shoshone, Southern Paiute, and Skull Valley Goshute rhetors.[45]

---

43. L. Simpson, 195.
44. L. Simpson, 50.
45. Reader, please don't get frustrated by my sometimes using *home Lands, sacred Lands,* and *Lands as relations* and sometimes using *homeland(s), sacred land(s),* and *land(s) relationships/relations/relationality*. I have done my best to stay true to the ways that authors and rhetors use language while also seeking to promote the use of the Lands as a conceptual enactment of the ecology of relations that make up Indigenous understandings and relations to places, animals, land, water, air, rocks, and so forth. It is all the more complicated because some of the Western Shoshone, Southern Paiute, and Skull Valley Goshute texts I use are public hearings that were transcribed in particular ways that reflect the worldview of the transcribers.

Home Lands

Home Lands are rooted in having lived in a place since time immemorial or for many generations. For many Indigenous peoples, "homeland" refers to a Native territorial base—a place of ancestral, traditional, or contemporary occupation, use, and governance. As Dina Gilio-Whitaker puts it:

> The very thing that distinguishes Indigenous peoples from settler societies is their unbroken connection to ancestral homelands. Their cultures and identities are linked to their origin places in ways that define them; they are reflected in language, place names, and cosmology (origin stories). In Indigenous worldviews, there is no separation between people and land, between people and other life forms, or between people and their ancient ancestors whose bones are infused in the land they inhabit and whose spirits permeate place.[46]

There are a variety of ways of thinking of home Lands among diverse Native peoples and nations—a homeland could be ancestral Lands stolen and occupied by settlers but that continue to hold value; it could be a contemporary reservation, whether located within or outside precontact ancestral or traditional Lands; it could be a region that is inside or outside a reservation; it could be a region with contiguous usage since time immemorial or a region that became a homeland after relocation; and it could be an imagined place of the past or future that sustains diasporic Native communities. James Clifford notes, "A feeling of connectedness to a homeland and to kin, a feeling of grounded peoplehood, is basic. How this feeling is practiced, in discursive, embodied, emplaced ways, can be quite varied."[47] While home Lands can mean different things to different Indigenous cultures, there is a commonality in the way that Indigenous peoples and nations fight to protect them. Robin Wall Kimmerer writes, "Whether it was their homeland or the new land forced upon them, land held in common gave people strength; it gave them something to fight for. And, so—in the eyes of the federal government—that belief was a threat."[48] Defense of home Lands, then, is a form of decolonization and radical resurgence that threatens the settler colonial state. The US federal government fights hard to continue to limit Indigenous peoples' and nations' relationships with home Lands, especially those outside of current reservation boundaries. As a rhetorical tactic that enacts and defends Indigenous relations

---

46. Gilio-Whitaker, *As Long as Grass Grows,* 27.
47. Clifford, "Varieties of Indigenous Experience," 205.
48. Kimmerer, *Braiding Sweetgrass,* 17.

with traditional and ancestral territories, home Lands appeals are a significant mode of survivance within structures designed to erase Indigenous peoples and nations from settler land. Western Shoshone, Southern Paiute, and Skull Valley Goshute peoples and nations use *homeland* and other terminologies to describe their relationship with the Lands proposed for nuclear waste storage.

Many Western Shoshone, Southern Paiute, and Skull Valley Goshute peoples continue to live within ancestral territories in the Great Basin, including those who live within reservation boundaries and those living in urban centers in the Great Basin, such as Las Vegas and Salt Lake City. Not all Western Shoshones, Southern Paiutes, and Skull Valley Goshutes live in the Great Basin, and those who do may not live within their particular family or band's ancestral territory. Indigenous nations and peoples within the Great Basin have often retained a portion of their ancestral home Lands. Unlike Native peoples and nations who endured forced relocations from their ancestral territories to wholly new regions of the continent—such as Cherokee, Chickasaw, and Choctaw nations who were forced to move to what is now Oklahoma—Indigenous peoples of the Great Basin were generally not forced to move outside the Great Basin. Yet, relocation still occurred with attempts to combine Indigenous peoples of different nations, kinship groups, and bands onto reservations, and efforts to radically reduce home Lands to small reservations within the ancestral territory. For example, while Western Shoshones populated the entire Great Basin region occupying parts of southeastern California, Nevada, Utah, and Idaho, their current Lands base is divided between a series of reservations created by settlers to contain and move them to smaller and less desirable places. While some Western Shoshone bands relocated to reservations outside of their traditional home Lands (in one case, a shared reservation with Northern Paiute peoples), some fought against BIA pressure to move away from their original territories.[49] Similarly, while Southern Paiute peoples lived within a region in what is now called southeastern California, southern Nevada, southern Utah, and northern Arizona, their current Lands base includes a series of reservations held by a series of tribal governments—a small fraction of their original home Lands. Skull Valley Goshutes considered much of what is now called Skull Valley—a valley extending from the Great Salt Lake to about Dugway, where the Stansbury and Cedar mountains converge—home Lands. Now, the Skull Valley Goshute Reservation consists of just 17,920 acres within the valley, created only after many unsuccessful attempts by the BIA to move them to the Uintah and Ouray Reservation in northeastern Utah (primarily populated by Utes and run by a

---

49. Crum, *Road on Which We Came.*

Ute tribal government).⁵⁰ Yet, these massive decreases in the size and scope of ancestral territories and reduction/relocation to smaller reservations do not negate claims to and relationships with the entirety of precontact traditional and ancestral home Lands.

It is not surprising, then, that arguments against the Yucca Mountain and Skull Valley nuclear waste sites commonly assert that these sites are within the home Lands of Western Shoshone, Skull Valley Goshute, and Southern Paiute peoples and nations. From a Western worldview, one of the key differences between the Yucca Mountain and Skull Valley PFS sites is that one is within current reservation boundaries (Skull Valley) and one is outside of current reservation boundaries (Yucca Mountain). From the perspective of Western Shoshone, Skull Valley Goshute, and Southern Paiute rhetors and their allies, however, this distinction is merely based in a settler colonial legal structure and not representative of past, present, and future relationships with home Lands. Because of deep attachments to home Lands, Indigenous Lands protectors seek to show how storing nuclear waste in these places would unduly burden and disrupt relations with Lands. The Indigenous Environmental Network, a long-standing nonprofit organization that supported Indigenous resistance to both sites, highlights Yucca Mountain and Skull Valley as homelands: "This disproportionate toxic burden—called environmental racism—has culminated in the current attempts to dump much of the nation's nuclear waste in the homelands of the Indigenous peoples of the Great Basin region of the United States. This action does not provide homeland security to our Indigenous peoples."⁵¹ This turn on the federal government's perspective that these sites would promote homeland security for Americans pivots toward calling on audiences to recognize Indigenous home Lands as distinct from the US.

Yucca Mountain

Yucca Mountain is undoubtedly Indigenous Lands. As demonstrated in chapter 2, Yucca Mountain and its surrounding area has a long history of human use and occupation by Western Shoshone and Southern Paiute peoples since time immemorial. So, it is not simply one part of a large traditional land base; it is a place where Western Shoshone and Southern Paiute peoples lived, worshipped, cultivated food, and buried ancestors. Even though the US government considers Yucca Mountain federal land gained through gradual

---

50. Crum, "Skull Valley Band."
51. Indigenous Environmental Network, "Indigenous Anti-Nuclear Statement," 1.

encroachment of the settler state, Yucca Mountain is still Indigenous home Lands. In the words of Vivienne Caron-Jake of the Southern Paiute Kaibab Band,

> To begin with, the Southern Paiute were placed, as were most tribal groups, communities, and nations, on this land as representatives of the Creator's people, and we were instructed to protect the land and other living creatures within it. We know ourselves to be the Nungwuh, the People. From time immemorial, these lands and my people have been inseparable. To belong is to have a fulfilled life. To know you belong is to continuously speak to this reality of belonging, to be thankful for the Creator's blessings, and to honor and respect all that is within your household, community, and tribe.[52]

Former Western Shoshone National Council chairperson Raymond Yowell similarly highlights how

> when the U.S. entered into the Ruby Valley Treaty of 1863 with the Western Shoshone Nation, the U.S. acknowledged the Shoshone's existence as a nation and recognized our rights to our homelands. Our rights as indigenous people were granted to us by the Creator of Life when we were placed in these lands countless generations ago, not granted by the invading Americans or any of their federal agencies. The Western Shoshone have never relinquished our indigenous rights to the U.S. or any other non-Shoshone government.[53]

Both Caron-Jake and Yowell recount being placed on these home Lands by the Creators. While Caron Jake emphasizes how to honor and respect one's home Lands, Yowell simultaneously rejects the federal government's claim to their Lands and asserts a Creator-given right to their home Lands. This, in turn, grounds resistance to nuclear waste storage.

An example of how Western Shoshones and Southern Paiutes invoked home Lands as a reason to reject the site comes from the public comment processes that accompanied the federal government's evaluation and eventual approval of the Yucca Mountain site. Despite numerous calls for government-to-government consultation, Western Shoshone, Southern Paiute, and allied Indigenous peoples used public hearings and public comment periods as a site of resistance. While the stated purpose of the hearings and comment peri-

---

52. Hebner and Plyler, *Southern Paiute*, xi.
53. Harney, *Way It Is*, 126.

ods was to evaluate the scientific suitability of the site, Indigenous rhetors eschewed this constraint and used the opportunity to display their relationship to Yucca Mountain as home Lands.[54] Members of the Las Vegas Paiute Tribe, the Lone Pine Paiute Shoshone Tribe, the Big Pine Paiute Tribe, the Western Shoshone National Council, the Western Shoshones, and the Paiute Tribes of Utah made statements that Yucca Mountain is a part of their home Lands since "time immemorial."[55] For example, Calvin Meyers, chair (at the time of comment) of the Las Vegas Paiutes, says, "I would like to welcome you to my homelands," and Western Shoshone Lois Whitney claims, "Yucca Mountain sits in the middle of my home land."[56] Rachel Johnson of the Lone Pine Paiute Shoshone Tribe declares, "We object to the proposed siting of the repository at Yucca Mountain. The proposed site is in the homelands of our people, lands we have occupied since time immemorial."[57] At a public hearing in Las Vegas, Edward Smith, chair (at the time of comment) of the Southern Paiute Chemehuevi Indian Tribe, argued that multiple nations share Yucca Mountain as part of their homeland:

> Our people, along with other Southern Paiute tribes and Western Shoshone and Owens Valley Paiute peoples have lived, traveled, worked, raised children, worshiped, harvested plants, animal, water and mineral resources and died in these lands for thousands of years. Our people were created on these lands. Our Creator gave us the sacred responsibility to live on, use and care for the land and all of its resources so that future generations would benefit from the many gifts that they provide to sustain life. These lands are part of our people and we are part of these lands. The two connected as one and that connection is everlasting, even though we have been forced throughout history to give up and move away from many areas of our traditional homeland. This land is and will always be Indian land.[58]

Articulating and defending Yucca Mountain as Indigenous home Lands is an important argument opposing the high-level nuclear waste site that enacts resistance to other ways of using and conceptualizing these Lands.

---

54. Endres, "Rhetoric of Nuclear Colonialism."
55. Harney, *Way It Is*; "Hearing for Site Recommendation Consideration"; "Science and Engineering Report"; and "Yucca Mountain Project Comments."
56. "Hearing for Site Recommendation Consideration," 102; and "Science and Engineering Report," 9.
57. "Public Hearing Session for a Geologic Repository," 11.
58. "Yucca Mountain Project Comments," 23.

The US government does not acknowledge the contested nature of Yucca Mountain and instead maintains that the Western Shoshones lost title to their home Lands that are outside of current reservation boundaries. In a DOE document that replies to the arguments presented in public hearings, like those quoted above, they replied: "The United States has met its obligations with the Indian Claims Commission's final award and, as a consequence, the aboriginal title to the land has been extinguished."[59] This dismissal of Western Shoshone and Southern Paiute articulations of Yucca Mountain as home Lands is not surprising coming from a settler government that labels the region a wasteland.[60] Yet, Western Shoshone and Southern Paiute peoples and nations continued to challenge the federal government's claims throughout the decades-long fight to protect their home Lands.

Overall, these appeals to stop the Yucca Mountain project because of its status as home Lands to Western Shoshones and Southern Paiutes are significant because they challenge the federal government's claim to the Yucca Mountain and introduce long-standing relationships to the Lands into the deliberative space. The comments highlighted in this section are directed to the US federal government via public comments and public hearings and therefore demonstrate to a non-Indigenous audience the importance of home Lands for Indigenous peoples. They call for decolonization and resurgence of Indigenous ways of knowing their home Lands.

Skull Valley

Recall the Skull Valley Goshute origin story in which coyote carries a basket of humans made on an island in the Great Salt Lake and distributes them around, with the hearty Goshutes escaping from the basket last.[61] As detailed in chapter 2, the Skull Valley Goshute nation successfully resisted relocation efforts until their reservation was created in 1912, to which they continue to

---

59. The Indian Claims Commission was created on August 13, 1946, to hear land claims filed by American Indians against the United States federal government. The commission did not have the authority to grant recovery of land, so rulings monetarily rewarded nations. The commission expired in 1978, but claims not yet resolved were transferred to the US Claims Court. As discussed in chapter 2, the Indian Claims Commission process for Western Shoshone nations was complicated and contested. US Department of Energy, "Site Recommendation," 201.

60. Endres, "From Wasteland to Waste Site."

61. Steward, "Some Western Shoshoni Myths."

be deeply attached.[62] As Leon Bear, former chairperson of the Skull Valley Goshute nation, put it:

> The Skull Valley Band of Goshute Indians have existed for thousands of years and have lived in the area containing our reservation. Our people chose not to migrate with the group that moved to Ibapah when the U.S. Government created a land base approximately 70 miles to the west of us. As traditionalists, we chose to stay with our families in Skull Valley; our wishes were recognized by the U.S. Government, and by executive orders issued in 1917 and 1918, the Skull Valley Reservation was created. There, we have lived and raised our families and carried on our traditional government. Our land and our values are very important to us and form the basis of our existence as an Indian tribe.[63]

The Skull Valley PFS interim high-level nuclear waste site would have been located on the small Skull Valley Goshute Reservation. Margene Bullcreek pointed to the exact location of the proposed site on several occasions when she hosted class visits to the reservation. The site was proposed for an area of the reservation not used for dwellings; it was across the small highway that cuts through the Skull Valley and through the Skull Valley Goshute Reservation. We often stopped along the highway before proceeding to the community center so that Margene could show us where the site would have been located. When considering the controversy within the Skull Valley Goshutes over the PFS site, the value of Skull Valley as home Lands is not in question. What is in contention is the question of how an interim high-level nuclear waste site would affect the home Lands.

Ohngo Gaudadeh Devia—the main group of Skull Valley Goshutes opposed to the interim nuclear waste site—rooted opposition in a defense of home Lands and the concomitant way of life. Bullcreek, the primary spokesperson in opposition to the Skull Valley PFS site, testified to the NRC: "Living with the fear that my ancestral homeland may become nothing more than a nuclear wasteland weighs heavy on my mind. I fear that the land of my ancestors will not be the land of my children's children because of the nuclear waste that will be brought upon the land and that may forever taint it."[64] Ohngo Gaudadeh Devia testifies: "The physical presence of the facility on the Skull Valley Goshutes' sacred homeland, and the continuous introduction into their homeland of highly radioactive spent nuclear fuel, will daily remind OGD

---

62. Crum, "Skull Valley Band."
63. Bear, "Prepared Statement of Leon D. Bear," 1.
64. Bullcreek, "Affidavit of Margene Bullcreek," 4.

members of these risks for at least twenty years. PFS proposes to cast shadows upon their lives for 7,000 sunrises."[65] These statements leave little doubt that the site would have consequences for the quality of the home Lands for some members. Concerns were not limited to the presence of nuclear waste in Skull Valley Goshute home Lands. OGD was also concerned about the possibility of a nuclear accident at the site:

> Moreover, members of OGD are concerned that even if the contamination resulting from a very severe transportation accident could be completely cleaned up, the cleanup process itself would have severe impacts on their community and their traditional life style, and their attitudes towards their traditional homeland could be permanently altered, tinged forever by uncertainty about the events they had already experienced and burdened by additional fears of future radioactive releases.[66]

In other words, OGD worried that an accident would essentially make their "ancestral homelands unlivable."[67] The disruption that the Skull Valley PFS site would cause to their way of life within their home Lands—whether an accident happened or not—led Bullcreek and OGD to view the PFS site as untenable.

One point came up often in the deliberations about the PFS site. The land surrounding Skull Valley is already toxic as a result of settler colonial policies that turned a perceived wasteland into a literal wasteland. Leon Bear and other proponents of the PFS site saw this as a key reason to move forward with the proposal because it is one of the few economic development opportunities available to a nation whose reservation is surrounded by tainted land. According to Bear: "We can't do anything here that's green or environmental. Would you buy a tomato from us if you knew what's out here? Of course not. In order to attract any kind of development, we have to be consistent with what surrounds us."[68] In another statement to the *Denver Post*, Bear emphasizes the importance of economic development over traditionalist values: "I'm a traditionalist to a certain point, but you can't go back and live in a wickup [a traditional Goshute dwelling made from sagebrush]. I was raised in the '70s, when it was all about promoting economic development. I was taught I could have a piece of the American pie."[69] Bear's reasoning is grounded in valuing

---

65. "Ohngo Gaudadeh Devia's Contentions," 4–5.
66. "Ohngo Gaudadeh Devia's Contentions," 12.
67. "Ohngo Gaudadeh Devia's Contentions," 37.
68. As cited in Nuclear Information and Resource Service, "Environmental Racism."
69. Riley, "Trainload of Debate."

Skull Valley Goshute home Lands as a source of economic development, for which storing nuclear waste was one of few viable solutions.

In contrast, Bullcreek told me and my students that even though much of the land surrounding the Skull Valley Goshute Reservation hosts toxicity, the line had been held at her reservation home Lands. An analysis of the Skull Valley PFS site by ally organization Nuclear Information Resource Service mirrors this thinking: "Their land-base is already surrounded by toxic industries, including biological and chemical weapons plants and incinerators, an aluminum chloride plant deemed the worst single air polluter in the country, and a low-level radioactive waste dump. Adding high-level nuclear waste to this toxic mix would be the final nail in the coffin for the traditional culture of the Skull Valley Goshutes."[70] Opposing the Skull Valley PFS site is important for resisting the settler notion of Skull Valley as wasteland and protecting the part of their home Lands that they still could.

While the focus of this book is primarily on those Skull Valley Goshute peoples who fought against their own government's decisions about nuclear waste siting, it is important to acknowledge that the Skull Valley Goshute government and other nuclear waste site supporters also view the reservation and Skull Valley as home Lands. This is not a contest between home Lands versus not-home Lands. I doubt there exists a Native nation that would not work to protect its home Lands. Rather, the stasis point between Skull Valley Goshute proponents and opponents centered on the question of how to best support the home Lands—through economic development or through traditional practices. The Skull Valley Goshute government saw the PFS site as an economic development opportunity that could provide jobs and revenue for tribal members, as well as opportunities to protect the home Lands.[71] Bullcreek, OGD, and allies insist that the PFS site would irreparably harm the home Lands and, in doing so, harm traditional values and practices that make Skull Valley Goshutes who they are. In her chapter about the PFS site in *All Our Relations*, LaDuke describes the tension between the promise of money for an impoverished Indigenous nation and the traditionalist "loyalty to an ancestral homeland."[72] Indeed, it is not uncommon to see contestation within Indigenous nations over resource and economic development characterized along the lines of traditionalists versus assimilationists. This is, of course, too simple a characterization that elides the complexity of intranational controversies about the use of Indigenous home Lands. The politics within Indigenous nations are just as complicated as those in any other country. Indigenous

---

70. Nuclear Information and Resource Service, "Nuclear Waste + Native Lands."
71. Bear, "Prepared Statement of Leon D. Bear."
72. LaDuke, *All Our Relations*, 106.

peoples and viewpoints are not homogenous, and the internal disagreements over how to protect Skull Valley Goshute home Lands and people are more typical than extraordinary.

Bullcreek and OGD invoked relationality with Skull Valley Goshute home Lands as a tactic of resistance to what they viewed as a problematic decision by their government officials. These arguments represent and draw from a traditionalist viewpoint about the risks posed to their home Lands by nuclear waste. Ultimately, these arguments became a part of the reason that the Department of the Interior reversed its earlier decision and reneged its support for the Skull Valley PFS site. The BIA, albeit an inherently flawed colonial structure of the settler state, sided with the preservation of the Skull Valley Goshute home Lands in its change of decision.

The BIA decision states: "The Secretary has the complex task of weighing the long-term viability of the Skull Valley Goshute reservation as a homeland for the Band (and the implications for preservation of Tribal culture and life) against the benefits and risks from economic development activities proposed for property held in trust by the United States for the benefit of the Band."[73] The BIA ultimately sided with preservation of Skull Valley Goshute home Lands. According to Honor the Earth, an organization that supported Bullcreek and OGD:

> While the state of Utah put its full muscle behind stopping the dump, the effort was primarily successful because of the consistent grassroots resistance on Skull Valley and from allies nationally. The stance of reservation-based and national Native groups on cultural and homeland protection became the very stance on which the BIA stood in rejecting the dump. The decision "recognizes our cultural perspective and lives as well as our sovereignty and the trust relationship between the federal government and our reservation community," said Margene Bullcreek, a leader of grassroots opposition to the dump. "This decision is not only highly important for Goshute people," added Tom Goldtooth, Executive Director of the Indigenous Environmental Network, "but also for all Indigenous people who face the same dilemma and who need protection against environmental justice."[74]

In the spirit of amplifying successful tactics of decolonization, the BIA's decision signaled success for Bullcreek and OGD; the BIA used some of Bullcreek's rhetorical tactics in its decision. While there were opportunities for PFS and

---

73. Honor the Earth, "Precedent Setting Decision."
74. Honor the Earth.

the Skull Valley Goshute government to appeal the decision, the PFS proposal ended with this decision, and there are no current plans to bring nuclear waste to the reservation. As noted in the Honor the Earth quote above, it is essential that this not be seen as a win by the state of Utah but as a win by Bullcreek and OGD. This win—preventing the Skull Valley PFS site—is but one in a long struggle for decolonization, resurgence, and survivance. It must be seen within the larger context of continued encroachment on Indigenous home Lands. But, for rhetorical scholars, an important takeaway is that the defense of home Lands successfully persuaded the BIA, making it a tactic worth considering for other struggles and contexts.

One cannot speak of the success of Bullcreek and OGD's campaign without noting that this was not seen as a win by the Skull Valley Goshute government that supported the PFS site. As I have argued elsewhere, the consequences of settler colonialism for the Skull Valley Goshute nation ultimately put the nation in an impossible position of choosing between economic development and protection of traditional practices in their home Lands. I chose to support Bullcreek and OGD in their efforts to stop the Skull Valley PFS site, but I did not make that choice lightly. I sought to understand the perspective of the Skull Valley Goshute government, seeing that economic development and sovereignty (as will be discussed in the next chapter) are also crucial to Indigenous survivance.

Sacred Lands

Home Lands cannot be easily separated from the sacred. As Dino Gilio-Whitaker contends, "The religious significance of a place is the spiritual glue that binds people to their homelands."[75] Sacred Lands are those relations that connect with the spiritual qualities of particular places (including all of the beings that reside with those places) with Indigenous peoples and nations. Closely related to appeals to home Lands are appeals to sacred Lands. For Western Shoshone, Southern Paiute, and Skull Valley Goshute peoples and nations, their home Lands are given by the Creator—they are inherently and inextricably also sacred Lands. Unlike many non-Native religions in America, Charles Wilkinson writes, "tribes usually are responsible for protecting the ancestral territories provided them by their creator."[76] Just like home Lands are not confined to current reservation territories, sacred Lands cover the

---

75. Gilio-Whitaker, *As Long as Grass Grows*, 136.
76. Wilkinson, *Indian Tribes as Sovereign Governments*, 50.

entire continent. According to LaDuke, "More than 75% of our sacred sites have been removed from our care and jurisdiction. Native people must now request permission to use their own sacred sites and, more often than not, find that those sites are in danger of being desecrated or obliterated."[77] As a result of various tangible threats to sacred Lands, Gilio-Whitaker adds, "Protecting sacred sites is one of the most difficult and pressing issues Native people now face."[78] Indigenous efforts to protect Yucca Mountain and Skull Valley are but two examples of a much wider phenomenon.

Some non-Indigenous readers may ask, Why are Indigenous Lands sacred? Gregory Cajete has devoted much of his career to understanding Indigenous spiritualities. He writes that "sacred orientation to place and space is a key element of the ecological awareness and intimate relationship that Indians have established with the North American landscape for 30,000 years or more."[79] Most Indigenous religions and spirituality are rooted in relationships with particular places, particular sacred Lands. While relationality will be addressed more fully in the next section, it is worth noting here that many Indigenous religions and spiritual practices involve communing with a specific rock formation, hot spring, cave with petroglyphs, or place where ancestors reside. The National Congress of American Indians recognizes the importance of sacred Lands.

> The National Congress of American Indians (NCAI) resolution SD 02 027 adopted a consensus that there was a "Zero tolerance for desecration, damage, or destruction of sacred places," and that among other things, there is a "recognition that sacred places are to be defined only as places that are sacred to practitioners of Native traditional religions. And that sacred places include land, (surface and subsurface), water and air, burial grounds, massacre sites, and battlefields, and spiritual commemoration, ceremonial, gathering and worship areas."[80]

Sacred Lands are key locations for spiritual practice.

Struggles to protect sacred Lands are pervasive for Indigenous peoples and nations because settler colonialism not only seeks to take away these Lands but also fails to adequately protect these sites from forms of encroachment that decrease the quality of spiritual experiences. The American Indian Religious Freedom Act purportedly affirms Indigenous nations' rights to practice

---

77. LaDuke, *Recovering the Sacred*, 14.
78. Gilio-Whitaker, *As Long as Grass Grows*, 129.
79. Cajete, "'Look to the Mountain,'" 3.
80. LaDuke, "Commentary."

their religions and access sacred Lands (including those outside of reservation territories) essential for conduct of religion, even if the nations have not maintained contiguous usage (difficult to do under settler colonial policies of removal, assimilation, and relocation). However, the legal and political systems' imbrication with settler colonialism limits the efficacy of the act, which maintains a colonial mindset about religion and religious sites and ignores the importance of Lands and particular places to a sacred site. For example, a church is a sacred site, but it is often seen as a building that could be placed anywhere and could be moved. Indigenous religious sites are rooted in particular places and ecological systems. LaDuke notes, "While the law [American Indian Religious Freedom Act] ensured that Native people could hold many of their ceremonies, it did not protect the places where many of these rituals take place or the relatives and elements central to these ceremonies."[81] If the place is not protected, then the religious practice is negatively affected. Storing nuclear waste within Yucca Mountain or within Skull Valley may not inhibit practicing ceremonies near the sites, but the sacred Lands themselves will be degraded because of the presence of nuclear waste.

Yucca Mountain

Western Shoshone and Southern Paiute peoples and nations appeal to the sacredness of Yucca Mountain and surrounding areas as a key part of their opposition to the site. Recall that Yucca Mountain is an area of contiguous usage by Western Shoshones and Southern Paiutes up until the region was appropriated as federal land in the 1950s. The Yucca Mountain area includes a plethora of cultural and spiritual qualities and places. Western Shoshone and Southern Paiute spiritualities are wholly attuned to sacred Lands. Interviews with Southern Paiute peoples reveal that Yucca Mountain is a site of puha, or spiritual power.[82] In an extended quotation, Richard Arnold of the Pahrump Paiutes describes puha:

> Puha, it's very hard to describe. Most would just call it power. Or try to define it as energy. It's something that goes way, way back; it's old, it's old stuff. It's good. It's fluid, it flows, it's all interconnected, it's there, if you need it, if you know how to use it, know how to talk to it. It can hear you. It can also get you. You have to be so careful with it. You have to go through a lot

---

81. LaDuke, *Recovering the Sacred*, 13.
82. Kuletz, *Tainted Desert*; and Stoffle et al., *Native American Cultural Resource Studies*.

just to be able to start that communication process. There are places it comes out; it's interconnected, related to those volcanoes. There's another one on the [Nevada] Test Site that's related too. Mount Charleston is another place, certain caves; a lot of it goes on the Salt Trail. Some of it goes on other types of songs, Silver Songs, Mountain Sheep Songs, Fox Songs, a whole bunch of different types of songs that tell you about puha. It's a hard thing to talk about, it really is, but it's there. It links us together; it's like a conduit of sorts. We believe there are three levels; we're in the middle, and there are extraordinary beings above and below us. Puha is a common thing between the three levels. When you do stuff, you have to appease each of these levels. If you get something out of balance with the bottom or upper level, it throws things way off kilter.[83]

Arnold goes on to explain how mountains, in particular, are a source of spiritual connection for Southern Paiute peoples:

I have been in places where you can hear the songs. They are there. It's the mountains that are singing to you. I've seen lots of things in my life, heard lots, but you could hear these songs just like we're talking here. Once again, our culture is so deep, so holistic, and if people would consider all those elements, it really makes sense, it really does. It's there, and if you're in tune or in sync with that stuff, you'll know it without a doubt. It's very alive and very well.[84]

Mountains and other spiritual sites remain active, yet they are under threat by settler colonialism. Corbin Harney writes, "The [Western Shoshone] spiritual grounds throughout the county are really important for us. We have to keep them alive, keep singing songs to them, because they're the ones that have kept us alive for thousands of years. And they're going to have to be used again by us, because we cannot afford to go with the modern way of life today."[85] These spiritual practices tend to be most strongly connected to traditionalists within particular Indigenous nations. According to the late Western Shoshone elder and activist Carrie Dann, "Traditional people still follow the old faith. You know like the spirit life and things like that. A lot of our indigenous people no longer practice that. But the traditional ones are—still practice that. They still believe in that."[86] While not practiced by all mem-

---

83. Hebner and Plyler, *Southern Paiute*, 178.
84. Hebner and Plyler, 179.
85. Harney, *Nature Way*, 48.
86. Dann, Nuclear Technology Oral History Project, 15.

bers of an Indigenous nation, traditional spiritual relationships are crucial to the maintenance of Indigenous cultures and religions against the onslaught of colonization and forced assimilation.

Various studies of the cultural and spiritual qualities of Yucca Mountain conducted during the tens of years that Yucca Mountain was being considered as a high-level nuclear waste site document Western Shoshone and Southern Paiute spiritual connections to Yucca Mountain.[87] While these studies were conducted through a flawed federal process for site selection based in the concept of resources as opposed to religious sites, they are nonetheless valuable not only because they document Western Shoshone and Southern Paiute spiritual connections to Yucca Mountain but also because they opened a restricted area to Western Shoshone and Southern Paiute peoples to reexperience. As Valerie Kuletz notes in her book, *The Tainted Desert*, when Yucca Mountain is viewed as a sacred site, "it becomes problematic to designate it as a burial tomb for toxic waste."[88]

According to the Indigenous Environmental Network, "the Western Shoshone is fighting to protect their lands, including the sacred Yucca Mountain."[89] Appeals to sacred Lands channel the qualities of a place.[90] These appeals rhetorically shift focus from the federal government's notion of land as resource, mountain as cavity for waste, and desert as lifeless to a different quality of the Lands: their sacredness. Affirming Yucca Mountain as sacred Land not only enacts survivance and argues for decolonization but also links the Western Shoshones and Southern Paiutes with a wide network of Indigenous peoples and nations seeking to protect sacred Lands. Throughout the many years in which Yucca Mountain was studied and considered as a waste site, Western Shoshone and Southern Paiute peoples and nations consistently affirmed the sacredness of Yucca Mountain as a mode of resistance. They talk about Yucca Mountain as a place linked to their spiritualities. Recognizing that each spirituality is distinct, the arguments are not identical across Western Shoshone and Southern Paiute comments.

According to former Western Shoshone National Council chief Raymond Yowell, "Yucca Mountain is a sacred site in our sovereign territory of the Newe Sogobia. The Bush administration has not consulted with our people on this serious issue that could endanger the future of our tribal nation."[91] Likewise,

---

87. Fowler, *Native Americans and Yucca Mountain*; Stoffle et al., *Native American Cultural Resource Studies*; and Stoffle, "Native Americans."
88. Kuletz, *Tainted Desert*, 139.
89. Indigenous Environmental Network, "Indigenous Anti-Nuclear Statement."
90. Endres, "Sacred Land."
91. Indigenous Environmental Network, "Yucca Mountain," 1.

Edward Smith of the Chemehuevi nation asserts, "Yucca Mountain is sacred to our people. It is part of the lands that our Creator gave to us."[92] Calvin Meyers of the Las Vegas Paiutes offers a detailed explanation about how transporting nuclear waste to Yucca Mountain would tangibly affect the spiritual qualities of their territory:

> The transportation of nuclear waste will go across a very important trail of ours that when we die, this is—this trail we go along to take us to the next place where we're supposed to be after this—after we pass this time. . . . We don't know what will happen to us. Will I be a Paiute then? Will I be able to go to the sacred place after I'm gone from here? That's a very important question for us. That's a very important question to a lot of people that are tribal people that have the land, that use the land, that have the land helping them do the things they need to do. . . . Without this land you have nothing, you can't go back and—you can't go anyplace. . . . Spirituality is something I hold dear, because without my spirituality, I am not a Paiute. Without being able to say that I can go to my hereafter, I can no longer say that I am a Paiute.[93]

These quotes express the sacred qualities of Yucca Mountain for Western Shoshone and Southern Paiute people. With varying levels of detail, they affirm how Yucca Mountain merits protection for the survivance of Western Shoshone and Southern Paiute peoples.

Settler colonialism is an environmental injustice because it severs sacred connections to Lands and, therefore, contributes to cultural genocide. As Western Shoshone Ian Zabarte writes, "The Western Shoshone Nation's cultural and religious relationship with the land, water, and all growing things within our ancestral lands and our fundamental belief that the interdependence and the protection of the land, water and all living things are a sacred duty under the Creator's Law and need to be understood by the Department of Energy."[94] Asserting and explaining the sacredness of Yucca Mountain to primarily non-Indigenous audiences in the federal government and publics is risky because it proposes a direct threat to the federal government's view of the land as resource that is appropriate for storing nuclear waste. Moreover, it exposes the radically different perspectives on Lands/land between Indigenous nations and the US nation. The Indigenous Environmental Network explicitly makes the connection between the different worldviews:

---

92. "Yucca Mountain Project Comments," 25.
93. "Hearing for Site Recommendation Consideration," 179–80.
94. Zabarte, "View of the Western Shoshone," 2–3.

According to the spiritual leaders and tribal elders of the Indigenous tribes of Western Shoshone and Paiute, the Yucca Mountain is sacred with the regional area having deep cultural and historical value to their peoples. President W. Bush and many leaders of Congress do not respect these deep spiritual values and cultural life-ways that have sustained the Indigenous peoples of this region since time immemorial. In the eyes of Indigenous peoples that follow the traditional teachings of our tribal ways, this President and people in Congress do not have a heart of love and compassion for Life and have clouded minds that put money above the health and safety of people and all Life.[95]

While the Yucca Mountain case highlights the differences in worldview between Indigenous and non-Indigenous rhetors, the Skull Valley PFS case pivots to differences of interpretation within one Indigenous nation.

Skull Valley

Margene Bullcreek points out that although Skull Valley may seem to be a lifeless wasteland to non-Indigenous people, there is great peace, spirituality, and vitality in the region.[96] She states in an interview: "Our reservation is sacred. This is the only land we have—the only thing the government left us after taking most of our country."[97] Recall that although their territory was massively reduced by the settler colonial government, the Skull Valley Goshute Reservation is within the Lands that the Creator gave them. For Skull Valley Goshute opponents of the PFS site, to bring nuclear waste to the reservation is to desecrate sacred Lands.

Bullcreek and OGD argue that storing nuclear waste in these sacred Lands would have irreversible consequences for the traditional way of life for Skull Valley Goshutes. In a statement to the NRC, Ohngo Gaudadeh Devia argues, "the organization [OGD] is also very concerned about the loss of traditional sacred sites and the effect this facility might have on traditional plant gathering and basically that the way of life of the Goshute Band will be forever changed should a nuclear accident occur."[98] This statement emphasizes that protecting sacred Lands is a matter of also preventing the loss of traditions

---

95. Indigenous Environmental Network, "Indigenous Anti-Nuclear Statement."
96. "Scoping Meeting," 50.
97. Nuclear Information and Resource Service, "Environmental Racism," 4.
98. Bullcreek, "Affidavit of Margene Bullcreek," 2.

and way of life, which is an essential tool in settler colonialism's attempt to erase Indigenous peoples and nations. In an interview, Bullcreek elaborates:

> Cedar and sage are sacred here. I cut willow branches over there to cradle my babies like my mother did, and my grandmother did, and her mother and her mother. Their bones are on this land. If you think it is desolate then you don't know the land. You don't know how to be still and listen. There is peace here. I felt I had to be outspoken or lose everything that has been passed down from generations. The stories that tell why we became the people we are and how we should consider our animal life, our air, things that are sacred to us. Leon Bear is trying to convince himself that what he is doing is right, but this waste will destroy who we are.[99]

In another statement, Bullcreek tells the NRC:

> But why should—so why should we be able to deal with the nuclear waste that's going to interfere. It's going to make—interfere into our lives of native—as Native Americans. We drink the water. We eat the wild plant life that are—this is all within the five mile scope of the EIS [environmental impact statement]. And we eat the wild animals, we eat the deer that comes—that's in our mountains. We have religious sites; we used the sage brushes as part of our sacred religious ceremonies. These are all sacred to us. We need to protect this. And also, I want to be able to say that we need to hold onto our traditions, because if this thing should ever—if the nuclear waste should control our lives, then we're not going to be able to be who we are. Who are we going to be? Are we going to be—is finally the government's going to make us—drive us in the melting pot that they have intended to do years ago?[100]

These extended quotes display the stakes of deciding whether to support the nuclear waste site. To Bullcreek, protecting remaining sacred Lands is an issue of survivance of the Lands and lifeways for Skull Valley Goshute peoples. Among those lifeways are the traditional spiritual practices of Skull Valley Goshute peoples that can only happen in Skull Valley. Bullcreek puts it simply: "We have our religious, sacred ceremonies that needs protected, to be protected."[101] Invoking the sacred qualities that could be lost if nuclear waste is brought to Skull Valley is a form of Indigenous Lands rhetoric that simultane-

---

99. Nuclear Information and Resource Service, "Environmental Racism."
100. "Scoping Meeting," 48.
101. "Scoping Meeting," 50.

ously asserts Indigenous knowledges and seeks to counter other framings of the Lands, particularly by settlers who often perceive it to be a wasteland and members of the Skull Valley Goshutes who supported the site.

Other Indigenous peoples offered support and solidarity with the Skull Valley Goshutes who were opposed to the PFS site. In one of the NRC hearings, Alberta Mason spoke in support of Bullcreek and Sammy Blackbear:[102] "My name is Alberta Mason. I'm Navajo from Window Rock, Arizona. I'm here in Provo, Utah, and I'm working with Margene Bullcreek and Sammy Blackbear. And I support their position in that to Native Americans we consider the Earth very sacred, and there are certain sites that are extremely sacred."[103] This quote illustrates how protection of sacred Lands is a topos, or point of argument, that is used widely by different Indigenous peoples and nations. Sacred Lands are not sacred for the same reasons, but the experience of protecting sacred Lands is common to many Indigenous peoples, leading to expressions of solidarity. Cory Hoopiiana, the vice president-elect of the Iosepa Historical Association at the time of speaking, indicates that Skull Valley is also sacred to Polynesian communities that relocated to Utah via conversion to the LDS religion:

> We actually have property out there in that region where they are proposing, about ten miles north of the Goshutes Indian Reservation. And we have spent a lot of time out there, primarily because that area is the first Polynesian town site ever established in the United States, or anywhere, for that matter. We have a lot of ancestors buried out there. That land is very sacred to us. We are in the process of building another monument to the first lady who expired out there. We have other plans to erect other monuments and we are trying to keep that land as sacred as we can.[104]

In this way, solidarity is expressed not only via the recognition of another Indigenous nation's sacred Lands but also through focusing on how the PFS site could harm nearby sacred Lands for non-Goshute Indigenous peoples.

While opponents of the PFS site express a way of knowing their sacred Lands that is different from and contrasted with non-Indigenous perspectives, they also convey a way of knowing the Lands that is different from that of the Skull Valley Goshute government and supporters of the PFS site. Bear

---

102. Margene Bullcreek and Sammy Blackbear were the two most vocal opponents of the PFS site and their government's support of it. Blackbear's concerns were mainly with governance and sovereignty and are therefore covered in detail in the next chapter.
103. "Limited Appearance Hearing," 12.
104. "Private Fuel Storage," 47.

describes how respect for Lands could be maintained with the PFS proposal. I quote him in extended form to display his voice and the reasoning:

> Our beliefs include respect and honor for our land and our values. It also includes the desire to be self-sufficient and to use our land base to benefit the health and welfare of our tribal members. We have studied various economic development programs, and we have spent more than eight years researching a spent nuclear fuel storage facility, which first came to our attention through the U.S. Government. We have studied the environmental effects of such a facility, taking into account our cultural and religious values, as well as archeological and religious sites. After thoughtful research and study, we have concluded that the storage facility currently proposed will have no adverse effects on any sacred or cultural sites or upon the wildlife that inhabits our reservation or upon our neighbors in the State of Utah. In fact, this storage project offers less environmental threat to the reservation, and the surrounding areas, than virtually any other industry that we might bring to the reservation. Because it is an interim storage facility and no fuel is handled on site, there is nothing to be released into the air, the water, or buried in our ground.[105]

This statement details Bear's perspective that economic development and self-sufficiency do not have to be in conflict with honoring sacred Lands. He cites studies that indicate the interim facility would not impact sacred sites, therefore arguing the proposal can support Skull Valley Goshute economic development without sacrificing the Lands. Likewise, Lawrence Bear underscored the utility of the reservation territory for supporting Skull Valley Goshutes: "And I have also heard a lot of people say, you know, our land's sacred. I believe our land is sacred, but then again, I say—somebody once said—not in this context, but this is what I say: It is not what we can do for our land; it is what our land can do for us. And that's what this is going to be about, and that is just what I would like to say."[106] Skull Valley Goshute proponents of the PFS site argue storing nuclear waste on sacred Lands is possible; nuclear waste can be stored safely without negative consequences for the Lands and spiritual lifeways. This differing view offers a point of stasis over whether nuclear waste will impact sacred Lands' connected spiritual practices. Responding to these arguments in favor of the site creates an extra argumentative burden for Bullcreek, Blackbear, and OGD. They not only have to convince the NRC and

---

105. Bear, "Prepared Statement of Leon D. Bear," 1.
106. "Public Meeting on the P Draft Environmental Impact Statement," July 27, 2000, 136–37.

BIA that the PFS site would harm Indigenous sacred Lands, but they also have to convince members of their own nation's government. Bullcreek attempts to do so this way: "They are waving this like it's economic development, like it's a really good deal, when it has poisoned us, when it has killed our natural awareness. Everybody is going to say 'we don't want this' later. But it is going to be too late."[107] Indigenous nations, like any other nation, are heterogenous and made up of individuals with different stances on controversial issues. As such, Indigenous Lands rhetorics in support of sacred Lands are directed to multiple audiences, including Native governments.

Similar to opposition to the Yucca Mountain site, Skull Valley Goshute opponents of the PFS site see the risks to their sacred Land as a form of environmental injustice. When I asked about how she conceived of environmental justice, Bullcreek responded:

> On the environmental justice, OK. That's the whole concept of my opposing the Private Fuel Storage because that's part of who we are as Indigenous people—was to be able to live our way of life without any interruptions that would make short of our living standards and what do we expect out of our environment that we consider as being sacred. And so environmental justice comes in when we have something like the PFS, coming in to disrupt our way of life and effects that it's going to have on us if there was going to be any type of mishap from this waste storage. And it seems like throughout the nation, that has to do with Indigenous people, it always has to deal with their environmental justice because it's disrupting their way of life. It's a small community usually—usually a small community that has to deal with this large corporation. And the large corporation does not consider the way of livelihood that we have as Indigenous people. They're just out for—to have gains for their own purposes.[108]

Yet, it is important to note that this is not the only lens for environmental injustices. Leon Bear argued that the state of Utah's attempts to stop the PFS site also constituted an environmental injustice by seeking to undermine the sovereignty and self-determination of the Skull Valley Goshute nation, a nation surrounded by numerous toxic sites with limited options for economic development.[109]

There is nothing new in the way that Western Shoshone, Southern Paiute, and Skull Valley Goshute nations and peoples fought to protect their sacred

---

107. Fahys, "Family Feud," 2.
108. Bullcreek, Nuclear Technology Oral History Project, 1.
109. Endres, "From Wasteland to Waste Site."

Lands. They join a long history and tradition of defense of sacred Lands by Indigenous peoples. According to Gilio-Whitaker, "Native peoples continue to fight for the protection of sacred sites within an inadequate and often unjust system."[110] Yet, there is value in appreciation and amplification of moments when sacred Lands have been protected. These moments deserve recognition, in part, because of what is at stake. In discussing the importance of the sacred to Indigenous peoples, LaDuke notes: "At stake is nothing less than the ecological integrity of the land base and the physical and social health of Native Americans throughout the continent."[111] This connection between sacred Lands and ecological integrity invokes the final interrelated tactic: relationality with Lands.

Lands as Relations

Relationality is central to Indigenous perspectives. Lands are home Lands and sacred Lands because of the kinships between Indigenous peoples and places. These are deep relationships with Lands in all of the complexity of that concept. Relationships exist between humans, plants, ancestors, animals, soils, rocks, water, air—all of the animate elements of a particular place. As Gilio-Whitaker notes, "This reciprocal relationship forms a sense of kinship with the land itself."[112] These kinship relationships rooted in reciprocity, responsibility, and respect take different forms across the diversity of Indigenous peoples and nations. Scholars have used different terms to describe these relations as connected to religion and spiritual practices, such as realist animism[113] and spiritual ecology—"an intimate relationship between themselves and their environment."[114] Regardless of the form taken or terminology used to describe them, relationships are the core of Indigenous ways of knowing, being with, and protecting Lands. Indigenous relationality with Lands is frequently used to stereotype Indigenous peoples as the supposed first environmentalists or as closer to nature. As Gilio-Whitaker notes, "Indigenous relationships with nature have been stereotypes and appropriated by dominant society in a multitude of ways (such as the ecological Indian), but in reality are rooted in a philosophical paradigm very different from that of dominant Western

---

110. Gilio-Whitaker, *As Long as Grass Grows*, 140.
111. LaDuke, *Recovering the Sacred*, 11.
112. Gilio-Whitaker, *As Long as Grass Grows*, 139.
113. Sheridan and Longboat, "Haudenosaunee Imagination."
114. Cajete, "'Look to the Mountain,'" 4.

society."[115] These paradigms may not be enacted by every Indigenous person, but examples of Indigenous peoples and nations not acting in alignment with these paradigms is not sufficient to discount them.

Lands as relations appeals recognize that Lands are alive. From the perspective of many Indigenous peoples, "everything the creator made is a living entity."[116] Western Shoshone elder Carrie Dann says: "To traditional indigenous people the earth is alive. It's a mother to all life."[117] Eunice Ohte of the Moapa Band of Paiutes puts it this way: "The land means everything to me. It feeds me. It clothes me. When I'm feeling bad, I can go there, and I can talk to her because I know she's older than me and I know she controls me and I don't have any control of her; so I have a lot of respect for the land . . . it is my prayers. It's what keeps me alive all this time, and my family."[118] According to Vine Deloria Jr., because they view the earth and everything on earth as living, Indigenous religions and cultures call for different relationships with the earth than Western perspectives that overvalue human agency.[119] Gilio-Whitaker writes, "Simply put, from an Indigenous perspective, nonhuman life forms have agency in a way that they do not in dominant Western cultures."[120] Kimmerer speaks of "a world with a democracy of species."[121] It is not only that more-than-human beings hold agency; Lands are also places of communion with ancestors. Deloria explains, "Most tribes were very reluctant to surrender their homelands to the whites because they knew that their ancestors were still spiritually alive on the land, and they were fearful that the whites would not honor the ancestors and the lands in the proper manner."[122] Relationality with Lands, then, is a key lifeway for Indigenous peoples and nations.

Relationality with Lands is also a matter of communication. The animate beings that constitute Lands have the ability to communicate with humans. Donal Carbaugh demonstrates a form of communication in the Blackfeet culture in which if humans listen, birds talk and places speak.[123] Carbaugh and Karen Wolf similarly describe a form of listening among the Apache that is deeply rooted in relationality:

---

115. Gilio-Whitaker, *As Long as Grass Grows*, 138.
116. Kidwell, Noley, and Tinker, *Native American Theology*, 127–28.
117. Dann, Nuclear Technology Oral History Project, 14.
118. As cited in Urban Environmental Research and Zabarte, *Tribal Concerns*, 36.
119. Deloria, "Comfortable Fictions."
120. Gilio-Whitaker, *As Long as Grass Grows*, 136.
121. Kimmerer, *Braiding Sweetgrass*, 58.
122. Deloria, *God Is Red*, 171–72.
123. Carbaugh, "'Just Listen.'"

Such a discourse, when properly active in an Apache way, brings into being a kind of consciousness, a way of living in the world where objects, animals, and other things, as well as people, become sources for messages. Note here, with this cultural discourse system, the consciousness is not contained within an individual exclusivity, but permeates animals and things, infusing the world with a unity that can speak if only consulted and heard in a proper way.[124]

Appeals to protect Lands as relations often report on forms of communication with more-than-human relations in the place being protected.

As a rhetorical tactic, Lands as relations are an articulation of Indigenous ways of knowing and being. Arguments against the Yucca Mountain and Skull Valley PFS sites are grounded Western Shoshone, Southern Paiute, and Skull Valley Goshute efforts to be in good relationships with Lands. Nuclear waste would disrupt those relations.

Yucca Mountain

Corbin Harney describes the Western Shoshone relationship to Lands this way: "This is the Native way: all of us are related to everything else, to the elements, to the animal life. We're all connected to the tree life too—you name it."[125] Likewise, Pahrump Paiute Richard Arnold narrates his "close relationship to the environment, to all the resources out there."[126] These relations are reciprocal. Harney reflects on what his grandmother told him: "If you don't take care of what's out there, like all the living things, you're going to wake up and they're not going to be there. If they're not there, you're not going to survive. You cannot survive without them, they cannot survive without you. So, we're all connected together as a life on this planet of ours."[127] Relationality with the more-than-human world is elemental to Western Shoshone and Southern Paiute lifeways, which are particularly enacted by traditionalists, elders, and other keepers of the culture. These ways of understanding relationality are interconnected with the animacy of all beings and the capacity for human communication with the more-than-human world.

Jessica Bacoch, former chair of the Big Pine Paiute Tribe of the Owens Valley Council, states, "The Paiute people regard the total ecosystem as a living

---

124. Carbaugh and Wolf, "Situating Rhetoric," 26.
125. Harney, *Nature Way*, 33.
126. Hebner and Plyler, *Southern Paiute*, 176.
127. Harney, *Nature Way*, 6.

entity and the spirits and beings that dwell there to this day are still meaningful to us. Many tribal people indigenous to the Yucca Mountain region have informed DOE officials that this area has special meaning and expressed opposition to the proposed Yucca Mountain project."[128] The animacy of the more-than-human world implies a communicative agency belonging to beings from rocks to plants to animals. As Harney tells it,

> Long ago, the land, the mountain, used to have more voice, a clearer voice, clearer than what it is today. The land, the rocks, they used to continue to tell us over and over again to take care of them and to ask us to do these things. But today we're lost . . . we just look at a mountain as if it's just there, nothing more. But the mountain's got a life to it. Everything's got a spirit, the mountain's got a spirit, and all the living things on the mountains have got a spirit.[129]

In this way, Yucca Mountain has spirit and capacities to communicate with those humans with the capacities to listen.

In an oral history interview, Western Shoshone Bennie Reilly Sr. talks about his wife, who is a healer. Although he does not have the special skill to talk to animals, he describes the times he has observed his wife talking to eagles:

> Lot of times, I see her talk to an eagle. I've seen her talk to an eagle on the side of the road and we'll stop, eagle'll be sitting there, she'll open her window and get out and talk to him, and they'll sit there and look at her, you know, turn their head around and all that, you know, and all that, listen for a while. Then they get up and take off. Or sometime they'll be sitting in a tree and they'll squawk back at her, this and that. That's a neat experience because they talk her language.[130]

Similarly, Arnold describes how elders would encourage communication with Lands:

> I remember when I was young, elders would say, "Listen to the wind. Listen to the water; it will talk to you. Listen to that land. Listen to those rocks." I remember being with some of these old folks and they'd say hurry up, pack

---

128. Bacoch, "Letter."
129. Harney, *Way It Is*, 45.
130. Reilly, Nevada Test Site Oral History Project, 28.

your stuff. There's no clouds, nothing. You'd hear the wind, listen to it, and sure enough, you'd hear it, know the rain is coming here.[131]

Although not every Western Shoshone and Southern Paiute person is able to listen to and communicate with the more-than-human world, it is a capacity that is enabled by Western Shoshone and Southern Paiute spirituality and relationality with Lands. These notions of relationality, reciprocity, animacy, and communication within the more-than-human world are central to Western Shoshone and Southern Paiute opposition to the Yucca Mountain site. According to Carrie Dann, "Some of that land, and especially Yucca Mountain, that's in the Western Shoshone area. That's on our lands and as a Western Shoshone people we don't want it [nuclear waste]. It is against, you know, what the rock has told us."[132] Opposition to the site was grounded in a sacred responsibility to protect their relationships with Yucca Mountain.

Opposition to Yucca Mountain is linked with opposition to other nuclear production processes that have disproportionately impacted Indigenous peoples and nations. Uranium mining in Indigenous Lands created a legacy of destruction. Based in interviews with Western Shoshone and Southern Paiute elders during the federal government's research into the Yucca Mountain site, anthropologist Richard Stoffle and colleagues summarize: "Radioactivity has been interpreted as 'the angry rock' by some elders" because it was taken without permission and used in ways it did not agree with.[133] Bringing it full circle, then, bringing radioactive waste to Yucca Mountain is problematic from the perspective of the mountain. As Edward Smith of the Chemehuevi nation states, "We believe that Yucca Mountain will become unhappy and angry if you put radioactive waste into it. The spirits living in the area will move away and eventually the land will be unable to sustain plants, animals, water, air, people, and life."[134]

In opposition to the Yucca Mountain site, Western Shoshones, Southern Paiutes, and their allies articulate the many ways that putting radioactive waste into Yucca Mountain would irreparably harm relationality with Yucca Mountain. Radioactivity threatens the more-than-human beings that Western Shoshone and Southern Paiute peoples rely on for wellness. According to Lorinda Sam, former environmental director for the Ely Shoshone Tribe, "As Western Shoshone people, we hold significant ties to the land. We use the land and

---

131. Hebner and Plyler, *Southern Paiute*, 176.
132. Dann, Nuclear Technology Oral History Project.
133. Stoffle et al., *Native American Cultural Resource Studies*, 15.
134. "Yucca Mountain Project Comments," 17.

its resources for our existence. The Yucca Mountain project can destroy our resources used by tribal members such as water, wood, grasses, pinion nuts, plant for food and medicinal uses by being exposed to radiation."[135] Similarly, Marlene Begay, a member of the Walker River Paiutes, says, "Putting nuclear waste in the land is polluting it and will kill Mother Earth. We have only one earth and one water. Everything is related. If we poison the earth, then we are poisoning ourselves."[136] Because of the relationality with Lands, damage to Yucca Mountain and to people cannot be separated. Because of this, it is crucial to treat Yucca Mountain with respect. Dann narrated, "Nuclear waste. It's wrong. Our stories talk about, you know, how different things will affect you. And if that comes from a rock, a rock has told us, you know, what to—how to treat a rock. And if we don't treat a rock in a respectful way, you know, you can destroy it."[137] Joe Kennedy, former chair of the Timbisha Shoshone Tribe, talks about the danger of mistreating Yucca Mountain:

> Our traditional ties go to Yucca Mountain, Yucca Mountain being a very spiritual place. There's a lot of stories, different stories about that mountain being the snake and, you know, that we were always told that, you know, you mistreat that mountain, that it may, someday it'll spew out poisons that'll affect all life as we know it.[138]

This tactic of Indigenous Lands rhetorics articulates why it is crucial to protect Yucca Mountain and prevent it from becoming a nuclear waste site. The tactic relies on testimony about the relationality between Western Shoshone and Southern Paiute peoples and the more-than-human beings at Yucca Mountain. These statements simultaneously enact Indigenous knowledges and lifeways and support their arguments against the site, illuminating the fundamental incommensurability between Native and Western relationships with Lands/land. In a clear articulation of the difference between Southern Paiute and Western perspectives, Calvin Meyers details, "You may go ahead and move out of Las Vegas, you can move clear across the country, where it may be safer, but I can't. My heart and soul comes from this earth, from right here, not very far away from where you guys want to destroy my land."[139]

---

135. "Yucca Mountain Public Hearing White Pine," 5.
136. "Public Comments on Site Recommendation," 17.
137. Dann, Nuclear Technology Oral History Project, 4.
138. Kennedy, Native American Forum, 18–19.
139. "US Department of Energy Public Hearing," October 12, 2001, 74.

Skull Valley

Although less prominent in the rhetorical tactics of Skull Valley Goshute opponents of the PFS site than other forms of Indigenous Lands rhetorics, Bullcreek and OGD's arguments against the PFS site do describe relationships of respect with Skull Valley Lands. Historian Dennis Defa wrote:

> The Goshute people are survivors. They have survived in a land that many see as a desert waste, with few resources or advantages. The Goshutes, however, see the land as their home, a home that has provided them with everything they needed. They knew to take care of their home, never upsetting a delicate balance of resource utilization and replenishment, and the land took care of them.[140]

Although not the words of a Skull Valley Goshute person, this historian's characterization is consistent with what I learned from Margene Bullcreek about her connection to her home Lands, representative of "the group's deep attachment to its traditional homeland."[141] In an oral history interview, Bullcreek describes it this way:

> Our sacredness and the spiritual beliefs that we have, we don't have materialistic types of beliefs, but we do believe in harmony with our, with the creatures or animals, the air. We believe the eagle is a sacred bird to us, and so the—I believe in the spiritualism of how I was brought up and to respect these things. I believe that there is healing in the plants; I believe that there is prayers that could be—that comes with the purification of the water in our ceremonies. I believe in the prayers that we have through ceremonies whether it's Sun Dance or other types of religious ceremonies that we have as indigenous people. And that's always been part of my family's belief and other indigenous peoples' belief that believe in that direction.[142]

A harmonious relationship with the Lands is based in a foundation of respect for the more-than-human world. The relationship is deeply connected to spirituality and the sacred. When Bullcreek states that the PFS facility would "damage our plant life, water, air, and spiritual atmosphere as well as future generations," she demonstrates that this damage threatens those more-than-

---

140. Defa, "Goshute Indians of Utah," 121.
141. Crum, "Skull Valley Band," 267.
142. Bullcreek, Nuclear Technology Oral History Project.

human beings and threatens a harmonious relationship built on respect.[143] Further, when Bullcreek argues "I am concerned that a release of radioactive waste would cause grievous injury to the people and the land," she expresses a concern for Lands in the same way she expresses concern for humans.[144] Bullcreek's arguments against the PFS site, then, express concern and respect for Lands as important relations. This form of Indigenous Lands rhetorics is an enactment of Indigenous knowledges that seeks to sustain traditional relationships and spirituality for the benefit of Lands, including the beings who are part of them.

As discussed above, the Skull Valley Goshute government representatives who advocated for the PFS site claimed that the site would not radically damage their spirituality and connection to homeland. According to Leon Bear, "This project was carefully chosen to minimize any interference with the tribal members who live on the reservation, to avoid interference with sacred or religious sites, and to avoid adverse effects on the wildlife and plant life existing on the reservation."[145] Moreover, his advocacy for the project pivoted to how the project would offer other pathways for relations with their homelands. He states: "The Skull Valley Band has deep respect for its cultural heritage and the land. We believe that this storage project offers a safe, clean industry to provide much needed economic development on our reservation, including jobs for members of the Band enabling some members to move back to the reservation, and preserving the Band's cultural heritage while protecting the land and its environment."[146] An important point here is the economic development provided by the PFS site would actually bring members back into everyday relationship with their homeland because they could move back to the reservation. In this way, Bear and other supporters of the PFS site explain the disagreement is not about the value of being in relationship with Lands but is about whether a nuclear waste facility—as an economic development opportunity—disrupts the Skull Valley Goshutes' relationship with their Lands.

CONCLUSION

Indigenous Lands rhetorics are central to both decolonization and resurgence. Rhetoricians have choices in their advocacy. They choose among the available means of persuasion in a given situation. Western Shoshone, Southern

---

143. LaDuke, *All Our Relations*, 105.
144. Bullcreek, "Affidavit of Margene Bullcreek," 2.
145. Bear, "Prepared Statement of Leon D. Bear," 1–2.
146. Bear, 1–2.

Paiute, and Skull Valley Goshute advocates could have chosen to argue on the grounds set by the federal government—the scientific suitability of the sites. Yet, they made a tactical choice to oppose the Yucca Mountain and Skull Valley PFS sites based in Indigenous Lands rhetorics. Indigenous arguments against Yucca Mountain and Skull Valley are an attempt at cultural preservation and resurgence that articulate Yucca Mountain and Skull Valley as unique Lands that will be damaged from nuclear waste. As Kyle Whyte argues, to place limitations on Indigenous relationships with Lands is fundamentally an environmental injustice.[147] Indigenous Lands rhetorics refuse to see Yucca Mountain or Skull Valley in the same way as the federal government does— as wasteland, resource, and object. Rather, they enact survivance and resurgence of Indigenous ways of knowing in a move toward decolonization. Of course, this is complicated in the Skull Valley Goshute nation, in which there is a fundamental disagreement about whether to support the PFS site. As I have argued elsewhere, both sides have arguments grounded in environmental injustices, the pursuit of sovereignty, and the value of lands.[148] Though I personally align more and have chosen to focus on the Skull Valley Goshute opponents of the PFS site in this chapter and book, it is important to recognize that the ongoing realities and consequences of settler colonialism are to blame for the many constraints faced by the Skull Valley Goshute nation. As discussed in chapter 1, nuclear waste was one of the only opportunities presented to a nation surrounded by other toxic wastes in a place perceived by settlers as a wasteland.

This chapter not only categorizes Indigenous arguments against storing nuclear waste within Yucca Mountain and Skull Valley into three tactics of Indigenous Lands rhetorics but also presents the radical incommensurability between Indigenous and settler perspectives on the value and use of Yucca Mountain and Skull Valley.[149] Tuck and Yang argue that "the opportunities for solidarity lie in what is incommensurable rather than what is common across these efforts."[150] Instead of seeking to reduce the incommensurability between Western and Indigenous ways of knowing and being with Lands/land, one goal of Indigenous Lands rhetorics is to seek solidarity from non-Indigenous peoples in their efforts to protect Yucca Mountain and Skull Valley.

---

147. Whyte, "Indigenous Experience."
148. Endres, "From Wasteland to Waste Site."
149. Endres, "Sacred Land."
150. Tuck and Yang, "Decolonization," 28.

CHAPTER 4

Indigenous National Interest Rhetorics

During a DOE public hearing in Amargosa Valley, Nevada, about the proposed Yucca Mountain high-level nuclear waste disposal site, Bill Helmer, a representative from the Environmental Office of the Timbisha Shoshone Tribe, argues:

> The Yucca Mountain project is illegally being proposed on Western Shoshone lands without Western Shoshone approval. This is a violation of the Treaty of Ruby Valley, and tribal sovereignty. In addition, the Western Shoshone National Council, of which the Timbisha Shoshone Tribe is a member, declared in 1995 that all Western Shoshone lands were a nuclear-free zone, thus barring the storage, use or disposal of all radioactive materials.[1]

Helmer's comment is reinforced by a Timbisha Shoshone Tribal Council resolution against the Yucca Mountain site, which states: "Therefore be it resolved that the Timbisha Shoshone Tribe strongly urges the Secretary of Energy to *not recommend* Yucca Mountain as a site suitable for the storage of high level nuclear waste."[2] Similarly, Jessica Bacoch, former tribal chairperson of the Big

---

1. "US Department of Energy Public Hearing," Amargosa Valley, October 10, 2001, 95.
2. Durham and Helmer, "Letter," 3.

Pine Paiute Tribe of the Owens Valley, writes in this public comment to the DOE:

> If Secretary [of Energy] Abraham determines that the Yucca Mountain site is suitable without addressing previous concerns by Tribes, then the United States Federal Government has failed to meet its trust responsibility with Native American Governments. Native American concerns must be addressed before submitting a recommendation to the President. Our people have called this beautiful part of the United States home for generations and we are the people who will have to live with the effects of a poorly planned nuclear repository at Yucca Mountain.[3]

These statements mirror many other Western Shoshone and Southern Paiute comments made during and after the decades-long Yucca Mountain siting process. Taken together, these examples express Western Shoshone and Southern Paiute government opposition to the Yucca Mountain site as enactments of inherent Indigenous sovereignty and nationhood. Indigenous governments making assessments about whether the Yucca Mountain repository would support their own interests as sovereign nations is an enactment of decolonization, inherent Indigenous sovereignty, and self-governance of Western Shoshone and Southern Paiute Lands and lifeways since time immemorial.

When former secretary of energy Spencer Abraham officially recommended that the US fulfill its legal obligation to store high-level nuclear waste by authorizing the Yucca Mountain site in 2002, his argument foregrounded the relationship between Yucca Mountain and the national interest of the US. According to Abraham: "Compelling national interests counsel in favor of proceeding with this project," including national security, energy security, homeland security, economic strength, and environmental protection.[4] Although Abraham notes that he took "particular note of comments and concerns raised by . . . Native American tribes," the official site recommendation document focused only on the national interest of the US as a whole and did not engage with the competing national interests of Western Shoshone and Southern Paiute nations that were expressed throughout the decision-making process.[5] The DOE did not conduct government-to-government negotiations but rather subsumed Native nations' concerns within the broad category of public comments, assimilating Western Shoshone and Southern Paiute inter-

---

3. Bacoch, "Big Pine Paiute Tribe," 3.
4. Abraham, "Recommendation," 1.
5. Abraham, 8.

ests within US national interest.[6] This move was enabled, in part, by the 1924 American Indian Citizenship Act, another attempt to assimilate Indigenous peoples into the US public and national interest.[7] Yet, many Indigenous peoples are also citizens of the many Indigenous nations that share boundaries with the US, meaning many Indigenous peoples have dual citizenship. In what Kevin Bruyneel has described as a third space of sovereignty, Indigenous peoples occupy a liminal space between two or more nations.[8] Sovereign Indigenous nations have their own national interests, and more often than not, those interests conflict with the US national interest. The Yucca Mountain siting controversy is an example of how Indigenous national interests compete with US national interest as a core condition of settler colonialism. In the case of Western Shoshone and Southern Paiute resistance to the Yucca Mountain site, Indigenous peoples and nations relentlessly push for nuclear decolonization through rhetorics that affirm inherent Indigenous sovereignty, self-governance, and national interests.

The controversy over the proposed Private Fuel Storage interim nuclear waste site within Skull Valley further illuminates the multifaceted relationship between US national interest and Native government national interests. In a 1998 letter to the Nuclear Regulatory Commission—the federal body empowered to grant a license for an interim nuclear waste facility—former Skull Valley Goshute chairperson Leon Bear argues the PFS project would support his nation through economic development, jobs, preservation of cultural heritage, and protecting Lands.[9] Unlike the Western Shoshone and Southern Paiute nations' opposition to the Yucca Mountain site, the Skull Valley Goshute government consistently supported the proposed PFS site and expressed how it would support the interests of the Skull Valley Goshute nation. Yet, Bear's arguments stand in contrast to those citizens of the Skull Valley Goshute nation who argued the site would not be in their national interest because it would degrade Lands, traditional lifeways, and spiritual practices necessary for the survivance of the Skull Valley Goshute peoples. According to Margene Bullcreek, the goals of the Ohngo Gaudadeh Devia

---

6. Endres, "Rhetoric of Nuclear Colonialism."

7. It is, of course, more complicated than this. The American Indian Citizenship Act is, like so many things, both enabling and constraining. It gave Indigenous peoples important rights while also taking away rights. For more on the act, see Wilkins and Stark, *American Indian Politics*; and Bruyneel, *Third Space of Sovereignty*.

8. Bruyneel, *Third Space of Sovereignty*.

9. Bear, "Prepared Statement of Leon D. Bear."

are to preserve and continue the cultural heritage of the Skull Valley Band of Goshutes. The organization has committed itself to protecting the way of life of its members, through its unique tribal culture, through protection of its physical surroundings and environment and through the Tribe's traditions. ... The organization's concern is that a nuclear waste storage facility sited so close to many of its members will irreversibly harm the environment. The organization is concerned about the negative impacts on wildlife and plant life that will result should there be a nuclear accident. The organization is distressed about the emotional health of all of those members close to the site.[10]

From this perspective, storing high-level nuclear waste on the reservation would put Skull Valley Goshute cultural and spiritual traditions at risk, therefore making it not in the interest of the Skull Valley Goshute nation. The Skull Valley Goshute government, Ohngo Gaudadeh Devia, and Bullcreek's statements on the Skull Valley PFS site demonstrate contestation within the Skull Valley Goshute citizenry about the best interests of their nation. This contestation is, of course, normal for any nation. Yet, it is a challenge for Indigenous nations to be seen as nations within a settler state that seeks to assimilate and eliminate them. Disagreements within the citizens of the Skull Valley Goshute nation, therefore, are an important enactment of sovereignty and self-governance.

The US federal government's position on the PFS site hinged on its trust relationship with the Skull Valley Goshute nation.[11] While the DOE was the primary government entity engaging with Indigenous peoples during the Yucca Mountain site deliberations, the Skull Valley PFS site deliberations primarily involved the BIA and the NRC, the latter of which granted a license to PFS in 2006 to run the facility within the Skull Valley Goshute Reservation. Despite initially approving a permit allowing the Skull Valley Goshutes to lease Land to PFS for an interim high-level nuclear waste site, the BIA reversed its decision in 2006, citing its trust responsibility to weigh preservation of Skull Valley Goshute homelands and lifeways against the economic benefits of the site for the Skull Valley Goshute peoples.[12] Although the BIA's decision was eventually overruled in a DC appellate court, the BIA's argument that its trust responsibility required it to make a determination about the best

---

10. Bullcreek, "Affidavit of Margene Bullcreek," 1–2.
11. The form of settler colonialism between the US and Native nations includes what the Supreme Court termed a "trust relationship" wherein the US is supposedly responsible to support tribal self-governance and the well-being of Native peoples and nations.
12. Bureau of Indian Affairs, "Record of Decision."

interests of the Skull Valley Goshute nation is an example of a constraint on Indigenous sovereignty within a settler state that views Indigenous nations as "domestic dependent" nations.[13] Although far from ideal, the PFS siting process used mechanisms to consider Skull Valley Goshute national interests that were not used in the Yucca Mountain siting process, underscoring inconsistencies in the US federal government's engagement with sovereign Indigenous nations.

The Yucca Mountain and Skull Valley PFS site controversies reflect inherent tensions between Indigenous national interests and US national interests. It is undoubtedly within the US national interest to find permanent and interim storage facilities for high-level nuclear waste in order to fulfill obligations set out in the Nuclear Waste Policy Act. Yet, what about Indigenous national interests? This chapter engages with the question of whether and how both sites fit with the national interests of Western Shoshone, Southern Paiute, and Skull Valley Goshute peoples and nations. In both cases, the US settler state constrained Indigenous sovereignty, self-governance, and nationhood, albeit in different ways. Western Shoshone, Southern Paiute, and Skull Valley Goshute peoples and nations, despite the differences in the specific sites, used a variety of tactics to exceed these constraints in order to support Indigenous national interests on their own terms.

This chapter focuses on enactments of Indigenous sovereignty and national interest as tactics of nuclear decolonization. There is nothing new about Indigenous nations and peoples defending and arguing for their sovereignty; this is a mode of survivance that has animated Indigenous peoples and nations since early interactions with the US settler state. Yet, this chapter amplifies Indigenous national interest rhetorics as significant rhetorical tactics in Indigenous Lands protection movements. Through retelling the stories of Indigenous resistance to the Yucca Mountain and Skull Valley PFS high-level nuclear waste sites, I offer an account of how arguments for and definitions of Native national interests support efforts toward nuclear decolonization and Indigenous-led futures with regard to nuclear waste. Indigenous national interest rhetorics exist within the third space of sovereignty.[14] Indigenous rhetors tactically move between Indigenous national interests and US national interests and Indigenous citizenship and US citizenship, working both within and without the structure of settler colonialism to use all available means of persuasion to advance Indigenous sovereignty and self-determination with

---

13. Recall that sovereign Native nations are officially treated as "domestic dependent nations" in a trust relationship with the US federal government. Wilkins and Lomawaima, *Uneven Ground*.

14. Bruyneel, *Third Space of Sovereignty*.

regard to nuclear waste siting. Indigenous peoples and nations not only argue for their national interests within a system designed to subsume Indigenous peoples into the US public but also debate internally about their own national interests and sometimes tactically use their status as US citizens to have a voice in decision-making processes that seek to exclude them.

National interests are a rhetorical construct. The national interest most simply refers to the goals and ambitions of a sovereign nation, which are dynamic and become the subject of deliberation. Rhetorical invocation of national interests is less likely to center on an explicit discussion of the meaning of the national interest per se than it is to center on assessing whether a particular policy, candidate, or impending decision falls within or outside the sometimes-nebulous concept of national interests. It is in these moments of political deliberation over particular policies that competing conceptions of the national interest may emerge within any nation. As a rhetorical construction, the national interest is at once elusive and unambiguous. As James Andrews argues,

> A nation's "interests" are, of course, a rhetorical construction. They are treated as if they have some kind of objective reality, but national interests must be defined and interpreted. Since the pursuit of national interests is often in direct conflict with particular individual interests, national interests must be justified in order to warrant the consequent sacrifices necessary to defend them.[15]

Appeals to national interests are deployed so often and differently that it can be difficult to pin down a precise definition; indeed, there is likely never one definitive definition of national interests that all citizens support. At the same time, US national interests are commonly associated with the values of patriotism, sacrifice, security, and the national good that "good citizens" ought to support. Appeals to national interests assume a communal understanding of the importance of supporting the national interest, even if that assumption breaks down in practice. While most rhetorical scholarship on national interests is focused on deliberation and contestation over US national interests, this chapter focuses on the national interests of Indigenous nations who share boundaries with the US.

In order to understand Indigenous national interest rhetorics, this chapter begins with a recounting of Indigenous sovereignty and nationhood and how it relates to rhetorical constructions of national interests. Then, I focus

---

15. Andrews, "Rhetorical Shaping," 41.

on how the US settler state positions nuclear waste in relation to articulations of US national interests. Next, I amplify tactical enactments of Indigenous sovereignty in support of Indigenous national interests as seen in Western Shoshone, Southern Paiute, and Skull Valley Goshute arguments about high-level nuclear waste sites proposed for their Lands. These rhetorics are one set of effective tactics for supporting Indigenous sovereignty in both instrumental and constitutive ways. I conclude with a discussion of the necessity of considering Indigenous national interests in any attempt to store nuclear waste.

INDIGENOUS SOVEREIGNTY AND NATIONAL INTERESTS

Indigenous sovereignty is core to decolonization. Western Shoshone, Southern Paiute, and Skull Valley Goshute sovereignties are core to nuclear decolonization efforts. Indigenous sovereignty, from their perspective, is not negotiable. As K. Tsianina Lomawaima writes, "Sovereignty is the bedrock upon which any and every discussion of [American] Indian reality today must be built."[16] Although the settler colonial state continually seeks to place limits on Indigenous sovereignty, it "was not delegated to them [Indigenous governments] by the federal or state governments—it is original and inherent power."[17] Sovereignty, in which Indigenous nations have control over the decisions, policies, and actions that relate to their peoples and Lands, is essential to survivance. Native peoples' and nations' arguments about the Yucca Mountain and Skull Valley PFS sites are rooted in the inherent sovereignty that Indigenous nations enact to make decisions about whether nuclear waste should be stored within their Lands.

At its most basic level, sovereignty is a form of power and authority to self-govern, self-define, and self-determine futures. Indigenous peoples and nations living within this continent prior to 1492 held inherent sovereignty, though it looked different across the many Indigenous governing systems used by the diversity of Indigenous peoples nations. Indigenous sovereignty was recognized by the earliest European settlers on this continent and continued to define the interactions between established Indigenous nations and the fledgling US through treaties and Supreme Court decisions that recognized Indigenous nationhood. Yet, despite a stated intention to support Native self-determination, the settler state limits Indigenous sovereignty and continues to see Indigenous peoples as colonized peoples who are minorities within the

---

16. Lomawaima, "Tribal Sovereigns," 3.
17. Wilkins and Stark, *American Indian Politics*, 38.

US. Indigenous nations "are rarely seen or then treated in the eye of the settler as that which they are and wish to be recognized as: nationals with sovereign authority over their lives and over their membership and living within their own space, which has been 'held for them' in the form of reservations."[18] The term *political sovereignty* is often used to describe how Indigenous sovereignty plays out within settler law and policy. Within the US, political sovereignty is granted by the laws of the US to Indigenous peoples and nations. When sovereignty is granted by another entity, it is dependent upon acknowledgment by the grantor and is, therefore, not true sovereignty. Recognition through political sovereignty egregiously and unilaterally limits the inherent sovereignty of Indigenous nations.

Three Supreme Court decisions under Chief Justice John Marshall in the early 1800s solidified the assumption that Indigenous political sovereignty is granted and introduced the concept of Indigenous nations as domestic dependent nations.[19] Jodi Byrd writes about the consequences of this designation:

> In a stunning moment of law-making and law-preserving violence, the U.S. government juridically transformed native nations from sovereign foreign states, whose governments and lands were independent of U.S. control, into domestic dependent nations existing within the boundaries of the United States and occupying, by grace of their guardian's permission, lands that rightfully belong to the United States. The impact of Marshall's opinion on behalf of the Court facilitated continued removals, forced diasporas, colonization, and assimilation through the establishment of a paternal relation between the United States and those peoples it deemed were its "children" or "wards."[20]

Domestic dependent status relegates Indigenous nations to a partial and contingent nationhood. The term also calls forth paternalistic images of Indigenous peoples as childlike dependents who need to be protected by the US federal government. Wallace Coffey and Rebecca Tsosie from the Native American Rights Fund highlight how "the concept of Indian tribes as 'domestic dependent nations' means that tribal governmental authority is to some extent circumscribed by federal authority."[21] They continue, "In a world where tribal political sovereignty is dependent upon federal acknowledgement,

---

18. A. Simpson, *Mohawk Interruptus*, 16.
19. Johnson & Graham's Lessee v. McIntosh; Cherokee Nation v. Georgia; Worchester v. Georgia.
20. Byrd, *Transit of Empire*, 198.
21. Coffey and Tsosie, "Rethinking the Tribal Sovereignty Doctrine," 192.

Indian nations will always be vulnerable to restrictions on their sovereignty, and perhaps even to the total annihilation of their sovereignty."[22] In a process of political colonization, the federal government, through legal statutes that "were passed in order to extend absolute U.S. control over jurisdiction, land tenure, national allegiance, and governance," maintains itself as the colonial center of power.[23] This creates a system in which the US government is "the ultimate decision-maker concerning the parameters of indigenous self-determination is the U.S."[24]

Recognizing the limitations of political sovereignty as defined through settler laws and policies, Coffey and Tsosie and John Borrows call for Indigenous nations to live by their inherent sovereignty.[25] Borrows, for example, calls on Indigenous nations to enact "an inherent, unextinguished, and continuing exercise of self-government" that challenges the imposition of political sovereignty onto Indigenous nations by the US federal government.[26] Coffey and Tsosie affirm, "Inherent sovereignty is not dependent on any grant, gift, or acknowledgment by the federal government. It preexists arrival of the European people and the formation of the United States. Cultural sovereignty is inherent in every sense of that word, and it is up to Indian people to define, assert, protect, and insist upon respect for that right."[27] Inherent sovereignty can contribute to decolonization through a constitutive redefinition of sovereignty that excises the settler state's political definition and emphasizes self-determination, self-governance, and Indigenous agency in creating meaningful futures for themselves. As Borrows notes, "This reinterpretation in understanding Native self-government suggests that the validation of our inherent sovereignty can be utilized to rejuvenate and endow our society with the power that it requires to emancipate our people from the structures of debilitating hierarchy and dominance."[28] Western Shoshone, Southern Paiute, and Skull Valley Goshute rhetors consistently enacted inherent sovereignty in their advocacy about high-level nuclear waste sites.

Western Shoshone, Southern Paiute, and Skull Valley Goshute nations and peoples also worked within the systems of political sovereignty and US citizenship to advance their positions. Because Indigenous political sovereignty

---

22. Coffey and Tsosie, 194.
23. G. Morris, "International Law," 69.
24. G. Morris, 65.
25. Borrows, "Genealogy of Law"; and Coffey and Tsosie, "Rethinking the Tribal Sovereignty Doctrine."
26. Borrows, "Genealogy of Law," 352.
27. Coffey and Tsosie, "Rethinking the Tribal Sovereignty Doctrine," 196.
28. Borrows, "Genealogy of Law," 353.

is generally limited to reservation Lands, Western Shoshone and Southern Paiute peoples and nations had to argue for their rights to be involved in the decision about Yucca Mountain, a place not within current reservation boundaries. While the Skull Valley Goshute government could choose to pursue an interim high-level nuclear waste site within their reservation (albeit subject to BIA and NRC approvals), Western Shoshone and Southern Paiute peoples had to advocate for government-to-government negotiations about a place that the US federal government does not recognize as Indigenous Lands. In doing so, they tactically used their positionality as members of the US public to gain access to spaces where they could make their voices heard.

Indigenous sovereignty is also tied to the concepts of nation and nationhood. While some Indigenous studies scholars have critiqued non-Indigenous concepts of political sovereignty, nation, and nationhood as forms of coloniality that impose settler notions of governance that may not align with Indigenous knowledges about political organization and governance,[29] assertion of Indigenous nationhood is also a powerful anticolonial tool. Indigenous nationhood is an anticolonial space, albeit complex and multiple, that enacts inherent Indigenous sovereignty.[30] Western Shoshone, Southern Paiute, and Skull Valley Goshute peoples and nations frequently invoke their status as sovereign nations to call for government-to-government negotiations over proposed waste sites, demanding that Indigenous national interests be part of decision-making.

Indigenous sovereignty is also linked to citizenship. Citizenship is a "primary technique of distributing rights and protections" within a nation.[31] Indeed, the ability to determine who is able to be a citizen is a key form of national power. Many Indigenous individuals living on reservations or in urban communities on this continent are citizens both of Indigenous nations and of the US.[32] Citizenship in the settler state is a direct attempt to assimilate Indigenous peoples into the US as an ethnic minority. As Byrd puts it, "Transforming American Indians into a minority within a country of minorities is the fait accompli of the colonial project that disappears sovereignty, land rights, and self-governance as American Indians are finally, if not quite fully, assimilated *into* the United States."[33] The 1924 Indian Citizenship Act was put

---

29. For example: Alfred, "Sovereignty."
30. Bruyneel, *Third Space of Sovereignty.*
31. A. Simpson, *Mohawk Interruptus,* 16.
32. This is not true for all Native peoples, some of whom are not enrolled as citizens in their Native nation, some of whom are members of non-federally recognized Native nations, and some of whom are enrolled as citizens in two or more Native nations as a result of mixed heritage.
33. Byrd, *Transit of Empire,* 135.

into place during the era of allotment and assimilation (1871–1928), during which it was the official policy of the federal government to assimilate Indigenous peoples into the US by ending treaty-making with Indigenous nations, transforming Indigenous reservation Lands into allotments, and granting US citizenship to Indigenous persons.[34] In the Termination era (1945–1961), the federal government used the Indian Citizenship Act as one justification for legislation that terminated more than fifty Indigenous governments and gave state governments more power to regulate Indigenous affairs. US citizenship, then, was granted to hasten the assimilation of Indigenous peoples into US society and the elimination of Indigenous sovereignty. It did not work completely, a testament to ongoing efforts to maintain sovereignty by Indigenous peoples and nations. While US citizenship works against Indigenous sovereignty and government-to-government relations, it can also afford Indigenous peoples rights that continue to be important for Indigenous survival (as I will discuss in more detail later). US citizenship, then, is complicated for Indigenous peoples and nations. As Audra Simpson notes, "All indigenous people certainly did not look at U.S. citizenship in the same light and very few saw it as unambiguously positive."[35] Western Shoshone, Southern Paiute, and Skull Valley Goshute Indigenous national interest rhetorics can include tactical use of US citizenship in moments when political sovereignty is constrained by the settler state.

As domestic dependent nations within the structure of political sovereignty and as dual citizens, Indigenous nations and peoples often work in the liminal third space of sovereignty to pursue their national interests.[36] Within this space, Indigenous peoples and nations work within the tensions between inherent and political sovereignty, Indigenous citizenship and US citizenship, and Indigenous national interest and US national interest. The third space of sovereignty can be both constraining and enabling. If Indigenous nations attempt to use US law and its notion of political sovereignty for the improvement of the nation or to assert sovereignty, they are stuck in a catch-22 where they have to accept the limited notion of political sovereignty granted by the US law in their quest for more self-determination within or outside the settler state. As Bruyneel puts it, "The ambiguous boundary imposed by the United States places a colonial bind on indigenous political choices, trapping indigenous people in a place neither here nor there. For indigenous politics, how-

---

34. Land allotments were assigned to each Indigenous male over the age of eighteen. The US then sold the remaining land to non-Indigenous people. Not all Indigenous nations' Lands were subject to allotment.
35. Bruyneel, *Third Space of Sovereignty*, 97.
36. Bruyneel.

ever, this same boundary has become the site of expression of a third space of sovereignty through postcolonial resistance."[37] Drawing on Simpson's theorization of a politics of refusal,[38] Bruyneel argues the third space is a productive location in which Indigenous sovereignty can exist alongside US sovereignty while also challenging it. As Vine Deloria Jr. describes it, Indigenous peoples and nations brilliantly work within both systems to govern themselves:

> In effect the tribes are pressing for complete independence from federal domination while retaining the maximum federal protection of the land base and services. With that goal, tribes shift back and forth to take advantage of every opportunity. The strategy has been to hit at every weak point that would yield more power to the tribe in the basic search for independence and to surrender certain powers where it was possible to give them up without losing any momentum in the basic movement.[39]

Indigenous peoples and nations engage in various decolonization and survivance movements that involve both working within and working outside the system of political sovereignty, working from their positions as US citizens at times, and at other times working as sovereign governments. These forms of resistance have created cracks in the structures of US settler colonialism, resulting in more control over decision-making and resources for many Indigenous nations.[40] Everything discussed up until now supports a key point: Indigenous governments have national interests. Indigenous national interest rhetorics are expressions of sovereignty and self-determination focused on what is best for the Indigenous nation, not for the US nation.

US NUCLEAR NATIONAL INTERESTS

Before demonstrating the ways that Western Shoshone, Southern Paiute, and Skull Valley Goshute peoples and nations articulate their own national interests in relation to the Yucca Mountain and Skull Valley PFS sites, it is important to understand how the settler state positions nuclear waste storage within the US national interest. More than simply a stasis point in political controversies, the US national interest is a powerful rhetorical device imbued with ideology. Here I am deliberately using *national interest* in the singular to

---

37. Bruyneel, 13.
38. A. Simpson, *Mohawk Interruptus*.
39. Deloria, *We Talk, You Listen*, 60.
40. Gedicks, *New Resource Wars*.

denote a dominant settler state articulation of the national interest. This, of course, belies the fact that there are many competing conceptions of national interest within the US settler state. The dominant national interest can be viewed as what Michael McGee called an ideograph: "an ordinary language term found in political discourse" that represents an abstracted "collective commitment to a particular but equivocal and ill-defined normative goal."[41] As a form of justification, an appeal to national interest within settler states is often tied to a utilitarian logic of providing the greatest good for the greatest number of people. The US national interest assumes that there will be undesirable consequences for some. To determine if these undesirable consequences are merited for a particular policy depends on showing that the desirable consequences for the nation outweigh the undesirable consequences for the sacrificing community. Previous research has shown the problematic nature of US national interest as a rhetorical strategy of gaining assent and limiting dissent for national policies.[42] When the settler state positions something as being in the national interest, it sets up a nearly impossible standard for counterarguments by shifting the burden of proof to opponents to somehow verify that harms to the sacrificing minority outweigh the benefits to the national interest. According to Matthew Glass, the US national interest / national security "imperative functions in American political life like a trump card. It normally overrides and outweighs other considerations in the development of policy and is especially difficult for ordinary citizens to call into question."[43]

Dominant US national interest is often related to national security and national sacrifice. National security is a subset of the national interest, even though the term *national security* may be invoked more often than *national interest*. *National security* is a powerful term that invokes patriotism and sacrifice in order to protect the nation from constructed and real threats. For example, in a letter to former president George H. W. Bush, former secretary of energy Abraham listed five compelling national interests that support opening a centralized national nuclear waste site in Yucca Mountain, and four of the five are national security issues.[44] While the construction of dominant US national interest has changed and evolved over time, one thing remains constant: when the national interest is invoked, a sacrifice is always implied. Whatever local interests conflict with the national interest are called upon to sacrifice for the good of the nation as a whole. As an interlocking set of terms,

---

41. McGee, "'Ideograph,'" 15.
42. Andrews, "Rhetorical Shaping."
43. Glass, *Citizens against the MX*, 93.
44. The five reasons are (in the order listed): (1) national security, (2) nonproliferation, (3) energy security, (4) homeland security, and (5) environmental protection. Abraham, "Letter."

the *national interest, national sacrifice,* and *national security* act as normative and seemingly objective frames through which US policies are defended. Indigenous peoples, when seen as US citizens or as a national sacrifice minority within the US nation, have little chance of overriding the dominant construction of national interest, in this case, to find a nuclear waste site.

From their inception, nuclear technologies have been inextricably linked to the intersecting discourses of US national interest, national security, and national sacrifice. Nuclearism is an ideology and a discursive system that follows four deeply interrelated master themes of discourse: mystery, entelechy, potency, and secrecy.[45] Implicit within these themes is the unquestioned assumption that nuclear weapons and nuclear power are crucial to the US national interest and US national security, which serves to normalize and justify all aspects of the nuclear production process.[46] In the US, therefore, nuclearism is always already in the national interest. This assumption has become so ingrained in common imagination that it is rarely questioned by anyone other than antinuclear activists.[47] Much dominant US nuclear rhetoric calls for the sacrifice of the communities affected by the legacies of the nuclear production process.[48] Decision-makers frame the harms to local populations and ecosystems from nuclear technologies as a national sacrifice to be borne by a minority segment of the nation that lives in proximity to sites of nuclear production in service to the majority of the nation that benefits from nuclear technology. The Great Basin, as a part of the larger western region, is seen as a "national sacrifice zone" because of its connection to the nuclear production process.[49] John Beck notes, "Much of the desert Southwest is today part of the American military's 'national sacrifice zone,' the crucible of US superpower status, the place where, since Pearl Harbor, hot and cold wars have been tested, monitored, enacted, or denied."[50] Although there is little evidence to suggest that the federal government ever officially called these regions national sacrifice zones, off-record comments reveal this attitude exists among some federal

---

45. Kinsella, "One Hundred Years of Nuclear Discourse."
46. Mathur, "Nuclearism."
47. Glass, *Citizens against the MX.*
48. Gallagher, *American Ground Zero*; Kuletz, *Tainted Desert*; and Taylor, "Nuclear Weapons."
49. Kuletz, *Tainted Desert*, 7. The term *national sacrifice zone* has been used by others both to describe nuclear colonialism and to describe other instances of oppression of underrepresented communities in the name of national interest. Across the nation, lands and communities that have suffered environmental degradation have been termed national sacrifice zones by environmental justice activists. Bullard, *Quest for Environmental Justice*; Endres, "Sacred Land"; Fast, "Water, History, and Sovereignty"; Hooks and Smith, "Treadmill of Destruction"; and Byrne and Hoffman, "'Necessary Sacrifice.'"
50. Beck, "Without Form and Void," 68.

government employees. For example, an article in the *New York Times* states, "Engineers at the Energy Department have privately begun calling such contaminated sites [nuclear weapons cleanup sites] 'national sacrifice zones.'"[51] In response to the use of and creation of nuclear wastelands in the western region of the US, activists have used the term *national sacrifice zone* to expose and attempt to fissure the ideology of nuclearism. In this sense, terming something a national sacrifice zone can also be a tool of resistance for activists seeking to reveal the injustices within nuclearism.

Nuclear waste is no exception to dominant national interest–oriented nuclear rhetoric. Although there is a pragmatic need for the US to do something about high-level nuclear waste, any proposed site for high-level nuclear waste disposal is not automatically in the US national interest. Rather, contestation over whether the Yucca Mountain or Skull Valley PFS sites are in the US national interest, whether national security is enhanced, and whether attendant national sacrifice is warranted form a primary point of debate in the controversies over these sites.

Unlike nuclear weapons and nuclear power, which are the desired outcome, or product, of the nuclear production process, nuclear waste is the unwanted by-product of nuclear production that requires safe disposal. As such, the relationship between nuclear waste and the US national interest is slightly different from the relationship between nuclear weapons/power and the US national interest. Whereas nuclear weapons supposedly protect the US from enemies and nuclear power presumably contributes to the nation's energy mix, nuclear waste itself is not a valuable product that contributes to the national interest. Rather, because the US faces a nuclear waste crisis, it is the nuclear waste storage facility, not the nuclear waste, that is the product of value.[52] It is, therefore, in the US nation's interest to find a permanent solution for nuclear waste. Former president George H. W. Bush supported the Yucca Mountain site in 2002, stating, "Proceeding with the [national high-level nuclear waste] repository program is necessary to protect public safety, health, and the Nation's security."[53] Permanent high-level nuclear waste storage is important not only to prevent radioactive emissions to promote health and environmental safety but also, more importantly, to secure the continued

---

51. Schneider, "Dying Nuclear Plants."
52. If reprocessing of nuclear waste was allowed in the US, nuclear waste could be seen as a product of value. Reprocessing is a way of reusing spent fuel (the by-product of nuclear reactors) by separating out the materials from spent fuel that can be reused for new fuel. Reprocessing is used in some countries, including the UK, Russia, China, and Japan. Reprocessing is currently not allowed in the US and remains controversial due to concerns about proliferation.
53. As cited in Vandenbosch and Vandenbosch, *Nuclear Waste Stalemate*, 44.

viability of nuclear technologies. Former president Barack Obama affirmed his commitment to addressing the US nuclear waste crisis by establishing the Blue Ribbon Commission on America's Nuclear Future, tasked with developing recommendations for permanent high-level nuclear waste disposal. That the commission is called "Blue Ribbon Commission on America's Nuclear Future" instead of, for example, "Blue Ribbon Commission on High-Level Nuclear Waste Disposal" exemplifies the logic that nuclear waste storage is in the US national interest because it is needed to continue to reap benefits from nuclear technologies. In his memo to the DOE when creating the commission, Obama specifies that permanent nuclear waste disposal is crucial to the US national interest because of the need to expand our reliance on nuclear energy.[54] Similarly, high-level nuclear waste from Cold War nuclear weapons production threatens continued development of nuclear weapons.[55] With highly visible controversies over radioactive leakages and the staggering amount of waste from nuclear production sites—Hanford, Rocky Flats, and Fernald, for example—there is a pressing need to ensure that high-level nuclear waste from nuclear weapons development is managed and stored in a safe manner. Importantly, and unsurprisingly, the BRC report still reinforces US national interest as more important than Indigenous national interests.[56] High-level nuclear waste, then, is itself a threat to nuclearism and the US national interest articulated therein.

Proponents of the Yucca Mountain and Skull Valley PFS sites suggest they support US national interest by "solving" the problem of nuclear waste to the benefit of the entire nation. Across the thirty years of controversy over the Yucca Mountain site, the argument that the site is in the US national interest occurs over and over in the corpus of texts I collected and reviewed. During the Yucca Mountain decision-making procedure, particularly the site authorization process run by the DOE, the federal government consistently argued that the Yucca Mountain site was not only technically sound but also in the US national interest. While the Nuclear Waste Policy Act specified that the site authorization decision be made solely on the scientific and technical suitability of the site, former secretary of energy Abraham introduced two additional criteria for site authorization: "Are there compelling national interests that favor proceeding with the decision to site a repository there? [And], are there countervailing considerations that outweigh those interests?"[57] Shifting the decision-making calculus from scientific and technical suitability alone to

---

54. Obama, "Memorandum."
55. Taylor, Kinsella, and Depoe, *Nuclear Legacies*.
56. Blue Ribbon Commission on America's Nuclear Future, *Draft Report*, xvi.
57. Abraham, "Recommendation," 9.

add weighing US national interest versus countervailing interests is a significant rhetorical move. This new frame explicitly situates the Yucca Mountain site within the US national interest and creates an argumentative burden on opponents to prove that the site is not. According to Abraham:

> [Authorizing the Yucca Mountain site] will advance our energy security by helping us to maintain diverse sources of energy supply. It will advance our national security by helping to provide operational certainty to our nuclear Navy. . . . It will help us clean up our environment by allowing us to close the nuclear fuel cycle and giving us greater access to a form of energy that does not emit greenhouse gases. And it will help us in our efforts to secure ourselves against terrorist threats by allowing us to remove nuclear materials from scattered above-ground locations to a single, secure underground facility. . . . I find that compelling national interests counsel in favor of taking the next step toward siting a repository at Yucca Mountain.[58]

Opposition arguments had to pinpoint sufficient disadvantages to the site that would outweigh the US national interest, as defined by the federal government. Perhaps it is no surprise that Abraham did not find countervailing interests outweighed the US national interest of authorizing the Yucca Mountain site. Yet, the expansion of the decision-making calculus to include national interest also created an opportunity for opponents of the site to bring in arguments that would not have been considered under a pure scientific and technical suitability framework.

Similarly, proponents of the Skull Valley PFS site laud its role in supporting the US national interest. According to PFS, "Not only is a safe, clean, temporary storage facility for spent nuclear fuel needed by the nation's generators of nuclear power electricity and their customers, it will solve a pressing national problem."[59] In this case, the Skull Valley Goshute government argues the nuclear waste site would also support the national interest of the Skull Valley Goshute nation by providing needed economic development and cultural revival. In both cases, not only is finding a solution to permanent storage of nuclear waste articulated with the US national interest, but also the specific sites are justified because of their role in supporting that interest. What this dominant framing doesn't account for is that Indigenous nations are nations with their own national interests.

---

58. Abraham, 31.
59. Private Fuel Storage, "Who Will Benefit." This website is now inactive, but it was active during the controversy.

INDIGENOUS NATIONAL INTERESTS IN HIGH-LEVEL NUCLEAR WASTE SITING

Existing outside the US nation and US national interests, Indigenous national interests call forth government-to-government relationality between the US and Indigenous nations and the likelihood of competing national interests. Although Indigenous nations—seen as domestic dependents under political sovereignty—still face a difficult argumentative burden to demonstrate how their national interest would outweigh the US national interest, there is an important distinction between being viewed as a minority and asserting sovereignty. There is not one way in which Indigenous national interests are understood. Rather, a comparison of the Yucca Mountain and Skull Valley PFS high-level nuclear waste siting decision processes reveals that Indigenous peoples and nations invoke national interests in myriad ways. Western Shoshone and Southern Paiute governments opposed the Yucca Mountain site in order to protect sovereignty and pursue cultural survival.[60] Although it is difficult to argue against the settler government's stated national interest, Western Shoshone and Southern Paiute opponents of the Yucca Mountain site used the site authorization public hearing process and other official and unofficial venues to introduce arguments about how the site would violate their national interests. In the case of the Skull Valley PFS site, the Skull Valley Goshute government highlighted how the PFS site would help fulfill economic, cultural, and environmental interests of the Skull Valley Goshute nation. Skull Valley proponents also sought to align Skull Valley Goshute national interests with the national interests of the US by providing a solution that would solve the national problem of nuclear waste while also allowing the Skull Valley Goshutes to pursue their own national interests. Skull Valley Goshute opponents of the site, however, challenged the national interests articulated by the Skull Valley Goshute government and offered a different vision. Ohngo Gaudadeh Devia and other Skull Valley Goshute opponents of the site asserted that the interest of the Skull Valley Goshute nation is to preserve traditional cultural practices within their Lands. In the next two sections, I focus on Western Shoshone, Southern Paiute, and Skull Valley Goshute national interest rhetorics in the Yucca Mountain and Skull Valley PFS siting controversies. To understand how the national interest circulates in public deliberation, rhetorical critics must be attentive to the multiple discursive manifestations it can take. While there are often explicit references to the "national interest" and its associated

---

60. It is important to note that while not all Western Shoshone and Southern Paiute individuals actively opposed the site, the governments all opposed the site. For more, see the discussion of this in chapter 2.

terms, national interest is also invoked without using these specific terms through references to, for example, cultural interest and economic interest.

Western Shoshone and Southern Paiute National Interests

Recall from chapter 3 that Yucca Mountain has been part of Western Shoshone and Southern Paiute Lands since time immemorial. As Western Shoshone elder Corbin Harney puts it, this relationship with the Lands along with the 1863 Treaty of Ruby Valley makes the Western Shoshones the rightful decision-makers and caretakers:

> That [Lands covered by the Treaty of Ruby Valley] was Shoshone land to begin with. This is something that they [settlers] should understand. They are the visitors here. They made all different kinds of rules like they're giving us something that belongs to them, but they know it didn't belong to them. We Shoshone people are the caretakers of this land. We should be the ones making the law, saying what they can do, what they can't do. They're the ones that say under the law, the treaty law as they call it, that they should be taking care of our land. Not to be giving it away and selling it. They haven't shown us that they own the land. They never have and they never will.[61]

Western Shoshones and Southern Paiutes of various nations—for instance, the Timbisha Shoshone Tribe and the Chemehuevi Indian Tribe—claim treaty-based, spiritual, and cultural connections to Yucca Mountain and the surrounding Lands. Western Shoshone and Southern Paiute peoples—both government representatives and individual citizens—have consistently communicated to the US federal government in meetings, protest events, and other venues that the Yucca Mountain facility is not in the national interests of the Western Shoshone and Southern Paiute governments.

For Western Shoshone peoples and nations, arguments about sovereignty and national interest are rooted in the 1863 Treaty of Ruby Valley. They argue Yucca Mountain and the surrounding Lands were not ceded to the US federal government. In the words of the Indigenous Environmental Network, an ally organization:

> If Congress approves Yucca Mountain for a nuclear waste dump, it will be another attack on the treaty rights of the Western Shoshone. . . . Rec-

---

61. Harney, *Nature Way*, 37.

ognition of Shoshone sovereign territory was formalized by the United States government when it signed the Treaty of "Peace and Friendship" of Ruby Valley in 1863 that guaranteed incoming settlers and military personnel safe passage through the Western Shoshone (Newe) Lands. These territorial boundaries under international law hold the same significance as those of Canada or Mexico. The Organization of American States (OAS) has repeatedly upheld Shoshone claims against the United States. The Western Shoshone is fighting to protect their lands, including the sacred Yucca Mountain. The Shoshone have claims against the United States for land that was stolen and illegally occupied in violation of the Treaty of Ruby Valley of 1863. Although extensive litigation has taken place, the United States has never to this day been able to show a document to back its current claim of ownership of this land. This Treaty is one of the few treaties made between the United States and Indigenous nations that did not cede any land.[62]

The treaty instead allowed the US federal government some rights to pass through Newe territory and the ability to pursue economic development within the territory.[63] Western Shoshone opposition to the Yucca Mountain site, then, is one of many struggles to demand that the federal government act in accordance with the Treaty of Ruby Valley. Carrie Dann, speaking at a public hearing in Crescent Valley, shows skepticism the US will act in line with the Treaty: "The constitution of the United States recognizes treaties as the supreme laws of the land. Okay. Then is it, or if it isn't then why did they write it into that? I mean I've seen laws broken by the federal government for 28 years and I find the federal government is very deceitful."[64] The Treaty of Ruby Valley, and the ways that the settler state violated it, is an important part of the national interests of Western Shoshones. Southern Paiute peoples and nations are not covered by the Treaty of Ruby Valley but nonetheless have their own legal bases that support their sovereignty.

A key foundation for Indigenous sovereignty is Indigenous self-governance. Western Shoshone and Southern Paiute peoples put their self-government practices on display by invoking Indigenous government leadership positions, government laws, and forms of decision-making about the Yucca Mountain site. Calvin Meyers, for example, states at a public hearing in Pahrump: "I am the Chairman of my reservation, on my Tribal Council. I have a lot of responsibility. I have all the responsibility of the United States President

---

62. Indigenous Environmental Network, "Indigenous Anti-Nuclear Statement."
63. Luebben and Nelson, "Indian Wars."
64. "US Department of Energy Public Hearing," Crescent Valley, October 10, 2001, 29.

does."[65] Recall as well the excerpt from a Timbisha Shoshone Tribe resolution in opposition to the site from the beginning of this chapter. In addition to displaying Indigenous governance practices, Western Shoshone and Southern Paiute peoples and nations called for government-to-government relationships between Indigenous nations and the US federal government. For example, according to Chad Smith, archaeologist for the Fort Mojave Indian Tribe, "Indian tribes must be consulted on a government-to-government basis, not through the public scoping process. You need to schedule consultations and negotiations with these governments."[66] Similarly, Richard Arnold, former Southern Paiute chair and spokesperson for the Consolidated Group of Tribes and Organizations,[67] states, "Government relations are extremely necessary and in doing so due to the trust responsibility and conducting government-to-government relations with those tribes, people should be able to respond to issues that are specific to the meeting at hand."[68] Lee Chavez of the Owens Valley Bishop Paiute Tribe emphasizes the importance of treating each Indigenous nation separately: "The DOE must meet with each tribal government personally."[69] Atef Elzeflawy of the Las Vegas Paiute Tribe talks about how the NRC met with the nation, which "sets an example for the Department of Energy or Assistant Secretary of Energy for the environmental programs to leave Washington and come to really take this government-to-government issue in their heart."[70] Government-to-government relations not only recognize the sovereign status of Indigenous nations but also allow for a deliberation across multiple national interests, not just the national interest of the US nation. While Indigenous national interests still face a difficult argumentative burden to prove to the settler state that, when in conflict, Indigenous national interests outweigh US national interests, the important point here is that government-to-government relations make space for the articulation of Indigenous national interests, a small but significant enactment of Indigenous sovereignty and nationhood.

---

65. "US Department of Energy Public Hearing," December 5, 2001, 74.
66. C. Smith, "Letter."
67. The Consolidated Group of Tribes and Organizations (CGTO) was created in the 1970s by Indigenous peoples and nations in the process of securing their rights under the American Indian Religious Freedom Act and preserving cultural resources at the Nevada Test Site. Though the CGTO is opposed to the Yucca Mountain site, a statement of opposition to the project by the CGTO is not comparable to the government-to-government consultation because, although it may contain members of tribal governments of the participating tribes, it is not an official government agency of these tribal governments.
68. "Yucca Mountain Project Comments," 3–4.
69. "Yucca Mountain Project Comments," 22.
70. "Yucca Mountain Project Comments," 30.

Yet, the DOE repeatedly failed to pursue government-to-government relationships with Western Shoshone and Southern Paiute nations. Urban Environmental Research and Ian Zabarte, now the principal man for the Western Bands of the Shoshone Nation, argue in a report on Indigenous concerns about the Yucca Mountain site: "The DOE generally failed to approach Native American tribes on a government-to-government basis that is the stated U.S. policy for relations with Native American tribes."[71] One key failure pointed out by Indigenous peoples and nations who participated in the public comment processes is that the DOE used a typical decide-announce-defend model of engagement that focused on securing acceptance of stakeholders, including Indigenous nations, for the already developed proposal to store nuclear waste in Yucca Mountain.[72] According to John Wells of the Western Shoshone National Council,

> The Western Shoshone has a fundamental problem with the DOE's disregard for the proper role of Native American nations based on our inherent sovereignty, historical relations, international treaties, and the US constitution. All too often consultation is consisting on brief conversations with individuals from a Native American community after decisions are made and policy is employed. The cultural differences needed to be resolved by the DOE are at least as serious and difficult to deal with as they were 200 years ago.[73]

Archaeologist Chad Smith similarly argues: "We feel that approval of the project is a foregone conclusion and the NEPA [National Environmental Policy Act] process is being abused by DOE. The attitude seems to have been, 'This is what we're going to do, now go out and do studies that o.k. it.'"[74] Alan Bacoch of the Big Pine Paiute Tribe of the Owens Valley adds:

> Tribes have set aside a lot of time and energy to participate in the suitability of the Yucca Mountain Project, yet we have received no response from the DOE on our comments to the DEIS [draft environmental impact statement] and our significant concerns have not been addressed. It now appears that our comments to the DEIS are considered irrelevant due to the fact that the Secretary of Energy may recommend the Yucca Mountain site regardless of the DEIS. Tribes cannot have confidence in an agency that seems to

---

71. Urban Environmental Research and Zabarte, *Tribal Concerns*, 16.
72. For more on decide-announce-defend decision-making, see Hendry, "Decide, Announce, Defend"; and Depoe and Delicath, introduction.
73. "US Department of Energy Public Hearing," September 5, 2001, 30.
74. C. Smith, "Letter."

consider approval of the Yucca Mountain site a foregone conclusion without tribal input.[75]

These statements, in one sense, are not unique. They express frustration at the typical decide-announce-defend model of participation, a common complaint of stakeholders beyond Indigenous nations. In a more important sense, though, these comments demonstrate the failure of the DOE to see Indigenous nations as nations, not only in the failure to conduct government-to-government negotiations but also in the lack of prior and informed consent for proposing a nuclear waste site in the Lands of sovereign Indigenous nations. The DOE's model of stakeholder engagement assumes at its core that participants are part of the US public and are communities within the US nation and that the challenge is merely to convince them to accept the DOE's plan.[76]

This is further exemplified through Western Shoshone and Southern Paiute resistance to the Consolidated Group of Tribes and Organizations (CGTO) standing in for government-to-government negotiations. The CGTO is an entity that the DOE used to do outreach with the various Indigenous nations and organizations determined to have a stake in the Yucca Mountain site. Yet, the CGTO is not an Indigenous government. Calvin Meyers, former chair of the Moapa Paiutes, points out: "The CGTO is not government to government. . . . Use of the Consolidated Group of Tribes and Organizations as government-to-government is wrong morally and ethically and I think legally because they didn't speak to the band of Paiute."[77] This statement and others like it function to demand government-to-government negotiation with each affected nation, in part because the CGTO could never represent the national interests of all Indigenous nations that would be impacted by storing nuclear waste inside Yucca Mountain. Arguments against the CGTO, then, support Indigenous sovereignty and national interest.

Western Shoshone and Southern Paiute nations and peoples refused to accept the failures in the DOE's approach and continued to call on the US federal government to consider Indigenous national interests at any opportunity. Western Shoshone Pauline Estevez explains,

> As to the government relationship, this is one way of doing it, you know. Come up here and we talk all this kind of stuff. So, then DOE can do their little checkmark and say, okay, we talked to some Indians out there, check that off. But it's not that easy because we'll always be heard. We're not going

---

75. "Yucca Mountain Project Comments," 17.
76. Endres, "Rhetoric of Nuclear Colonialism"; Endres, "Sacred Land."
77. "Yucca Mountain Project Comments," 7.

to stop. Even if there is money shoved down our throats in the wrongful act that is going to happen, that is very wrong to the indigenous people of this continent."[78]

Estevez's comment demonstrates survivance and resilience in the face of the DOE's flawed process. In an oral history interview, Ian Zabarte explains how Western Shoshone peoples make their own opportunities to be involved: "I'm not even involved with the Yucca Mountain site. There's no invitation for Western Shoshone, at least the Western Shoshone National Council, to be involved. We create our own opportunities, we do our own research on radiation health effects, and we defend our own lands as well as we can."[79] This refusal to stop fighting for the national interest of the Western Shoshones may not be the sole contributor to discontinuing the Yucca Mountain project, but it played an important role. Furthermore, the refusal itself is an act of sovereignty.[80]

Calls for government-to-government relations do, to an extent, fall within what Glen Coulthard and others have termed a politics of recognition that can position Indigenous sovereignty as dependent on the settler state's recognition, another form of granted political sovereignty.[81] Yet, despite the constraints of recognition, Indigenous nations calling for government-to-government relations are also enacting inherent Indigenous sovereignty in a constitutive performative rhetoric that is an end in itself regardless of the outcome of the deliberations with the settler state.[82] Despite the critique of recognition, there is value in continuing to call for government-to-government relations. This is the only way for Indigenous national interests to be a part of the deliberation. Otherwise, the federal government excludes Indigenous concerns by assimilating them within the US public and national interest.[83] Although Indigenous advocates were not always successful in the realization of their demands for government-to-government relations, their insistence on continuing to call for them within public hearings is a tactic of survivance. Moreover, public hearings include audiences outside those who convene the meetings.[84] So, even if the DOE does not listen or act on what Indigenous peoples and nations call

---

78. "US Department of Energy Public Hearing," Amargosa Valley, October 10, 2001, 10.
79. Zabarte, Nuclear Technology Oral History Project.
80. A. Simpson, *Mohawk Interruptus*.
81. Coulthard, *Red Skin, White Masks*; A. Simpson, *Mohawk Interruptus*; and Byrd, *Transit of Empire*.
82. Lake, "Enacting Red Power."
83. Endres, "Rhetoric of Nuclear Colonialism."
84. Hunt, Paliewicz, and Endres, "Radical Potential."

for in public hearings, the ideas presented are heard by the other people present and may also be subsequently distributed to other audiences.

While calling for government-to-government interactions was one of the most prominent arguments presented in support of Indigenous sovereignty and national interest, Western Shoshone and Southern Paiute peoples and nations also discussed the many ways the Yucca Mountain site would go against their national interests. Chapter 3 offers a detailed analysis of how the site's impact on Lands is one significant way that the site is not in Western Shoshone and Southern Paiute national interests. Here, I briefly illuminate some of the other ways that Western Shoshone and Southern Paiute peoples and nations articulated their national interests in relation to the site. Barbara Durham and Bill Helmer, Timbisha Shoshone tribal administrator and environmental director at the time of writing a letter to the DOE, state: "It is the responsibility of the Western Shoshone of this generation to protect future generations, not poison them."[85] They go on to offer specific ways that the project would affect their nation:

> In conclusion, the Timbisha Shoshone Tribe will be directly affected by the proposed Yucca Mountain project. Since the Furnace Creek parcel of the Tribe is down-gradient from the groundwater of Yucca Mountain, the predicted radionuclide leakage from the storage casks will eventually reach the Timbisha Shoshone. Also the proposed Carlin/Caliente Bonnie Claire rail corridor alignment for the transport of high level nuclear waste bisects the Scotty's junction trust land of the Timbisha Shoshone Tribe in Nevada. If built, the proposed Yucca Mountain project would adversely affect future members of the Timbisha Shoshone Tribe as well as all living things at the site vicinity and along the proposed transportation corridors.[86]

These comments tell us that the Yucca Mountain project would not protect future generations and, therefore, is not in the interest of the Timbisha Western Shoshones, who are a sovereign nation that needs to consider its own survival. Arguments for the ways that the Yucca Mountain site would impact Native nations and peoples were not limited to Western Shoshone and Southern Paiute peoples. Ally Indigenous governments also spoke about how the project was outside of the interests of Indigenous peoples and nations in the vicinity of Yucca Mountain. According to the Hopi Tribal Council's comments on the draft environmental impact statement:

---

85. Durham and Helmer, "Letter."
86. Durham and Helmer.

Another implication [of the Yucca Mountains site] is the condemnation of Nevada to serve as a "national sacrifice area." There is a perception in the eastern portion of the United States, and probably also in the coastal west, that Nevada is empty, and therefore it won't matter if regions within that State are made toxic for millennia. However, the Mohave Desert is a complex ecosystem with integrity, just like any other ecosystem. There are plants and animals, birds and insects, that are important to the future of the region, the country, and therefore, the planet. There are also people who live in Nevada, including the tribal peoples who claim Yucca Mountain as their own.[87]

This comment also pivots toward how the Yucca Mountain site is also not in the interest of the state of Nevada, nor the US, nor the planet. In resisting the notion of a national sacrifice area, the Hopi Tribal Council speaks for the interests not only of the Indigenous nations and peoples in the region but also of the planet.

Western Shoshone and Southern Paiute peoples and nations, along with Indigenous ally nations and organizations, used Indigenous national interest rhetorics to ensure that Indigenous sovereignty, self-governance, and national interests are a part of deliberations about the Yucca Mountain project. While my own previous work focused primarily on how the federal government excluded Indigenous nations and peoples from deliberation and participation in decision-making,[88] here I deliberately seek to amplify and commemorate the insistent national interest rhetorics that enact survivance, resurgence, and decolonization. The repetition of calling for government-to-government interactions and insisting that Indigenous national interests be a part of the conversation channels generations of Indigenous peoples and nations who have survived and protected Lands against the relentless onslaught of settler colonialism. These rhetorics matter, not just because in this case they contributed to the Yucca Mountain site's demise but also because they are acts of inherent Indigenous sovereignty.

Returning to the concept of the third space of sovereignty, Western Shoshone and Southern Paiute people also worked from the positionality of US citizens to make their national interests heard. From the perspective of Indigenous nations and those who support decolonization, government-to-government relations are the gold standard for Indigenous-US relations because they recognize Indigenous sovereignty and national interests. Yet, government-to-government relations are far from the norm. In cases where the US settler

---

87. Hopi Tribal Council, "Letter."
88. Endres, "Rhetoric of Nuclear Colonialism."

state refuses to engage in government-to-government negotiations, Indigenous nations and peoples use their status as US citizens to gain access to deliberations. Recall the quote from Deloria above indicating that Indigenous nations and peoples use every tactic at their disposal to support their national interests. When Western Shoshone and Southern Paiute nations were denied government-to-government negotiations, they showed up in force at hearings and events designed to engage *the public* in decision-making. Indeed, most of the textual examples highlighted above were part of the official processes of public participation run by the DOE. Although the Nuclear Waste Policy Act mandates that "affected tribes" be consulted on a government-to-government basis,[89] the DOE used public comment periods and the CGTO as a stand-in for government-to-government consultations. Although Indigenous nations and peoples specifically and repeatedly requested government-to-government negotiation before, during, and after the public comment periods, the federal government did not grant these requests, leaving Indigenous peoples and nations to express their arguments during the public comment period, therefore effectively redefining government-to-government consultation as participation in the public comment period. Despite these requests, the DOE framed the decision-making process so that if Western Shoshone and Southern Paiute nations wanted to submit "official" and "legitimate" arguments against the site, they had to use the public comment period; as its name implies, the public comment period names its participants as part of the US public.

A consequence of subsuming Western Shoshone and Southern Paiute peoples within the public comment period is that they were also subsumed into the US national interest. The DOE, then, viewed Western Shoshone and Southern Paiute objections to the site within the general category of US public objections, which could then be weighed against the proposed US national interest of going forward with the Yucca Mountain site. After the site authorization public comment period, for example, the DOE compiled all of the public comments and responded to them in a comment summary report.[90] Abraham used this and other information to produce the Yucca Mountain site recommendation report submitted to the president.[91] While the comment summary report included Indigenous objections to the site, former secretary of energy Abraham's more widely read site authorization report did not reference Indigenous objections to the site. Rather, Abraham's report incorporated Western Shoshone, Southern Paiute, and other Indigenous arguments within

---

89. US Department of Energy, "Nuclear Waste Policy Act," 8.
90. US Department of Energy, "Site Recommendation."
91. Abraham, "Recommendation."

the general category of *public* opposition to the site. In Abraham's response to public comments, he referred to participants in the public comment period using the vague terms "critics," "the public," and "opponents."[92] There is only one sentence in the report that indicates that Indigenous peoples and nations might have been involved in the decision-making process: "My predecessors and I invited and encouraged public, governmental, and tribal participation at all levels."[93] However, Abraham neither stated whether Indigenous peoples or governments actually participated nor acknowledged the Indigenous public comments that criticized the process for not inviting government-to-government negotiations and that described how the Yucca Mountain site is not in the national interest of Western Shoshone and Southern Paiute peoples. Abraham's response to the public comment period elided arguments about the competing national interests of Indigenous nations.

This definition of Indigenous peoples and nations as within the US public is significant because it allows the federal government to use the national interest and national sacrifice as a justification for the Yucca Mountain site. The national interest of the Western Shoshones to regain control of their treaty Lands is a threat to the Yucca Mountain project. The national interest of the Southern Paiutes to prevent degradation of a sacred homeland is also a threat to the Yucca Mountain project. Indigenous claims to treaty rights and spiritual connections to Yucca Mountain threaten the US federal government's ability to address high-level nuclear waste, especially given that Western Shoshone and Southern Paiute nations do not want to use their Land to support the nuclear production process. When Indigenous peoples are recognized as sovereign nations in government-to-government interactions, these arguments must be considered. However, if Indigenous peoples and nations are named as part of the US public, then not only do their arguments about treaty rights and national interest not fit within the constraints of the public participation process but also their objections to the site can be redefined as coming from a minority ethnic group within the nation that is asked to sacrifice their land for the greater good of the nation as opposed to sovereign nations with their own national interest.

Yet, the federal government could not completely ignore or erase Indigenous nations and peoples from the process. Western Shoshone and Southern Paiute peoples demanded to be heard. They used the venue provided to them as members of the public and citizens of the US to insist on Indigenous sovereignty, demand government-to-government relations, and articulate

---

92. Abraham, 32–45.
93. Abraham, 32.

their national interests. Through these public venues, Western Shoshone and Southern Paiute peoples and nations may not have convinced the DOE to change their approach, but their concerns reached wider audiences. Indigenous national interest rhetorics, in the case of the Yucca Mountain site, used any means necessary to enact sovereignty, call for government-to-government relations, and advocate for their own national interests.

Skull Valley Goshute National Interests

The relationship between the US national interest and Skull Valley Goshute national interests is complicated because there was a disagreement among the members of the nation about whether the PFS site would be in their interest. A variety of stakeholder groups, including the nuclear industry, the PFS corporation, the federal government, the Skull Valley Band of Goshute Nation, Ohngo Gaudadeh Devia, the state of Utah, and environmental groups, weighed in on the proposal and how it affected US national interest as well as Skull Valley Goshute national interests. Although there were also many stakeholders involved in contestation over the Yucca Mountain site, the contour of the controversy generally presented a conflict between US national interest and Western Shoshone and Southern Paiute national interests. What sets apart the Skull Valley PFS site controversy is that Skull Valley Goshutes actively debated whether the PFS nuclear waste site was in the national interest of the Skull Valley Goshute nation. To further complicate the discourse, other stakeholders variously defined Skull Valley Goshutes as citizens within the US national interest or as citizens of the Skull Valley Goshute nation with their own national interest. The federal government and nuclear industry defined the Skull Valley Goshutes as a sovereign nation with its own national interest, albeit subject to the constraints of political sovereignty. The Utah state government and some environmental groups defined the Skull Valley Goshutes as part of the state of Utah, thereby eliding their sovereign status and their right to pursue a proposal that the Skull Valley Goshute government deemed within its national interest. Skull Valley Goshute opponents of the site maintained their sovereignty but tactically used their status as citizens of the US to gain access to the NRC hearings and to maintain alliances with non-Native environmentalists and the state of Utah.

The Skull Valley Goshute government sought to partner with the Private Fuel Storage corporation by entering into a lease that would have allowed PFS to run a high-level nuclear waste site within Skull Valley Goshute Reservation Lands. This lease, although subject to approval by the BIA, is an act of political sovereignty and self-determination by the nation. According to former Skull Valley Goshute council chairperson Leon Bear,

> The thing about the Skull Valley Band of Goshutes is that the Skull Valley Band has a treaty since 1863. We have executive orders that were put into place in 1917 and 1918 reserving the property that we now own, which we have sovereignty over, which we regulate and have our laws and orders on. So the fact that the Skull Valley Band is into this issue and has come together with PFS to license or to put a lease together for the land is appropriate.[94]

In addition to arguing that it is a sovereign right to pursue the PFS project, the Skull Valley Goshute government consistently argued that the Skull Valley PFS site would support Skull Valley Goshute national interests, particularly in terms of economic development and cultural preservation. Recall from chapter 3 that the proposed PFS site is one of the few opportunities for economic development because Skull Valley Goshute Lands are already widely considered to be a wasteland due to a preponderance of toxic facilities surrounding the reservation. Mary Allen, former vice-chair of Skull Valley Goshutes, states:

> [The PFS facility] will benefit us with education, schools, housing and health for our people. Also other economic development, because when we have this facility, with the monies we get, we'll develop some more economic development for our people and provide more jobs because that's what we need. A lot of people have been away from the reservation because there's not many jobs. So, this would be a good opportunity for many to come and live on the reservation and work on the reservation. And it will help us with our culture too. A long time ago when my grandfather was chairman, vice-chairman, and secretary, everybody would do things together; it was like a big family. Everybody would speak their native language and right now that's disappearing. So, that's what we need to bring back for our future and the children.[95]

These statements not only articulate sovereignty with the Skull Valley Goshute nation's decision to lease to PFS but also link this sovereign decision with the national interest of the Skull Valley Goshutes to seek out economic development opportunities while also preserving culture. This is an important enactment of sovereignty.

---

94. "Scoping Meeting," 33.
95. Private Fuel Storage, "Voices: Mary Allen."

While the main crux of Leon Bear and the Skull Valley Goshute government's argument is that the site is in their national interest, they also argued that the site benefits the US nation by addressing the high-level nuclear waste crisis. According to Danny Quintana, attorney for the Skull Valley Goshutes, "It's in the national interest to build this facility."[96] This move positions the Skull Valley Goshute national interests in coalescence with US national interests by helping to address the nuclear waste crisis in the US while also benefiting the Skull Valley Goshute nation. Unlike the Yucca Mountain site, the US could recognize the Skull Valley Goshute national interest in a way that did not subsume Skull Valley Goshute interests within the US national interest.

Opponents of the site not only contested whether the site was in the Skull Valley Goshute national interest but also accused the Skull Valley Goshute government of acting out of line with the interest of its citizens. Margene Bullcreek and Sammy Blackbear were two of the most vocal opponents of the Skull Valley PFS site. Recall from chapter 3 that opponents argued having a nuclear waste facility on the Skull Valley Goshute Reservation would violate cultural and spiritual practices, as well as potentially harm the Lands. Opponents also questioned the logic that they should sacrifice for the US national interest. According to Bullcreek, "It's not our responsibility, as traditionalists, to sacrifice our land for the problem of nuclear waste that U.S. Companies have created."[97] She similarly states in an NRC hearing: "I am a Native American, and I am a caretaker. I am a caretaker for my Reservation. I am not—we are not here to save the nation for our sacrifice. We are already sacrificing."[98] In direct contradiction to the Skull Valley Goshute government's argument, Skull Valley Goshute opponents argued the project would not be in the national interests of Skull Valley Goshute peoples.

Marginalized members of the Skull Valley Goshutes attempted to maintain a focus on upholding sovereignty while also calling into question the governing practices of the Skull Valley Goshute council. For example, opponents accused Bear and other members of the Skull Valley Goshute government of acting against the interests of its citizens by selling their sovereignty to PFS. As Blackbear puts it, "They're [PFS] trying to use our own sovereignty against us, and that's only because Leon sold it to them. . . . Our own sovereignty against our own people. And that's when enough was enough."[99] Bullcreek agrees: "Sovereignty isn't selling your independence and your heritage to the

---

96. Moulton, "NRC Lets Utah."
97. Nuclear Information and Resource Service, "Beware of 'Private Fuel Storage.'"
98. "Public Meeting on the P Draft Environmental Impact Statement," July 27, 2000.
99. *Skull Valley.*

highest bidder."[100] These statements reference how PFS would benefit from the sovereign status of the Skull Valley Goshutes because the PFS site would be subject to different processes and regulations than a municipality or state government. Other Indigenous peoples and nations spoke in support of the Skull Valley Goshute opponents, noting that the Skull Valley Goshute council was abusing its sovereignty. For example, John Kennedy, general counsel for the Confederated Tribes of the Goshute Reservation, states:

> We recognize the sovereign status of the Skull Valley Band. We recognize that they have authority with respect to their tribal lands, just as any Indian tribe would have. But at the same time, we emphasize that all Indian tribes, in exercising their sovereign rights, also need to be careful about their sovereign responsibilities. And we feel that in this instance, that has not been the case.[101]

These accusations of the misuse of sovereignty are linked with opponents' arguments that Bear and the Skull Valley Goshute government engaged in corruption, stating that they never got to vote on the proposal and that Bear signed the lease with PFS in secret.[102] Bullcreek and Blackbear charged that Bear only shared financial resources from the PFS proposal with proponents of the site and denied resources and services to dissidents.[103] In relation to these accusations of corruption, Leon Bear was put on probation for tax fraud charges that emerged from a leadership corruption case. Three additional Skull Valley Goshute government officials also pleaded guilty of using tribal funds for illegal purposes during the time of the PFS controversy. Further, Bear canceled four elections for new governmental executive council members; he claimed it was due to a lack of quorum, but opponents claimed that it was to prevent opponents of the PFS proposal from being elected.[104] The BIA stepped in and ran an election in 2006, in which Lawrence Bear, a relative of Leon Bear, was elected as the new Skull Valley Goshute chairperson.[105] These arguments attempt to maintain the sovereign status of the Skull Valley Goshutes via shifting from definitional stasis (Are Skull Valley Goshutes sovereign?) to a qualitative stasis (Are the sovereign acts of the Skull Valley Goshute government just?). Leon Bear maintained that a majority of the band sup-

---

100. Nuclear Information and Resource Service, "Environmental Racism."
101. "Scoping Meeting," 37.
102. Spangler, "Foes of Goshute."
103. Fahys, "Family Feud"; and Fahys, "Goshutes Who Have Opposed."
104. Fahys, "Would-Be Goshute Leader."
105. Henetz, "Goshutes Elect"; and Henetz, "Skull Valley."

ported the proposal and that he did not violate sovereignty, coerce Skull Valley Goshute citizens, or act outside the interest of the nation. On the contrary, he argued that the Skull Valley Goshute opponents, the state of Utah, environmentalists, and other opposition to the site did not recognize the sovereign status of the Skull Valley Goshutes and their self-determination in deciding to pursue the PFS site as a form of economic development.

Skull Valley Goshute opponents of the project also argued that Private Fuel Storage was acting against the national interests of Skull Valley Goshutes. Although PFS explicitly affirmed the sovereign status of the Skull Valley Goshute nation, opponents argued that PFS specifically targeted an Indigenous nation in order to use its sovereign status to bypass state of Utah opposition and have more control over the regulation of the project. According to Margene Bullcreek, "PFS is a large corporation targeting our small, traditional Native American Reservation for this dangerous project and taking advantage of our sovereignty."[106] Sammy Blackbear also vilifies PFS: "Pretty much everything you name, they've [PFS] done illegally, and we don't like it. So that's why, not only myself but other tribal members are bringing PFS to task. Not only them but the Bureau of Indian Affairs."[107] The connection between PFS and the Bureau of Indian Affairs is significant because the BIA's trust relationship with the Skull Valley Goshute nation empowered it to authorize the lease between PFS and the Skull Valley Goshute nation, which it did in 1997. Opponents called on the BIA to reverse its approval of the lease, which the BIA eventually did in 2006 based, in part, on the arguments that opponents had made to the BIA about the PFS site's impact on cultural sustainability of the Skull Valley Goshute nation. Opponents argued that PFS's motive for recognizing Native sovereignty was colored by the benefits that would come to PFS by working with a sovereign Native nation over local municipal and state governments. According to Kevin Kamps of the Nuclear Information and Resource Service, an ally to Ohngo Gaudadeh Devia,

> The lease agreement signed by Chairman Bear and PFS requires that the tribe "use its sovereign status to support and promote this Lease and Project," and that the tribe "not at any time, pass any law, rule or regulation which could adversely affect or burden this Lease or the Project." The lease also forbids the tribe from setting any environmental protection standards that are stronger than federal standards. The agreement, in effect, forfeits

---

106. As cited in Nuclear Information and Resource Service, "Beware of 'Private Fuel Storage.'"

107. As cited in *Skull Valley*.

control of the reservation dumpsite to PFS, and regulation to the federal NRC.¹⁰⁸

In other words, the PFS site benefits from locating their waste site on an Indigenous reservation that has a different relationship with the federal government. Other opponents of the site positioned PFS as the main villain in this story. According to Tom Goldtooth, director of the Indigenous Environmental Network:

> We recognize the sovereignty of the Skull Valley Tribal Council to make decisions on behalf of their people, but the Tribe is in this situation to begin with because of unjust policies that have negatively impacted their inherent rights to maintain a healthy, economically viable community. The Tribe is not the enemy here, Private Fuel Storage is.¹⁰⁹

By calling PFS the enemy, these comments not only demonstrate that PFS was not seeking to promote the national interest of the Skull Valley Goshutes but more importantly highlight the precarity of Indigenous sovereignty within a settler state.

Skull Valley Goshute and allied Indigenous opponents of the PFS faced a difficult rhetorical bind in arguing against the sovereign decision of the Skull Valley Goshutes. On its face, the decision of the Skull Valley Goshute government to sign a lease with PFS to build a nuclear waste site on the reservation is difficult to contest by those who support Indigenous sovereignty and self-determination. Skull Valley Goshute and other Indigenous opponents of the PFS site managed this difficulty by arguing (1) that Leon Bear and the Skull Valley Goshute government are not using sovereignty responsibly and are hence acting against the national interest of the nation and (2) that PFS is the real enemy that is manipulating and buying off the leadership of the nation. For example, the Indigenous Environmental Network states: "We particularly call upon tribal governments and intertribal organizations to measure their responsibilities to our peoples, not in terms of dollars, but in terms of maintaining our spiritual traditions and assuring our physical, mental, spiritual well being. It is our responsibility to assure the survival of all future generations and be true caretakers for our Mother Earth."¹¹⁰ As most of the rhetoric affirms the sovereign status of the Skull Valley Goshute nation, the debate focused instead on whether the PFS site would be in the interest of the citi-

---

108. Nuclear Information and Resource Service, "Environmental Racism."
109. As cited in Nuclear Information and Resource Service.
110. Indigenous Environmental Network, "Indigenous Anti-Nuclear Statement."

zens of the Skull Valley Goshute nation and whether the Skull Valley Goshute government was working in the interest of its own citizens.

Yet, it was not just Skull Valley Goshute opponents of the PFS site who were in a double bind. The Skull Valley Goshute nation was also in a double bind similar to what Dina Gilio-Whitaker describes for Indigenous nations involved in resource extraction:

> Things get ethically complicated when Native nation governments willingly choose to engage in resource extraction—especially fossil fuels—given the harm they cause, both in the extracting and in the production of climate-changing greenhouse gases. The need to escape poverty and assert sovereignty, weighed against cultural obligations to protect land, forces tribes into what can seem like an impossible double bind. It is a realm of difficult choices that exists beyond binaries of black and white and right and wrong, necessitated by the unforgiving and unrelenting demands of capitalism.[111]

In other words, settler colonialism forces Indigenous nations into a series of impossible choices. Byrd notes that settler colonialism succeeds, in part, "by pitting indigenous people against each other, or making them fight for scraps to avoid the larger structuring problems of settler colonialism."[112] While contestation over what constitutes the national interest within the Skull Valley Goshute nation is an act of sovereignty and self-governance, even those acts can be influenced by settler colonialism, creating many impossibilities and binds within Indigenous sovereignty and self-governance.

Skull Valley Goshute opponents, who felt that their voice was limited by their own governmental leaders and processes, sought out additional venues in which they could resist the PFS site. They shifted between defining themselves as citizens of the Skull Valley Goshute nation and as citizens of the US in order to gain access to venues for airing their grievances. Unlike the Yucca Mountain case wherein Western Shoshones and Southern Paiutes actively sought government-to-government consultation, the Skull Valley PFS site is based in BIA and NRC recognition of the sovereign status of the Skull Valley Goshute government. On the one hand, Skull Valley Goshute opponents, invoking their status as Skull Valley Goshute citizens, called on the BIA to intervene in what they saw as unjust governmental practices and appealed to the BIA to reverse its earlier decision to approve the lease between PFS and the Skull Valley Goshute nation. On the other hand, Skull Valley Gos-

---

111. Gilio-Whitaker, *As Long as Grass Grows*, 69.
112. Byrd, *Transit of Empire*, 150.

hute opponents of the site used their status as members of the US public to participate in NRC public meetings about the proposed site and to file a contention—under the organization Ohngo Gaudadeh Devia—in opposition to the site with the NRC.[113] The Skull Valley Goshute government had already worked directly with the NRC to register its support for the PFS site, so the opponents' only option was to file their opposition via the public hearing process, tactically using their status as members of the US public to gain access to air their complaints to the NRC.

The division within the Skull Valley Goshute peoples over the PFS site started as a disagreement over whether a nuclear waste facility should be allowed on the reservation. The rhetoric of both proponents and opponents includes underlying assumptions about national interest and sovereignty as significant points of contestation. In arguments about whether the PFS site would serve the national interest of the Skull Valley Goshute peoples, proponents and opponents disagreed about the roles of economic development and cultural preservation within the interest of the Skull Valley Goshutes, and opponents questioned whether the Skull Valley Goshute government was truly working toward the best interest of its citizens. While all Skull Valley Goshutes affirmed the importance of Indigenous sovereignty, the debate about the PFS site raised questions about the quality of sovereignty, whether outside forces were manipulating Skull Valley sovereignty, and whether the actions of the Skull Valley Goshute government were a just use of sovereignty. Ohngo Gaudadeh Devia attempted to uphold the importance of sovereignty as a concept while simultaneously showing that the application of sovereignty in the particular case was problematic. Opponents of the Skull Valley Goshute government's decision also tactically used their positionality as both members of the Skull Valley Goshute nation and members of the US public to argue against the site in a variety of venues. In comparison to the Yucca Mountain site controversy where Western Shoshone and Southern Paiute peoples had to struggle to make their own national interest central to the deliberation, the Skull Valley Goshute national interest was a prominent party in the PFS controversy, revealing the contextual nature of Indigenous national interest rhetorics. The Skull Valley Goshutes, however, were not the only stakeholders that invoked national interest in this controversy. The story of the PFS controversy is further complicated by consideration of the ways that Private Fuel Storage argued that the waste site would meet both the US national interest and the Skull Valley Goshute national interests.

---

113. "Ohngo Gaudadeh Devia's Contentions."

Private Fuel Storage, in reaction to delays in the federal government's progress in opening a permanent high-level nuclear waste site, proposed their own temporary interim storage site in Skull Valley, to be used until the federal government opened Yucca Mountain or another permanent storage site. PFS, in this case, speaks for the nuclear industry's need for a solution to nuclear waste and its support of a temporary interim storage site that would relieve the burden on the nuclear industry to temporarily store the spent fuel on nuclear reactor sites. PFS and other nuclear industry representatives argued the Skull Valley PFS site was in the US national interest because the lack of a national high-level nuclear waste storage facility threatens the nuclear industry and the future of nuclear power. According to PFS, "Not only is a safe, clean, temporary storage facility for spent nuclear fuel needed by the nation's generators of nuclear power electricity and their customers, it will solve a pressing national problem, and will offer economic benefits to its host community, the surrounding county and the state."[114] While acknowledging the site would benefit the nuclear industry, PFS stressed it would also contribute to solving the national problem of nuclear waste, wherein spent fuel rods are stored on-site in storage pools and casks that are at or near capacity at numerous nuclear power plants in the US. Furthermore, according to PFS, the site would advance the national interest of the Skull Valley Goshutes via economic development and cultural preservation. The now inactive PFS website included the following:

> The lease of 820 acres of desert land on the Skull Valley Reservation to Private Fuel Storage LLC (PFS) will provide the Tribe with
>
> - Preference in hiring tribal members who qualify for jobs at the facility;
> - Revenue for tribal government initiatives, including
>   ▷ Private healthcare for all tribal members; the closest Indian Health Services are currently more than 200 miles away,
>   ▷ Education and training,
>   ▷ Housing,
>   ▷ Improved infrastructure for future development,
>   ▷ A cultural center;
> - Job potential in related manufacturing businesses.
>
> In addition, the PFS project will give members of the Tribe who currently live near their work in Grantsville, Tooele, Salt Lake City, and other areas,

---

114. Private Fuel Storage, "Who Will Benefit."

a reason to move back to the Reservation. This will enable the Tribe to preserve its culture, which is disappearing as members scatter to pursue education and work opportunities.[115]

To bolster its argument, the PFS website included quotations from Skull Valley Goshute proponents, such as the following statement by Leon Bear:

> For a long time the tribe has been pretty much distressed over revenues that they don't have, lack of infrastructure of the tribal government. And we were looking for economic benefits or development for the tribe out there that would provide revenue for us. And we feel, we really believe that this is one economic project that would benefit us greatly. It will allow our tribal government to provide social programs for our tribal members, housing needs, health needs. The fact is that these things are not provided to the Skull Valley Band through the federal agency, the BIA, the state of Utah, or any other government. And it looks like we're going to have to provide these things on our own.[116]

PFS's recognition of the sovereign status of the Skull Valley Goshute nation is, in one sense, a tangible triumph for Indigenous struggles for self-determination and recognition of their sovereign status. Whereas the nuclear industry's advocacy in favor of the Yucca Mountain site conflicted with the national interest of Western Shoshone and Southern Paiute peoples and nations, its advocacy of the Skull Valley PFS site supported the national interest of the government of the Skull Valley Goshute nation.

One possible explanation for this inconsistency is that the nuclear industry simply sought to advance its own interest in opening a high-level nuclear waste site and drew from the available arguments that fit each particular case. The sovereign status of the Skull Valley Goshute nation provides tangible benefits for PFS in their pursuit of an interim high-level nuclear waste storage site. In the case of the monitored retrievable storage program (from which the Skull Valley PFS site evolved), the Office of the Nuclear Waste Negotiator specifically targeted Indigenous nations to host facilities because of a perception their sovereign status and dire economic circumstances would allow for an easier approval process.[117] Reflecting on the MRS program, Robert Vandenbosch and Susan Vandenbosch contend, "In the U.S. federal system, Indian

---

115. Private Fuel Storage, "PFS Project Benefits the Nation."
116. Private Fuel Storage, "Voices: Leon Bear."
117. Gowda and Easterling, "Voluntary Siting and Equity"; and Gowda and Easterling, "Nuclear Waste."

tribes have sovereignty, and governors could not veto the participation of Indian tribes in the nuclear waste facility siting program. This makes them attractive venues for siting many facilities prohibited by state law."[118] PFS never publicly admitted to this motive for working with the Skull Valley Goshute nation. Yet, opponents of the site attribute this motive to PFS; recall that Skull Valley Goshute and other Indigenous opponents of the site accused PFS of using the Skull Valley Goshutes' sovereignty to bypass obstacles and attain its own ends. Although it may be impossible to discover whether or not PFS actively targeted the Skull Valley Goshute nation for political expediency, it is important to analyze PFS's support of Indigenous sovereignty and national interest as both a positive recognition of Indigenous national interest in a political milieu in which Indigenous sovereignty and struggles are more often unrecognized and a problematic invocation of Skull Valley Goshute national interest as a means to attaining the corporation's interest in addressing waste, the main problem for continued nuclear power development.

The federal government also played an important role in the PFS controversy, albeit different from the role it played in the Yucca Mountain controversy. The Yucca Mountain site was proposed via a process initiated by the Nuclear Waste Policy Act, which mandates the federal government assume responsibility for storing spent fuel rods and other high-level nuclear waste from the nuclear energy industry. As such, the act obliges the federal government to select, operate, and regulate a national repository. In the case of PFS, a privately run interim storage facility, the federal government's primary role was regulatory. The BIA was responsible for managing its trust responsibility to the Skull Valley Goshute nation, and more specifically for adjudicating the lease negotiated between the Skull Valley Goshutes and PFS. The NRC was responsible for adjudicating the license for the high-level nuclear waste site. The BIA (enforcer of the trust relationship) had to decide if the site would benefit the Skull Valley Goshute national interest. Initially, in 1997, the BIA provisionally approved the lease (pending an environmental impact statement and NRC licensing), stating that the project fit within the national interest of the Skull Valley Goshutes.[119] Later, in 2006, the BIA reversed their earlier decision and denied the lease, stating that the project would violate their trust responsibility to the Skull Valley Goshutes. The BIA's decision was made by weighing "preservation of tribal culture and life against the benefits and risks from economic development."[120] The decision concludes, "It is not consistent with the conduct expected of the prudent trustee to approve a proposed lease

---

118. Vandenbosch and Vandenbosch, *Nuclear Waste Stalemate*, 98.
119. Bureau of Indian Affairs, "Record of Decision."
120. Gehrke, Fahys, and Burr, "Interior Dumps N-Waste Plan."

that promotes storing high-level spent fuel on the reservation."[121] In these statements, the federal government through the auspice of the Department of the Interior and the BIA exercised its trust responsibility to deny the lease. Not surprisingly, Skull Valley Goshute opponents of the site viewed the decision as a victory and Skull Valley Goshute proponents of the site viewed the decision as a loss. On the one hand, this decision demonstrates the concept of political sovereignty, in which Indigenous sovereignty is always circumscribed by the US federal government. In an effort to uphold its trust responsibility and support the cultural preservation of the Skull Valley Goshutes, the BIA overrode the decision of the Skull Valley Goshute government. On the other hand, the BIA decision could be seen as a corrective to the faulty leadership practices of the Skull Valley Goshute government wherein government representatives were not acting in the interest of its members. Either way, the BIA acted in line with its role in a system of political colonialism when determining the national interest of the Skull Valley Goshute nation in relation to the PFS site.

The NRC had to decide if licensing a temporary high-level nuclear waste storage facility would be in the US national interest. The commission recognized the sovereign status of the Skull Valley Band of Goshute nation during its deliberations and the Skull Valley Goshute government was involved throughout the process. Skull Valley Goshute opponents who wanted to speak out against the views of their government participated in the NRC public hearings and submitted an official contention, not explicitly as Skull Valley Goshute citizens but as members of the public and interested parties. Skull Valley Goshute opponents spoke as individuals in NRC-sponsored public hearing meetings and filed a contention with the NRC as an organization (Ohngo Gaudadeh Devia). The NRC process, therefore, allowed for both government-to-government engagement between the Skull Valley Goshute nation and the US government and for individual Skull Valley Goshutes to engage through procedures set up for the general US public. For example, at a March 8, 2002, NRC public hearing, Michael Farrar from the NRC convened the meeting by stating, "This is the chance for the public here to say its piece."[122] As a petitioner, Ohngo Gaudadeh Devia submitted one of five contentions to the NRC; others were submitted by the state of Utah, the Skull Valley Goshute government, the Confederated Tribes of the Goshute Reservation, and a group of local business entities operating in the Skull Valley designated as "Castle Rock" by the NRC. The NRC contention process, in addition to public hearings, allowed Skull Valley Goshute people to voice their concerns to the NRC

---

121. Bureau of Indian Affairs, "Record of Decision," 19.
122. "Private Fuel Storage," 5.

in a situation where relying only on government-to-government interaction would have limited their voices. Skull Valley Goshutes responded differently to government decisions based on their stance on the PFS site. While Skull Valley Goshutes always held to their sovereign status, they shifted between their positions as Skull Valley Goshute citizens and US citizens to respond to the federal government's position.

The state of Utah vehemently opposed the PFS site and argued against the site based on state interest but generally neglected to consider the national interest of the Skull Valley Goshute nation. For example, former US congressional representative Jim Hansen stated, "I believe this is bad public policy, dangerous to our national security and the economy of Utah, fundamentally unsafe, and possibly illegal. This proposal is even worse when you consider that none of the waste is generated in Utah and not one watt of this power is used by the people of Utah."[123] The assertion in this statement that the PFS site is located in Utah is incorrect. Although the Skull Valley Goshute Reservation Lands are surrounded by Utah, the reservation is not a part of the state but a sovereign nation. Moreover, the state put up a sign on the state road to Skull Valley that restricted nuclear waste from being transported on the road as one of its strategies for preventing the site; if it could not stop the site because it was located on the Skull Valley Goshute Reservation, it could prohibit nuclear waste from traveling to the site (see figure 10). The state of Utah's opposition to the site focused mainly on protecting the people of Utah, with little consideration for the Skull Valley Goshute nation's desire to store the waste. This led to tensions between the state of Utah and the Skull Valley Goshute nation.

Like the state of Utah, local and national environmental groups opposed to the PFS site also argued that it violated the US national interest. These environmentalist groups worked in coalition with the Skull Valley Goshute opponents, often releasing coauthored press releases and coordinating protest actions together. Across the discourse, these groups sometimes defined the Skull Valley Goshutes as part of the US public and sometimes defined them as citizens of their own sovereign nation. A press release from Public Citizen and Nuclear Resource and Information Service states:

> As a national security risk, this site threatens the health and safety of the public—not just for Utah, but for the entire country, because the dangerous radioactive waste would travel on our railways through highly populated regions across the United States, only to be moved again in the future. Further, there are no nuclear power plants within Utah's borders, yet Utah's

---

123. "Public Meeting on the P Draft Environmental Impact Statement," July 28, 2000, 197.

FIGURE 10. A sign erected by the state of Utah expressing opposition to storing high-level nuclear waste within Skull Valley. Photo taken by Danielle Endres.

residents are being targeted to bear the burden of 80 percent of the country's commercial high-level radioactive waste. Sited on an impoverished Indian reservation riddled by corruption, controversy and tribal tensions over the proposed dump, this private storage site illustrates how environmental justice is once again being ignored by federal agencies and aggressive energy companies that are more concerned with turning nuclear power into a profitable venture, rather than protecting public health and safety.[124]

This statement asserts that the PFS site would be located on an "Indian reservation" but also that Utah's residents are being targeted for this storage. In another example, a press release from the Nuclear Research and Information Service details,

Public interest groups and Indigenous spokespersons today charged that the U.S. Nuclear Regulatory Commission (NRC) is exacerbating the nation's nuclear waste problems—and endangering national security—by preliminarily approving a so-called temporary waste dump in Utah known as Private

---

124. Public Citizen and Nuclear Information and Resource Service, "On Verge of Approval."

Fuel Storage. . . . The groups declared PFS a national security risk because the high-level nuclear waste would travel on railways through highly populated regions across the United States with little to no preparation or training for states and cities.¹²⁵

In these two examples, the environmental groups that opposed the PFS site are most concerned with arguing whether the site is in the US national interest. While they recognize their coalition with Indigenous peoples (they do not specifically mention the Skull Valley Goshutes) in their messages, they do not consider the national interest of the Skull Valley Goshutes in their arguments against the site. Their arguments assimilate Skull Valley Goshutes into the US public.

In sum, the controversy over the Skull Valley PFS site furthers an understanding of the many-sided discourse of national interest that involves the nuclear industry, the federal government, the Skull Valley Goshute nation, the state of Utah, and environmental groups. Skull Valley Goshutes primarily define themselves as members of a sovereign nation with its own national interests, but this national interest is contested among Skull Valley Goshute citizens. Further, in certain instances, it was tactically advantageous for Skull Valley Goshute individuals opposed to the PFS site to act as members of the US public, using this role as an entry point for advocating for their own perception of national interest in opposition to the Skull Valley Goshute government's construction of the national interest. While the federal government and PFS defined the Skull Valley Goshutes as a nation with its own national interest, these definitions work within an overarching system of settler colonialism. To further complicate the discourse of national interest in relation to the PFS site, the state government of Utah and environmental groups focused more on national and state interest—viewing the Skull Valley Goshute Reservation as within Utah or part of the US national interest—to the neglect of considering the Skull Valley Goshute community as a sovereign nation with its own national interest.

CONCLUSION

Indigenous national interest rhetorics are multiple and context dependent, but at their core, these rhetorics uphold, demand, and enact inherent sovereignty within a settler structure of political sovereignty designed to constrain

---

125. Nuclear Information and Resource Service, "Opposition."

Indigenous self-determination. Indigenous national interest rhetorics respond to the slipperiness of settler colonialism's attempts to constrain Indigenous sovereignty, therefore showing up differently in diverse struggles. Across the differences between the Yucca Mountain and Skull Valley PFS sites, Indigenous rhetors relentlessly asserted sovereignty and unique national interests by whatever means they could. Depending on the specific situation and context, Indigenous national interest rhetorics took the form of demanding government-to-government relations, illuminating dissonance between Indigenous national interests and the US national interest, aligning with the US national interest, or contesting the way their own government defined national interest. While Western Shoshone, Southern Paiute, and Skull Valley Goshute peoples and nations consistently defended their status as sovereign nations with their own national interests, there are also moments where they worked from their positionalities as US citizens and perceived members of the US public. When calls for government-to-government relations were not recognized, Western Shoshone and Southern Paiute nations and peoples showed up in force at public hearings. When Skull Valley Goshute people opposed the decision of their own government, they appealed to the BIA as Skull Valley Goshute citizens and to the NRC as US citizens. The liminal third space of sovereignty is both enabling and constraining for Indigenous survivance and decolonization.

Yet, the stories in this chapter underscore that Indigenous political sovereignty within a settler colonial system is ultimately circumscribed by the federal government's authority through the domestic dependent and trust relationships with the federal government. Whether Indigenous nations agree with or contest the US national interest, the settler state views the national interests of these nations as substrate to the US national interest, except for the rare cases in which Indigenous national interests align with the US national interest (the Skull Valley Goshute government's support of the PFS site). The federal government's (through the DOE) definition of Indigenous as part of the US public in the case of Yucca Mountain and the federal government's (through the BIA) overturning of the decision of the Skull Valley Goshute government show how the settler state uses its power to define and control Indigenous sovereignty—when it is recognized and when it is not. Even if readers agree with the BIA's decision to support the Skull Valley Goshute opponents by denying the lease of the PFS site, this example still falls within the overarching system of political colonialism. Ultimately, it was the federal government (the DOE and the BIA) that decided the fate of the Yucca Mountain and PFS sites. Considering that colonialism is endemic and that resistance to it is still constrained within an overarching system of political colonialism, Coffey and Tsosies's call for a shift in paradigm to inherent sovereignty offers a more productive lens for understanding Indigenous national interest rhetorics.[126] While the exercise of inherent sovereignty does not replace the system of political sovereignty, it shifts focus to deliberate performances of Indigenous national interest as constitutive of an alternate identity outside the colonial system. Inherent sovereignty is not directed against the US federal government or political colonialism but is directed at Indigenous peoples and nations as an affirmation of self-determination.

---

126. Coffey and Tsosie, "Rethinking the Tribal Sovereignty Doctrine."

CONCLUSION

Decolonization Tactics for Survivance

An enduring memory from my decades-long engagement with nuclear colonization and nuclear decolonization was formed early in the research project. As a graduate student, I traveled to the Yucca Mountain Information Center in Las Vegas to access Department of Energy documents about the Yucca Mountain Project. I went to the center every day for a few days, combing through binder after binder of public comments and public hearing transcripts. On one of the days—I don't remember which—one of the employees at the center asked me about my project. I told her that I was focused on analyzing the arguments made by Native peoples and nations against the Yucca Mountain site. She immediately responded something to the effect of having seen Native peoples give testimony at the hearings that she described as "so quaint." I remember very little about the rest of the conversation, but those two words—"so quaint"—have stuck with me all these years not only because they made me angry in the moment but also because of how dismissive they were, channeling common stereotypes of Native peoples and nations as old-fashioned, stuck in the past, and strangely exotic. In a way, my desire to change that woman's mind, to show her that Indigenous resistance to Yucca Mountain was not quaint, and to share with her the sophistication, brilliance, and power of Western Shoshone and Southern Paiute arguments against the site is one of motivations that drove my research project. Nuclear decolonization is, regardless of how settlers might perceive it, anything but quaint.

Nuclear decolonization is a movement created by and for Indigenous peoples and nations. It is an insistent and powerful mode of Indigenous survivance that enacts Lands protection, sovereignty, and resurgence. In their resistance to the Yucca Mountain and Skull Valley PFS high-level nuclear waste sites, Western Shoshone, Southern Paiute, and Skull Valley Goshute peoples and nations used Indigenous Lands rhetorics and Indigenous national interest rhetorics to not only contribute to preventing two nuclear waste sites but, more importantly, to enact nuclear decolonization. These rhetorics are rooted in deep connections to the Great Basin and two specific places: Yucca Mountain and Skull Valley. They are rooted in intertwined Indigenous pasts, presents, and futures with these places and the right to self-determine and self-govern whether and how to engage with nuclear waste. Although presented in detail here as a set of rhetorical tactics that worked in two specific struggles over nuclear waste siting, nuclear decolonization is much more. It is a distinct form of mobilization to protect Lands and sovereignties. It is an everyday way of being for many of the Western Shoshones, Southern Paiutes, and Skull Valley Goshutes highlighted in this book and others who have spent much of their lives raising awareness about and resisting the harmful consequences of the nuclear production cycle for Native peoples and nations.

My retelling of how Western Shoshone, Southern Paiute, and Skull Valley Goshute peoples and nations fought to protect their Lands from nuclear waste simultaneously works to particularize and localize one mode of Indigenous social change while also demonstrating how this story is one of many in a constellation of stories of successful and ongoing movements for Indigenous sovereignties and Lands.[1] Nuclear decolonization, then, is one part of a larger story of Indigenous decolonization, survivance, and resurgence on this continent that began in 1492, lives in the present, and will animate the future until Indigenous peoples and nations are free again. Indigenous theories and practices of social change are a core and enduring presence in this place, what settlers named the US, that have persistently prevented settler colonialism's goal—to eliminate the Native—from becoming complete.[2] The ongoing presence of Indigenous movements for social change and decolonization is something to commemorate. For non-Indigenous people seeking to be allies or

---

1. Other examples include Estes, *Our History*; Keeler, *Edge of Morning*; Jacob, *Yakama Rising*; Estes and Dhillon, *Standing with Standing Rock*; Dhillon, *Prairie Rising*; The Kino-nda-niimi Collective, *Winter We Danced*; LaDuke, *Winona LaDuke Chronicles*; Josephy, Johnson, and Nagel, *Red Power*; and T. Johnson, Champagne, and Nagel, "American Indian Activism."

2. Ned Blackhawk retells the story of the US as one in which the enduring presence, agency, and survival of Native peoples and nations is an essential part of the history of this continent. Blackhawk, *Rediscovery of America*.

comrades in Indigenous decolonization, these movements are something to stand alongside, amplify, and disseminate. This is why this book retells stories of nuclear decolonization. Telling these stories is important, not only because of my accountability to the peoples and places who asked me and others to share them but also because they illuminate a vital star in the beautiful constellation of Indigenous social change.

In the remainder of this conclusion, I focus on four key implications that I hope readers can take from this book. First, I speak to my colleagues in rhetorical studies, and more broadly communication studies. I argue that doing Indigenous rhetorics communication research, especially as a non-Indigenous scholars like myself, requires commitments to thinking about theory and method in ways that are grounded in Indigenous knowledges and sovereignties. Second, in dialogue with interdisciplinary scholarship and environmental justice advocates, I situate nuclear decolonization within a broader conversation about the importance of Indigenizing environmental justice. The stories in this book highlight the importance of sovereignty and Lands to Indigenous environmentalisms and antinuclearisms and argue that nuclear decolonization is a distinct form of antinuclear mobilization that cannot be subsumed within broader environmental and antinuclear movements. Third, I articulate the policy implications for nuclear waste siting that come from listening to Western Shoshone, Southern Paiute, and Skull Valley Goshute actors. As the country, and world, continue to struggle to find places to store nuclear waste, I offer a series of tangible policy steps that would bring more justice to the process of waste siting decisions. Finally, I address the peoples and places I worked with during my engagement with nuclear decolonization. I speak not only to my collaborators, participants, and others in the movement for nuclear decolonization but also to Native Lands protectors working on a variety of campaigns.

INDIGENOUS RHETORICS: THEORY AND METHOD

For rhetorical scholars, nuclear decolonization offers a theoretical resource and critical lens. As noted in the introduction chapter, nuclear decolonization is a bottom-up theory created by and for Indigenous peoples and nations. As Michael Lechuga writes, "The expressions and actions of activists should be seen as complex thought, in real time, that is making sense of and immediately responding to oppression."[3] Nuclear decolonization need not be made sense of

---

3. Lechuga, "Anticolonial Future," 382.

through the canon of Western rhetorical theory nor through continental theories of power. Rather, the rhetoric of nuclear decolonization is based in Indigenous knowledges and constituted through series of rhetorical tactics invented by brilliant, dedicated Lands protectors. While I have outlined some contours of the rhetorical tactics within this theory that I learned through engagement with and listening to Western Shoshone, Southern Paiute, and Skull Valley Goshute peoples and nations, there is ample room for more engagement and expansion of the dynamics of nuclear decolonization as a rhetorical phenomenon. For instance, one topic not included in this book is the way that Western Shoshone, Southern Paiute, and Skull Valley Goshute peoples and nations navigated between Indigenous sciences and Western sciences to argue against the scientific suitability of the Yucca Mountain and Skull Valley PFS sites. I hope to see nuclear decolonization unpacked in future academic work about the relationship between nuclear technologies and Indigenous peoples and nations, particularly in a continued shift in focus from critiquing the strategies of colonization to amplifying the tactics of decolonization.

The articulation of nuclear decolonization rhetoric also intersects with a broader surge of theorization in rhetoric about anticolonialisms, particularly in relationship with Indigenous, Black, Latine, Asian American, African, and Asian rhetorics that have and continue to assert self-determination in response to forms of colonization.[4] This surge in anticolonial theorizing and praxis is valuable and productive for our field. This book contributes to the project of localizing and particularizing structures and practices of decolonization in specific Western Shoshone, Southern Paiute, and Skull Valley Goshute struggles to protect Lands and sovereignties from nuclearism's entanglement with settler colonialism. Yet, although nuclear decolonization is a specific theory and praxis rooted in particular peoples and places, there are also fruitful possibilities for learning from practitioners of nuclear decolonization toward continuing to nuance rhetorical studies' appreciation of pluriversal rhetorics and anticolonial pathways.[5]

---

4. Some examples include Ono, *Contemporary Media Culture*; Wanzer-Serrano, *New York Young Lords*; Schwartz-DuPre and Scott, "Postcolonial Globalized Communication"; Na'puti, "Rhetorical Contexts of Colonization"; Hasian, "Colonial Hermeneutics of Suspicion"; Shome, "Postcolonial Approaches to Communication"; Lechuga, "Anticolonial Future"; Olaniyan, "Know Your History"; de Onís, "Energy Colonialism"; Vats, "(Dis)Owning Bikram"; Sowards, "#RhetoricSoEnglishOnly"; Asante and Hanchey, "Decolonizing Queer Modernities"; Agyeman Asante, "#RhetoricSoWhite and US Centered"; Tarin, "Buen Vivir"; Olson and Casas, "Felipe Guaman Poma de Ayala's"; Cortez, "Of Exterior and Exception"; Atallah et al., "Transnational Research Collectives"; Dutta, "Whiteness, Internationalization, and Erasure"; and deTar, "Why 'Anticolonial'?"

5. Cushman, Baca, and García, "Delinking."

As Indigenous rhetorics and Indigenous communication continue to grow and deepen, this book offers one example for resisting dominant disciplines of knowledge construction that operate in complicity with settler colonialism.[6] As Tiara Na'puti argues, to unsettle the field of rhetorical studies requires changing the ways rhetorical scholars think about the purposes and processes of research, the theories we use, and our relationships with our research. By mobilizing an Indigeneity analytic, she argues that rhetorical studies, and I would add communication studies, can open new pathways and possibilities for work that is rooted in the wisdoms and innovations within Indigenous knowledges.[7] This book specifically engages with the question of whether and how non-Indigenous scholars might do Indigenous communication research that seeks to center Indigeneity. This is not an uncontroversial topic. There are a range of perspectives from arguments that non-Indigenous, and specifically white, scholars should stop doing Indigenous research to arguments about the best, most ethical ways for non-Indigenous researchers to do this work. One need only peruse academic Twitter to find robust examples of the diversity of opinions about this question. I, of course, argue that it is possible for non-Indigenous people to engage in ethical research that can serve Indigenous peoples and nations.[8] Because of my focus on Indigenous movements for social change, many of which actively call on non-Indigenous audiences to work in solidarity, there is a role for non-Indigenous scholar activists in Indigenous decolonization movements. That role cannot be taken lightly but rather requires reflection, accountability, and discomfort.

I brought some specific commitments to this research project as a non-Indigenous settler seeking to uplift and stand with Indigenous advocates for nuclear decolonization. From where I sit now, having had many years to reflect on how my research approach changed and adapted over time, in some cases based on mistakes and missteps, I would call my process of research a part of a growing focus on Indigenous communication methods.[9] Indigenous communication methods are an approach to research based in anticolonial, place-based, and community-based relations that seek to serve the needs of Indigenous peoples and nations. This approach builds from rich scholarly conversations about and examples of ethical, respectful, and collaborative

---

6. For more on the settler colonial academy, as well as ways to engage in resistance, see la paperson, *Third University Is Possible.*

7. Na'puti, "Speaking of Indigeneity."

8. I am very grateful to have been able to have many conversations with Taylor N. Johnson and Jessica Chaplain about our shared experiences as white settler women doing Indigenous rhetorics research and teaching. Some of our conversations are reflected here: T. Johnson and Endres, "Decolonizing Settler Public Address."

9. For one example, see Cordes, "Revisiting Stories and Voices."

Indigenous research methods.[10] While I am in no position to lay out a definitive Indigenous communication research method that can be applied to other studies and projects, here I want to linger on three practices that guided my work: reliance on public texts, anticolonial inductive fieldwork, and reflexivity grounded in comradeship.

As I argued in the introduction, I made a deliberate effort to base my analysis on the public rhetoric of nuclear decolonization advocates. That is, I sought to access, document, and analyze the rhetorical tactics that Western Shoshone, Southern Paiute, and Skull Valley Goshute peoples designed for distribution to public, including non-Indigenous, audiences. These showed up in public hearing comments, email list alerts, press releases, memoirs, organizational websites, protest events, gatherings within Indigenous Lands, and more. Some of these texts came from government repositories (e.g., public hearings), but I accessed and saved the large majority of them through my engagements in what is now known as rhetorical fieldwork.[11] I attended events in person not only to engage in participant observation of in situ rhetorics that might otherwise remain undocumented but also to listen to, learn from, and see how nuclear decolonization tactics were created and distributed. I joined email lists that allowed me to keep track of developments, learn about events where I could lend my support, and read newsletters and press releases. In some cases, I worked with participants to document and further share their stories through oral history interviews.[12] These texts, like many social movement texts, are designed to be shared in an effort to raise awareness and grow the movement. Amplifying those texts through a rhetorical analysis is one small way to extend the reach of those efforts with academic audiences and students, while recognizing the important critique that academic publications can be inaccessible to many audiences and limited to a small readership. For rhetoricians interested in engaging with Indigenous decolonization movements, a focus on public texts offers a way to engage with texts that are already being produced and readied for distribution. Yet, a reliance on public texts does not imply a business-as-usual approach to rhetorical analysis. When committing to anticolonial and Indigenous research methods, an approach to engaging with public texts still involves relationship-building, navigating

---

10. This rich literature can by no means be characterized by a mere footnote. Rather than seeking a comprehensive list of citations, I offer three touchstones for Indigenous research methods: Kovach, *Indigenous Methodologies*; Wilson, *Research Is Ceremony*; and L. Smith, *Decolonizing Methodologies*.

11. Endres et al., "In Situ Rhetoric."

12. Stored and available for use at the J. Willard Marriott Library at the University of Utah. The easiest way to find them, though, is on my website: https://www.danielleendres.com/nuclear-west-oral-histories.

(mis)trust, articulating political commitments, serving Native peoples' and nations' needs, and processes of informed consent.

When I read Lechuga's essay on changing the way rhetoricians do social movement rhetoric toward anticolonial futures, I was struck by his call for scholars to

> not privilege the theoretical canon of research, but to start by observing and working with activists who are developing an on-the-ground-theory for meeting violent power where it occurs. This, of course, requires a skill set for relationship-building outside of the academy where the anticolonial interests of the activist are shared by researcher.[13]

Part of the reason this quotation spoke to me was that I always saw myself as pursuing what I would describe now as a radically inductive mode of research engagement, one that required deep engagement with rhetorical practices before applying or developing theory. While Lechuga's argument is not simply about doing inductive research, there is an important connection between a rhetorical critic being committed to an inductive orientation and the ability to start with listening as opposed to theory. Yet, inductive research can and often does still privilege the notion of an academic making sense of what they have observed with their expertise and knowledge of external theories—they might start with in situ observation, but they then apply existing theories to explain the rhetorical practices. I have done this in previous work by applying a Foucauldian theory of power to nuclear colonialism and resistance to it. Lechuga's argument importantly intervenes in this form of inductive research by seeing theory as internally developed by on-the-ground activists as opposed to externally imposed by an academic. This changes an academic's role from distiller of knowledge to that of an archivist, collaborator, storyteller, or amplifier. Inspired by Lechuga's prodding, this book presents nuclear decolonization as an Indigenous theory and practice, one that I have been privileged to be able to watch and learn from over the past twenty-something years. What I am calling anticolonial inductive fieldwork is a process during which I engaged in a series of relationships that allowed me to build an archive and tell a story of nuclear decolonization as both theory and a set of tactics built from the bottom up by decades of Indigenous peoples and nations doing the work of decolonization, survivance, and resurgence.

A final aspect of my research process has been engaging in an ongoing process of reflexivity about my role as a white settler woman, my motivations

---

13. Lechuga, "Anticolonial Future," 384.

for this research, and my responsibilities to Western Shoshone, Southern Paiute, and Skull Valley Goshute peoples and nations. While the preface lays out parts of my story and motivations for doing this research, reflexivity is a process that infuses an entire research project. As a practitioner of rhetorical fieldwork, ongoing reflexivity about my political commitments, my positions of earned and unearned privilege, and the ways that my positionality inevitably frames my writing and interpretations is an essential component of my research.[14] Indigenous research methods have taught me, as Shawn Wilson puts it, "that 'checking your heart' is a critical element in the research process."[15] Checking my heart has entailed seeing moments of discomfort, pain, and uncertainty as opportunities for learning, coming to the research with a good heart and good motives "that benefit everyone involved," embracing the moments of joy and comradery that come from working toward social change, and working to maintain relations, even as many of my original contacts have passed on.[16] What has kept me working on this project for over twenty years is a conviction that I had something to contribute to this movement, not as an expert but as a comrade.[17] Jaskiran Dhillon describes the possibilities and challenges of striving to be "a politicized ally—a comrade—to Indigenous peoples in their struggles for justice and freedom in the settler colonial present"; she writes of a form of "reflexive relationality" that is rooted in responsibility, accountability, and care.[18] One way I have tried to engage reflexively is by noticing my relationship to white guilt and channeling those feelings into tangible actions to stand with Indigenous peoples and nations and challenge settler colonialism not only in relation to nuclear decolonization but in all areas of my work and life. Another way I have done this is by learning about the violent history of how white women, in particular, have done harm, acted in complicity with settler colonialism, and worked against the interests of Indigenous peoples and nations, leading me to ask myself over and over again: How is this work serving Western Shoshone, Southern Paiute, and Skull Valley Goshute peoples and nations?[19] Striving to follow a path of relational reflexivity and comradeship is difficult work; it would be easier to fall back on my privilege and run away, as I have sometimes wanted to do. Yet, I have come to embrace the difficulty, discomfort, and worry about messing

---

14. Middleton et al., *Participatory Critical Rhetoric.*
15. Wilson, *Research Is Ceremony,* 60.
16. Wilson, 60.
17. Dhillon, "Notes on Becoming a Comrade."
18. Dhillon, 41.
19. Grande, "Whitestream Feminism"; Moreton-Robinson, *Talkin' Up*; M. Jacobs, *White Mother*; and Arvin, Tuck, and Morrill, "Decolonizing Feminism."

up as moments of checking my heart. As Dhillon notes, "It is naïve to assume we won't make mistakes, that there will not be moments of fracture and dissention. But I believe we can find our way through these moments if our thoughts and actions are informed by accountability and a sincere desire to 'stand with' our Indigenous comrades."[20] It is important to pause here on the complicated relationship between intentions and consequences. Because good intentions can still have harmful consequences, reflexivity also requires attention to and accountability for the consequences of one's research practices. Reflexivity in Indigenous communication research is an ongoing process that is essential if one's goal is to not just research about Indigenous people and nations for one's own benefit but to do what little one can to create fissures in settler colonialism and support Indigenous decolonization. Taken together, these practices inform an approach to Indigenous rhetorics and communication scholarship that resists imposing theory onto Indigenous peoples and nations, sees Indigenous social movements as theory, and embraces reflexive research processes that are accountable to relationships and communities.

INDIGENIZING ENVIRONMENTAL JUSTICE

Nuclear decolonization is a distinct form of sovereignty and Lands protection that works in the intersections of Indigenous decolonizations, Indigenous antinuclearisms, Indigenous environmentalisms, and Indigenized environmental justices. For interdisciplinary environmental and nuclear studies scholars as well as environmental justice advocates, this book positions nuclear decolonization as a specific type of Indigenized environmental justice movement.[21] This case study in the complex intersections between environmental (in)justice, nuclear technologies, and Indigenous nations demonstrates that nuclear decolonization cannot be subsumed within mainstream antinuclear or environmental movements, nor within mainstream nuclear studies or environmental studies, both of which have some grounding in settler colonialism. Nuclear decolonization does work toward and engages in strategic coalition with antinuclear and pro-environmental goals, but it is ultimately about sovereignty and protecting Indigenous Lands and lifeways from the environmental injustices of settler colonialism.

While nuclear decolonization is a form of environmental justice advocacy, it is important to note that mainstream environmental justice discourses

---

20. Dhillon, "Notes on Becoming a Comrade," 51–52.
21. Gilio-Whitaker, *As Long as Grass Grows*.

can exclude Indigenous sovereignty and decolonization by seeing Indigeneity as a racial category or a class-based category, not a political category. Settler colonialism is undoubtedly entangled with racialization, racism, and racial capitalism, so this is not to say that race does not play a role in environmental injustices faced by Indigenous peoples and nations.[22] Rather, Dina Gilio-Whitaker argues that environmental justice scholarship and policy need to be Indigenized to take seriously and provide benefit to Indigenous peoples and nations and to affirm the centrality of Lands and sovereignties to Indigenous environmental justice. An Indigenized environmental justice framework "must acknowledge the political existence of Native nations and be capable of explicitly respecting the principles of Indigenous nationhood and self-determination."[23] An environmental justice framework that cannot account for the sovereignty of Native governments has no hope of adequately supporting Indigenous national interests, goals, and futures.[24] Likewise, an environmental justice framework that cannot attend to Lands as an entire ecology of sacred relations, agencies, and communications between humans and more-than-human beings has little chance of both preventing and offering reparations for the forms of cultural genocide that come from preventing Indigenous peoples from being in good relations with their Lands relatives.[25] The takeaway here is that scholars and activists working in the space of environmental justice must recognize that environmental justice looks different for Indigenous peoples and nations.

NUCLEAR WASTE SITING POLICY

This book also has broader social significance for ongoing national and international deliberations about nuclear waste. The study of nuclear waste storage is important because waste is the inevitable by-product of all nuclear technology. The amount of high-level nuclear waste from nuclear energy and the nuclear weapons production process in need of permanent disposal is staggering. Yet, decisions about where to store nuclear waste or any form of toxic waste are difficult and rife with controversy.[26] Some advocates fundamentally

---

22. Moreton-Robinson, *White Possessive*; and Byrd, *Transit of Empire*.
23. Gilio-Whitaker, *As Long as Grass Grows*, 12.
24. T. Johnson, "Indigenous Publicity."
25. Whyte, "Indigenous Experience."
26. Bickerstaff, "'Because We've Got History Here'"; Clarke, *Native Americans and Nuclear Waste*; Easterling and Kunreuther, *Dilemma of Siting*; G. Johnson, *Deliberative Democracy*; Leonard, "Sovereignty, Self-Determination"; and Solomon and Li, "Environmental Equity."

oppose the use of nuclear power or other nuclear technologies that produce radioactive waste and advocate for radical changes in public consciousnesses; some decry the capitalist system in which industry is allowed to pollute with few checks on growth and environmental destruction; and some argue that poor and marginalized communities are targeted for sites of nuclear waste and pollution. Others are less critical of nuclear technologies, believing that they are necessary to the national interest or that government regulation sufficiently checks nuclear pollution and waste. Whether the resulting technologies of nuclear production—nuclear weapons and nuclear power—are ultimately beneficial or harmful for society also remains controversial.

Regardless, there is no denying that the US still desperately needs a place to permanently store high-level nuclear waste, preferably before the government makes any decisions about expanding its reliance on nuclear energy or continued development of nuclear weapons. Former president Barak Obama's Blue Ribbon Commission on America's Nuclear Future expressed a need for developing voluntary sites for both interim and permanent nuclear waste disposal, and the Department of Energy's Office of Nuclear Energy continues to work toward a consent-based siting process.[27] Now is an important time to reflect on the past problems in nuclear waste siting processes and the successes of Indigenous peoples and nations who challenged the Yucca Mountain and Skull Valley PFS. This book offers a series of cautionary tales and stories of hope that should be considered as the nation continues to deliberate about high-level nuclear waste siting.

I offer two arguments about needed changes in US nuclear waste policy to support nuclear decolonization. Neither is a silver bullet, but both offer tangible ways to improve how the settler government interacts with Indigenous peoples and nations. First, recognition of inherent Indigenous sovereignty and use of government-to-government relations must be a part of any efforts to involve Indigenous communities in nuclear waste siting decisions. Because the entire continent is Indigenous Lands, any nuclear waste site that is proposed must include government-to-government interactions between the US and the Indigenous peoples and nations on whose Lands a site is proposed. Supporting nuclear decolonization does not mean that Indigenous Lands cannot be used for a nuclear waste site. What it does mean is that no community, including Indigenous nations, should be in a position where storing nuclear waste is the only viable form of economic development. So, in addition to the mandate of government-to-government negotiations from the beginning of any proposed site, recognition of inherent Indigenous sovereignty also entails

---

27. Blue Ribbon Commission on America's Nuclear Future, *Report to the Secretary.*

actions outside of the scope of nuclear waste siting to support Indigenous self-determination and futures. While dismantling settler colonialism so that Indigenous peoples and nations will not face the sort of double bind faced by the Skull Valley Goshute nation is a tall order, it is essential for fully involving Indigenous peoples and nations as entities who can self-determine their futures in relation to nuclear waste.

Second, free, prior, and informed consent is essential for any proposal to store nuclear waste within Indigenous Lands. As already discussed, the US government's current approach to high-level nuclear waste is a consent-based process. This is a marked improvement from the processes that were used for the Yucca Mountain and Skull Valley PFS sites. Consent-based siting was proposed by the Blue Ribbon Commission, in part based on decades of research highlighting the failures of the Yucca Mountain siting process. While the Blue Ribbon Commission and a recent Government Accountability Office report both emphasize consent-based siting as key to addressing nuclear waste,[28] a free and prior informed consent model emphasizes the right of any Indigenous nation to give or withhold consent for any policy that would affect their Lands and rights. The word *free* is important because it refers to the ability to self-determine without threats of force, and the word *prior* signals that consent must happen at the very start of a decision-making process. There is some reason to be skeptical of the DOE's current consent-based siting process, in part because the monitored retrieval storage program in the late 1980s and early 1990s has been criticized for targeting Indigenous nations with no other economic development opportunities.[29] A shift to a free and prior informed consent model for decision-making would ensure that Indigenous sovereignty, self-determination, and agency are involved from the very start of any proposed site and that consent can be withdrawn at any point in the process.

SPEAKING TO INDIGENOUS LANDS PROTECTORS

To those Western Shoshones, Southern Paiutes, and Skull Valley Goshutes who so generously contributed to this project over the years, shared stories, invited me to events, and hosted me on your Lands, I hope that this retelling of your stories does justice to the immense contributions you made to your communities. Thank you.

---

28. US Government Accountability Office, "Commercial Spent Nuclear Fuel"; and Blue Ribbon Commission on America's Nuclear Future, *Report to the Secretary.*
29. Gowda and Easterling, "Nuclear Waste and Native America."

I hope this story of how tactics of nuclear decolonization worked to stop the Yucca Mountain and Skull Valley Goshute high-level nuclear waste sites serves as a site of inspiration, productive memory, and collaboration for Native Lands protection and sovereignty movements. As noted above, nuclear decolonization is one part of a larger constellation of Indigenous decolonization movements. Indigenous peoples fighting hydraulic fracturing (i.e., "fracking"), oil pipelines, and toxic pollution might find productive similarities with the cases of nuclear decolonization presented in this book. Similar to the Indigenous Environmental Network's report on *Indigenous Resistance against Carbon,* which reports that Indigenous mobilization has "stopped or delayed greenhouse gas pollution equivalent to at least one-quarter of annual U.S. and Canadian emissions," this book participates in a web of stories of survivance and successful decolonization campaigns.[30] By studying two successful instances of nuclear decolonization, this book significantly enhances understanding of opportunities for tactical resistance within settler colonialism.

The stories I have told and the research I have done is one way of documenting forms of activism that may otherwise be lost or not widely distributed. While archives can be exclusionary spaces based on decisions about what is worthy to save and whose voices count in an oppressive society, this book seeks to act as a different kind of archive that collates a series of texts and retells stories of successful decolonial activism. Nuclear decolonization is worthy of an archive and, as Rebecca Solnit says, activists need to actively remember those successes that sustain progressive activism against the dominant interests that seek to erase these wins.[31] I want to be very clear that I do not declare nuclear colonization over and recognize the need for constant vigilance in the struggles against nuclear colonialization and other manifestations of settler colonialism. Yet, to maintain vigilance, it is important to describe, reflect on, and remember what has worked to enact nuclear decolonization. I hope that this archive of nuclear decolonization contributes in some small way to the past, present, and future of Indigenous decolonization and sovereignty.

AN INVITATION

In the end, nuclear decolonization is a theory and praxis by and for Indigenous peoples and nations. Yet, there are roles for non-Indigenous people to support nuclear decolonization. This book is one small effort to do so by tell-

---

30. Indigenous Environmental Network and Oil Change International, *Indigenous Resistance against Carbon,* 1. See also The Red Nation, *Red Deal.*
31. Solnit, *Hope in the Dark.*

ing the stories of Western Shoshone, Southern Paiute, and Skull Valley Goshute successful resistance to the Yucca Mountain and Skull Valley PFS nuclear waste sites. I invite each of you, my readers—both Indigenous and non-Indigenous—to make efforts to share these stories and find ways to uplift Indigenous decolonization efforts.

BIBLIOGRAPHY

Abraham, Spencer. "Letter to the President Recommending Yucca Mountain as a Nuclear Waste Repository." February 14, 2002. http://nuclearfiles.org/menu/key-issues/nuclear-energy/issues/yucca-mountain/letter-to-the-president_salp_ocrwm_doe_gov.pdf.

———. "Recommendation by the Secretary of Energy Regarding the Suitability of the Yucca Mountain Site for a Repository under the Nuclear Waste Policy Act of 1982." February 2002. http://nuclearfiles.org/menu/key-issues/nuclear-energy/issues/yucca-mountain/secretary-of-energy-recommendation_sar_ocrwm_doe_gov.pdf.

"Agreement-in-Principle between the Shoshone Bannock Tribes and the United States Department of Energy." September 25, 2017. https://www.id.energy.gov/insideneid/PDF/AIP%20 2017%20-%20FINAL%20-%20signed%20original%20_09252017%20(2).pdf.

Agyeman Asante, Godfried. "#RhetoricSoWhite and US Centered: Reflections on Challenges and Opportunities." *Quarterly Journal of Speech* 105, no. 4 (2019): 484–88. https://doi.org/10.1080/00335630.2019.1669892.

Alfred, Gerald Taiaiake. "Sovereignty: An Inappropriate Concept." In *The Indigenous Experience: Global Perspectives*, edited by Roger Maaka and Chris Andersen, 322–36. Toronto: Canadian Scholars' Press, 2006.

Andrews, James R. "The Rhetorical Shaping of National Interest: Morality and Contextual Potency in John Bright's Parliamentary Speech against Recognition of the Confederacy." *Quarterly Journal of Speech* 79 (1993): 40–60. https://doi.org/10.1080/00335639309384018.

Arvin, Maile, Eve Tuck, and Angie Morrill. "Decolonizing Feminism: Challenging Connections between Settler Colonialism and Heteropatriarchy." *Feminist Formations* (2013): 8–34.

Asante, Godfried, and Jenna N. Hanchey. "Decolonizing Queer Modernities: The Case for Queer (Post)Colonial Studies in Critical/Cultural Communication." *Communication and Critical/Cultural Studies* 18, no. 2 (2021): 212–20. https://doi.org/10.1080/14791420.2021.1907849.

Atallah, Devin G., Urmitapa Dutta, Hana R. Masud, Ireri Bernal, Rhyann Robinson, Michelle Del Rio, Celine Voyard, et al. "Transnational Research Collectives as 'Constellations of Co-Resistance': Counterstorytelling, Interweaving Struggles, and Decolonial Love." *Qualitative Inquiry* 28, no. 6 (2022): 681–93. https://doi.org/10.1177/10778004211068202.

Bacoch, Jessica. "Big Pine Paiute Tribe of the Owens Valley Comments on the US Department of Energy's Yucca Mountain Preliminary Site Suitability Evaluation [Public Comment #551914]." October 10, 2001.

———. "Letter to the Department of Energy." October 3, 2002. http://www.ocrwm.doe.gov/documents/sr_comm/sr_pdf/330076.pdf.

Barad, Karen. "After the End of the World: Entangled Nuclear Colonialisms, Matters of Force, and the Material Force of Justice." *Theory & Event* 22, no. 3 (2019): 524–50.

Barker, Holly M., José Antonio Lucero, and Trisha T. Pritikin. "Loom of the Future: Nuclear Decolonization and UW." Seattle: University of Washington, 2022. https://jsis.washington.edu/wordpress/wp-content/uploads/2022/03/22_TF_JSIS-495D_Barker_Lucero.pdf.

Barringer, Felicity. "Uranium Exploration near Grand Canyon." *New York Times*, February 7, 2008, sec. Washington. https://www.nytimes.com/2008/02/07/washington/07canyon.html.

Bear, Leon. "Prepared Statement of Leon D. Bear, Chairman of the Skull Valley Band of Goshute Indians." Nuclear Regulatory Commission, June 2, 1998.

Beck, John. "Without Form and Void: The American Desert as Trope and Terrain." *Nepantla: Views from South* 2, no. 1 (2001): 63–83.

Benally, Timothy, Chenoa Bah Stillwell, and Phil Harrison. *Memories Come to Us in the Rain and the Wind: Oral Histories and Photographs of Navajo Uranium Miners and Their Families.* The Navajo Uranium Miner Oral History and Photography Project. Jamaica Plain, MA: Red Sun Press, 1997.

Bickerstaff, Karen. "'Because We've Got History Here': Nuclear Waste, Cooperative Siting, and the Relational Geography of a Complex Issue." *Environment and Planning A* 44, no. 11 (2012): 2611–28. https://doi.org/10.1068/a44583.

Biello, David. "Nuclear Blasts May Prove Best Marker of Humanity's Geologic Record [in Photos]." *Scientific American*, February 10, 2015. http://www.scientificamerican.com/article/nuclear-blasts-may-prove-best-marker-of-humanity-s-geologic-record-in-photos/.

Black, Jason Edward. *American Indians and the Rhetoric of Removal and Allotment.* Jackson: University Press of Mississippi, 2015.

———. "Native Resistive Rhetoric and the Decolonization of American Indian Removal Discourse." *Quarterly Journal of Speech* 95, no. 1 (2009): 66–88. https://doi.org/10.1080/00335630802621052.

Blackhawk, Ned. *The Rediscovery of America: Native Peoples and the Unmaking of U.S. History.* New Haven, CT: Yale University Press, 2023.

Blue Ribbon Commission on America's Nuclear Future. *Draft Report to the Secretary of Energy.* July 29, 2011. http://brc.gov/sites/default/files/documents/brc_draft_report_29jul2011_0.pdf.

———. *Report to the Secretary of Energy.* January 2012. https://www.energy.gov/ne/articles/blue-ribbon-commission-americas-nuclear-future-report-secretary-energy.

Borrows, John. "A Genealogy of Law: Inherent Sovereignty and First Nations Self-Government." *Osgoode Hall Law Journal* 30, no. 2 (1992): 291–353.

Boyd, Julia A. "Black Rainbow, Blood-Earth: Speaking the Nuclearized Pacific in Albert Wendt's Black Rainbow." *Journal of Postcolonial Writing* 52, no. 6 (2016): 672–86. https://doi.org/10.1080/17449855.2016.1165279.

Brayboy, Bryan McKinley Jones. "Toward a Tribal Critical Race Theory in Education." *The Urban Review* 37, no. 5 (2006): 425–46. https://doi.org/10.1007/s11256-005-0018-y.

Bruyneel, Kevin. *The Third Space of Sovereignty: The Postcolonial Politics of U.S.-Indigenous Relations*. Minneapolis: University of Minnesota Press, 2007.

Buescher, Derek T., and Kent A. Ono. "Civilized Colonialism: Pocahontas as Neocolonial Rhetoric." *Women's Studies in Communication* 19, no. 2 (2001): 127–53.

Bulkeley, Deborah. "Goshute Leader Calls N-Waste Rulings 'Thin.'" *Deseret News*, September 14, 2006. https://www.deseret.com/2006/9/14/19974037/goshute-leader-calls-n-waste-rulings-thin.

Bullard, Robert D., ed. *The Quest for Environmental Justice: Human Rights and the Politics of Pollution*. San Francisco: Sierra Club Books, 2005.

Bullard, Robert D., and Glenn S. Johnson. "Environmentalism and Public Policy: Environmental Justice: Grassroots Activism and Its Impact on Public Policy Decision Making." *Journal of Social Issues* 56, no. 3 (2000): 555–78. https://doi.org/10.1111/0022-4537.00184.

Bullcreek, Margene. "Affidavit of Margene Bullcreek before the Nuclear Regulatory Commission." Nuclear Regulatory Commission, November 22, 1997. https://www.nrc.gov/docs/ML1310/ML13109A375.pdf.

———. Nuclear Technology in the American West Oral History Project, March 18, 2008. Tape No. U-1865. Everett L. Cooley Collection, University of Utah Marriott Library Special Collections Department.

Bureau of Indian Affairs. "Record of Decision for the Construction and Operation of an Independent Spent Fuel Storage Installation (ISFSI) on the Reservation of the Skull Valley Band of Goshute Indians (Band) in Tooele County, Utah," September 7, 2006. https://deq.utah.gov/Pollutants/H/highlevelnw/opposition/docs/2006/09Sep/ROD%20PFS%2009072006.pdf.

Butrim, Lauren, Jessica Collins, Cole DeGideo, Anais Gentilhomme, Desiree Gross, Karlee Heath, James Kim, Erin Kitano, Xinlei Liu, and Kayla Magers. "Ippen Dron, All of Us Together: A Collection of Tools to Address US Nuclear Colonialism in the Republic of the Marshall Islands." 2017.

Byrd, Jodi A. *The Transit of Empire: Indigenous Critiques of Colonialism*. Minneapolis: University of Minnesota Press, 2011.

Byrne, John, and Steven M. Hoffman. "A 'Necessary Sacrifice': Industrialization and American Indian Lands." In *Environmental Justice: International Discourses in Political Economy—Energy and Environmental Policy*, vol. 8., edited by John Byrne, Leigh Glover and Cecilia Martinez. New York: Routledge, 2002.

Cajete, Gregory. "'Look to the Mountain': Reflections on Indigenous Ecology." In *A People's Ecology: Explorations in Sustainable Life*, 1–20. Santa Fe, NM: Clear Light, 1999.

Carbaugh, Donal. "'Just Listen': 'Listening' and Landscape among the Blackfeet." *Western Journal of Communication* 63, no. 3 (1999): 250–70. https://doi.org/10.1080/10570319909374641.

Carbaugh, Donal, and Karen Wolf. "Situating Rhetoric in Cultural Discourses." In *Rhetoric in Intercultural Contexts*, edited by Alberto Gonzalez and Dolores Tanno, 22:19–30. International and Intercultural Communication Annual. Thousand Oaks, CA: Sage Publications, 1999.

Chamberlain, Kendra. "Nuclear Colonialism: Indigenous Opposition Grows against Proposal for Nation's Largest Nuclear Storage Facility in NM." *The NM Political Report*, November 14, 2019. https://nmpoliticalreport.com/2019/11/14/nuclear-colonialism-indigenous-opposition-grows-against-proposal-for-nations-largest-nuclear-storage-facility-in-nm/.

Cherokee Nation v. Georgia, no. 30 US 1 (U.S. Supreme Court 1831).

Churchill, Ward. "A Breach of Trust: The Radioactive Colonization of Native North America." *American Indian Culture and Research Journal* 23, no. 4 (1999): 23–69. https://doi.org/10.17953/aicr.23.4.w66221q604409252.

———. "Cold War Impacts on Native North America: The Political Economy of Radioactive Colonization." *A Little Matter of Genocide: Holocaust and Denial in the Americas 1492 to the Present,* 289–362. San Francisco: City Lights Publishers, 1997.

———. *A Little Matter of Genocide: Holocaust and Denial in the Americas 1492 to the Present.* San Francisco: City Lights Books, 1997.

———. "Nuclear Trust: The Radioactive Colonization of Native North America." *Dark Night Field Notes,* no. 14 (1998): 32.

———. "Radioactive Colonization: A Hidden Holocaust in Native North America." In *Struggle for the Land: Indigenous Resistance to Genocide, Ecocide, and Expropriation in Contemporary North America,* 261–328. Monroe, ME: Common Courage Press, 1993.

Churchill, Ward, and Winona LaDuke. "Native America: The Political Economy of Radioactive Colonialism." *Insurgent Sociologist* 13, no. 3 (1986): 51–78.

———. "Native America: The Political Economy of Radioactive Colonialism." *IWGIA Yearbook 1991,* no. 68 (1991): 25–67.

———. "Native North America: The Political Economy of Radioactive Colonization." In *The State of Native America: Genocide, Colonization, and Resistance,* edited by M. Annette Jaimes, 241–66. Boston: South End Press, 1992.

———. "Radioactive Colonization and the Native-American." *Socialist Review,* no. 81 (1985): 95–119.

Clarke, Tracylee. "The Construction of Goshute Political Identity: Negotiation of Voice Regarding Nuclear Waste Policy Development." *Frontiers in Communication* 2 (2017). https://doi.org/10.3389/fcomm.2017.00002.

———. "Goshute Native American Tribe and Nuclear Waste: Complexities and Contradictions of a Bounded-Constitutive Relationship." *Environmental Communication* 4, no. 4 (2010): 387–405. https://doi.org/10.1080/17524032.2010.520724.

———. *Native Americans and Nuclear Waste: Narratives of Conflict.* Saarbrücken: VDM Verlag, 2008.

Clary-Lemon, Jennifer. "Gifts, Ancestors, and Relations: Notes toward an Indigenous New Materialism | Enculturation." *Enculturation: A Journal of Rhetoric, Writing, and Culture,* November 12, 2019. https://www.enculturation.net/gifts_ancestors_and_relations.

Clary-Lemon, Jennifer, and David M. Grant, eds. *Decolonial Conversations in Posthuman and New Material Rhetorics.* Columbus: The Ohio State University Press, 2022.

Clifford, James. "Varieties of Indigenous Experience: Diasporas, Homelands, Sovereignties." In *Indigenous Experience Today,* edited by Marisol de la Cadena, and Orin Starn, 197–224. New York: Routledge, 2007.

Coffey, Wallace, and Rebecca A. Tsosie. "Rethinking the Tribal Sovereignty Doctrine: Cultural Sovereignty and the Collective Future of Indian Nations." *Stanford Law & Policy Review* 12, no. 2 (2001): 191–221.

Cole, Daniel. "Writing Removal and Resistance: Native American Rhetoric in the Composition Classroom." *College Composition and Communication* (2011): 122–44.

Congressional Research Service. "Nuclear Waste Storage Sites in the United States." May 3, 2019; updated April 13, 2020. https://fas.org/sgp/crs/nuke/IF11201.pdf.

Conquergood, Dwight. "Performance Studies: Interventions and Radical Research." *TDR (1988)* 46, no. 2 (2002): 145–56.

Cordes, Ashley. "Meeting Place: Bringing Native Feminisms to Bear on Borders of Cyberspace." *Feminist Media Studies* 20, no. 2 (2020): 285–89. https://doi.org/10.1080/14680777.2020.1720347.

———. "Revisiting Stories and Voices of the Rogue River War (1853–1856): A Digital Constellatory Autoethnographic Mode of Indigenous Archaeology." *Cultural Studies ↔ Critical Methodologies* 21, no. 1 (2021): 56–69. https://doi.org/10.1177/1532708620953189.

Cordes, Ashley, and Leilani Sabzalian. "The Urgent Need for Anticolonial Media Literacy." *International Journal of Multicultural Education* 22, no. 2 (2020): 182–201. https://doi.org/10.18251/ijme.v22i2.2443.

Cortez, José M. "Of Exterior and Exception: Latin American Rhetoric, Subalternity, and the Politics of Cultural Difference." *Philosophy & Rhetoric* 51, no. 2 (2018): 124–50. https://doi.org/10.5325/philrhet.51.2.0124.

Coulthard, Glen Sean. *Red Skin, White Masks: Rejecting the Colonial Politics of Recognition*. Minneapolis: University of Minnesota Press, 2014.

Crum, Steven J. *The Road on Which We Came: A History of the Western Shoshone*. Salt Lake City: University of Utah Press, 1994.

———. "The Skull Valley Band of the Goshute Tribe: Deeply Attached to Their Native Homeland." *Utah Historical Quarterly* 55, no. 3 (1987): 250–67.

Cushman, Ellen. "Toward a Rhetoric of Self-Representation: Identity Politics in Indian Country and Rhetoric and Composition." *College Composition & Communication* 60, no. 2 (2008): 321–65.

Cushman, Ellen, Damián Baca, and Romeo García. "Delinking: Toward Pluriversal Rhetorics." *College English* 84, no. 1 (2021): 7–32.

Danielsson, Bengt, and Marie-Therese Danielsson. *Poisoned Reign: French Nuclear Colonialism in the Pacific*. 2nd ed. Ringwood, Vic., Australia: Penguin Books, 1986.

Dann, Carrie. Nuclear Technology in the American West Oral History Project, March 18, 2008. Tape No. U-2031. Everett L. Cooley Collection, University of Utah Marriott Library Special Collections Department.

Davis, Mike. "Utah's Toxic Heaven." *Capitalism Nature Socialism* 9, no. 2 (1998): 35–39. https://doi.org/10.1080/10455759809358792.

de Certeau, Michel. *The Practice of Everyday Life*. Berkeley: University of California Press, 1984.

Defa, Dennis. "The Goshute Indians of Utah." In *History of Utah's American Indians*, edited by Forrest Cuch, 73–122. Salt Lake City: Utah State Division of Indian Affairs / Utah State Division of History, 2000.

Deloria, Vine, Jr. "Comfortable Fictions and the Struggle for Turf: An Essay Review of The Invented Indian: Cultural Fictions and Government Policies." *American Indian Quarterly* 16, no. 3 (1992): 397–410. https://doi.org/10.2307/1185800.

———. *God Is Red: A Native View of Religion*. Golden, CO: Fulcrum Publishing, 2003.

———. *We Talk, You Listen: New Tribes, New Turf*. Lincoln: University of Nebraska Press, 2007.

Denzin, Norman K., Yvonna S. Lincoln, and Linda Tuhiwai Smith. *Handbook of Critical and Indigenous Methodologies*. Los Angeles: Sage, 2008.

de Onís, Catalina M. "Energy Colonialism Powers the Ongoing Unnatural Disaster in Puerto Rico." *Frontiers in Communication* 3 (2018). https://doi.org/10.3389/fcomm.2018.00002.

———. *Energy Islands: Metaphors of Power, Extractivism, and Justice in Puerto Rico*. Oakland: University of California Press, 2021.

Depoe, Stephen, and John W. Delicath. Introduction to *Communication and Public Participation in Environmental Decision Making*, edited by Stephen P. Depoe, John W. Delicath, and Marie-France Aepli Elsenbeer, 1–10. Albany: SUNY Press, 2004.

deTar, Matthew. "Why 'Anticolonial' International Rhetorical Studies?" *Rhetoric & Public Affairs* 24, no. 1 (2021): 191–206.

Dhillon, Jaskiran. "Notes on Becoming a Comrade: Indigenous Women, Leadership, and Movement(s) for Decolonization." *American Indian Culture and Research Journal* 43, no. 3 (2020): 41–54. https://doi.org/10.17953/aicrj.43.3.dhillon.

———. *Prairie Rising: Indigenous Youth, Decolonization, and the Politics of Intervention*. Toronto: University of Toronto Press, 2017.

Dickson, Mary. "The People Speak: When the Public Is Not Welcome." *Catalyst*, January 31, 2007. http://166-70-249-138.ip.xmission.com/component/k2/item/144-the-people-speak-when-the-public-is-not-welcome.

Dunbar-Ortiz, Roxanne. *An Indigenous Peoples' History of the United States*. Boston: Beacon Press, 2014.

Durham, Barbara, and Bill Helmer. "Letter to the Department of Energy [Public Comment #551862]." September 2001.

Dutta, Mohan J. "Whiteness, Internationalization, and Erasure: Decolonizing Futures from the Global South." *Communication and Critical/Cultural Studies* 17, no. 2 (2020): 228–35. https://doi.org/10.1080/14791420.2020.1770825.

Easterling, D., and Howard Kunreuther. *The Dilemma of Siting a High-Level Nuclear Waste Repository*. New York: Springer, 1995.

Edwards, Nelta. "Nuclear Colonialism and the Social Construction of Landscape in Alaska." *Environmental Justice* 4, no. 2 (2011): 109–14.

Endres, Danielle. "Animist Intersubjectivity as Argumentation: Western Shoshone and Southern Paiute Arguments against a Nuclear Waste Site at Yucca Mountain." *Argumentation* 27, no. 2 (2013): 183–200. https://doi.org/10.1007/s10503-012-9271-x.

———. "Environmental Criticism." *Western Journal of Communication* 84, no. 3 (2020): 314–31. https://doi.org/10.1080/10570314.2019.1689288.

———. "Environmental Oral History." *Environmental Communication* 5, no. 4 (2011): 485–98.

———. "From Wasteland to Waste Site: The Role of Discourse in Nuclear Power's Environmental Injustices." *Local Environment* 14, no. 10 (2009): 917–37. https://doi.org/10.1080/13549830903244409.

———. "The Most Nuclear-Bombed Place: Ecological Implications of the US Nuclear Testing Program." In *Tracing Rhetoric and Material Life: Ecological Approaches*, edited by Bridie McGreavy, Justine Wells, George F. McHendry Jr., and Samantha Senda-Cook, 253–88. Palgrave Macmillan, 2018.

———. "The Rhetoric of Nuclear Colonialism: Rhetorical Exclusion of American Indian Arguments in the Yucca Mountain Nuclear Waste Siting Decision." *Communication and Critical/Cultural Studies* 6, no. 1 (2009): 39–60. https://doi.org/10.1080/14791420802632103.

———. "Sacred Land or National Sacrifice Zone: The Role of Values in the Yucca Mountain Participation Process." *Environmental Communication* 6, no. 3 (2012): 328–45. https://doi.org/10.1080/17524032.2012.688060.

Endres, Danielle, Aaron Hess, Samantha Senda-Cook, and Michael K. Middleton. "In Situ Rhetoric: Intersections between Qualitative Inquiry, Fieldwork, and Rhetoric." *Cultural Studies ↔ Critical Methodologies* 16, no. 6 (2016): 511–24. https://doi.org/10.1177/1532708616655820.

Endres, Danielle, and Samantha Senda-Cook. "Location Matters: The Rhetoric of Place in Protest." *Quarterly Journal of Speech* 97, no. 3 (2011): 257–82. https://doi.org/10.1080/00335630.2011.585167.

Engels, Jeremy. "'Equipped for Murder': The Paxton Boys and 'the Spirit of Killing All Indians' in Pennsylvania, 1763–1764." *Rhetoric & Public Affairs* 8, no. 3 (2005): 355–81.

Estes, Nick. *Our History Is the Future: Standing Rock versus the Dakota Access Pipeline, and the Long Tradition of Indigenous Resistance.* London: Verso Books, 2019.

Estes, Nick, and Jaskiran Dhillon, eds. *Standing with Standing Rock: Voices from the #NoDAPL Movement.* Minneapolis: University of Minnesota Press, 2019.

Fahys, Judy. "Family Feud: Goshutes Split over Nuclear Waste Site." *Salt Lake Tribune*, August 18, 2002.

———. "Goshute Says Feds, State Let the Tribe Down." *The Salt Lake Tribune.* September 14, 2006. https://archive.sltrib.com/article.php?itype=NGPSID&id=4334759.

———. "Goshutes Who Have Opposed Nuclear Waste Are out in Cold." *Salt Lake Tribune*, January 6, 2003.

———. "Would-Be Goshute Leader Sentenced in Theft Case." *Salt Lake Tribune*, November 29, 2005.

Fan, Mei-Fang. "Environmental Justice and Nuclear Waste Conflicts in Taiwan." *Environmental Politics* 15, no. 3 (2006): 417–34. https://doi.org/10.1080/09644010600627683.

———. "Nuclear Waste Facilities on Tribal Land: The Yami's Struggles for Environmental Justice." *Local Environment* 11, no. 4 (2006): 433–44. https://doi.org/10.1080/13549830600785589.

Fanon, Frantz. *The Wretched of the Earth.* New York: Grove Press, 1963.

Fast, Robin Riley. "Water, History, and Sovereignty in Simon J. Ortiz's 'Our Homeland, a National Sacrifice Area.'" *Studies in American Indian Literatures* 30, no. 3–4 (2018): 36–53.

Fattah, Geoffrey, and Suzanne Struglinski. "Pressure Used to Stop Nuclear Dump, Lawsuit Says." *Deseret News,* July 19, 2007. https://www.deseret.com/2007/7/19/20030489/pressure-used-to-stop-nuclear-dump-lawsuit-says.

Feldblum, Sammy. "New Mexico on Track to House U.S. Spent Nuclear Fuel, despite Concerns." *National Geographic,* July 30, 2019. https://www.nationalgeographic.com/environment/2019/07/new-mexico-nuclear-waste-storage/#close.

Final Environmental Impact Statement: Long-Term Management of Defense High-Level Radioactive Wastes (Research and Development Program for Immobilization), Savannah River Plant, Aiken, South Carolina. Washington DC: US Department of Energy, November 1979. https://www.energy.gov/sites/prod/files/EIS-0023-FEIS-1979.pdf.

Fowler, Catherine S. *Native Americans and Yucca Mountain: A Revised and Updated Summary Report on Research Undertaken between 1987 and 1991.* Reno, NV: Cultural Resource Consultants, October 1991.

Fowler, Catherine S., and Don D. Fowler. "Notes on the History of the Southern Paiutes and Western Shoshonis." *Utah Historical Quarterly* 39, no. 2 (1971): 95–114.

Fox, Sarah Alisabeth. *Downwind: A People's History of the Nuclear West.* Lincoln, NE: Bison Books, 2014.

Gallagher, Carole. *American Ground Zero: The Secret Nuclear War.* New York: Random House, 1994.

Gard, A. Rowan. "Looking for Light on the Dark Side of the American Dream—Exploring the Painful Legacy of Nuclear Colonialism in Paradise." *International Journal of Research in Sociology and Anthropology* 3, no. 4 (2017): 32–42.

Gedicks, Al. *The New Resource Wars: Native and Environmental Struggles Against Multinational Corporations.* Montreal: Black Rose Books, 1994.

Gehrke, Robert, Judy Fahys, and Thomas Burr. "Interior Dumps N-Waste Plan." *The Salt Lake Tribune*, September 8, 2006. http://archive.sltrib.com/article.php?id=4304740&itype=NGPSID.

Gilio-Whitaker, Dina. *As Long as Grass Grows: The Indigenous Fight for Environmental Justice, from Colonization to Standing Rock.* Reprint ed. Boston: Beacon Press, 2020.

Glass, Matthew. *Citizens against the MX: Public Languages in the Nuclear Age.* Chicago: University of Illinois Press, 1993.

Gowda, M. V. Rajeev, and Doug Easterling. "Nuclear Waste and Native America: The MRS Siting Exercise." *Risk: Health, Safety & Environment* 9, no. 3 (1998): 229–58.

———. "Voluntary Siting and Equity: The MRS Facility Experience in Native America." *Risk Analysis* 20, no. 6 (2000): 917–30. https://doi.org/10.1111/0272-4332.206084.

Grande, Sandy. "Whitestream Feminism and the Colonialist Project: Toward a Theory of Indigenista." *Red Pedagogy: Native American Social and Political Thought* (2004): 123–57.

Gray, Robin R. R. "Rematriation: Ts'msyen Law, Rights of Relationality, and Protocols of Return." *Native American and Indigenous Studies* 9, no. 1 (2022): 1–27. https://doi.org/10.1353/nai.2022.0010.

Grinde, Donald A., and Bruce Elliott Johansen. *Ecocide of Native America: Environmental Destruction of Indian Lands and Peoples.* Santa Fe: Clear Light Books, 1998.

Grossman, Zolton. *Unlikely Alliances: Native Nations and White Communities Join to Defend Rural Lands.* Seattle: University of Washington Press, 2017.

Hamel-Green, Michael. "Networking against Nuclear Colonialism: The Nuclear Free and Independent Pacific Movement, 1975–95." *Developing Alternatives: Community Development Strategies and Environmental Issues in the Pacific.* Melbourne: Victoria University of Technology, 1996.

Hardeen, George. "Shirley Acknowledges Navajo EPA Staff for Church Rock Uranium Mine Site Cleanup." *Navajo-Hopi Observer*, May 8, 2007. https://www.nhonews.com/news/2007/may/08/shirley-acknowledges-navajo-epa-staff-for-church-/.

Harney, Corbin. *The Nature Way.* Las Vegas: University of Nevada Press, 2009.

———. *The Way It Is: One Water, One Air, One Mother Earth.* Nevada City, CA: Blue Dolphin Publishing, 1995.

———. "Yucca Mountain: No Place for Nuclear Waste." Nuclear Information and Resource Service, October 24, 2000. https://www.nirs.org/yuccaltrbycorbin102400/.

Hasian, Marouf. "Colonial Hermeneutics of Suspicion, the Spectacular Rhetorics of the Casement Report, and the British Policing of Belgian Imperialism, 1904–1908." *Critical Studies in Media Communication* 30, no. 3 (2013): 224–40. https://doi.org/10.1080/15295036.2012.670877.

Hauser, Gerard A. "Attending to the Vernacular: A Plea for an Ethnographical Rhetoric." In *Rhetorical Emergence of Culture,* edited by Christian Meyer and Felix Gerke, 157–72. New York: Berghahn Books, 2011.

"Hearing for Site Recommendation Consideration of the Yucca Mountain Site for Geologic Disposal of Spent Nuclear Fuel and High-Level Radioactive Waste." Las Vegas, NV, December 12, 2001.

Hebner, Logan, and Michael Plyler. *Southern Paiute: A Portrait*. Logan: Utah State University Press, 2010.

Hecht, Gabrielle. *Being Nuclear: Africans and the Global Uranium Trade*. Cambridge, MA: The MIT Press, 2012.

Hendry, Judith. "Decide, Announce, Defend: Turning the NEPA Process into an Advocacy Tool Rather Than a Decision-Making Tool." In *Communication and Public Participation in Environmental Decision Making*, edited by Stephen P. Depoe, John W. Delicath, and Marie-France Aepli Elsenbeer, 99–112. Albany: SUNY Press, 2004.

Henetz, P. "Goshutes Elect New Tribal Leadership." *Salt Lake Tribune*, October 25, 2006.

———. "Skull Valley: Former Leader out as Goshutes Elect a New Slate." *Salt Lake Tribune*, October 25, 2006.

"Henry Red Cloud of Oglala Lakota Tribe on Native American Anti-Nuclear Activism, Uranium Mining, and the Recession's Toll on Reservations." *Democracy Now*, September 30, 2010. http://www.democracynow.org/2010/9/30/henry_red_cloud_of_oglala_lakota.

Hess, Aaron. "Critical-Rhetorical Ethnography: Rethinking the Place and Process of Rhetoric." *Communication Studies* 62, no. 2 (2011): 127. https://doi.org/10.1080/10510974.2011.529750.

Honor the Earth. "Precedent Setting Decision Stops Skull Valley Goshute Nuclear Waste Dump: A Victory for Environmental and Energy Justice" (press release). September 21, 2006. http://www.honortheearth.org/skullvalley.htm.

Hooks, Gregory, and Chad L. Smith. "The Treadmill of Destruction: National Sacrifice Areas and Native Americans." *American Sociological Review* 69, no. 4 (2004): 558–75. https://doi.org/10.1177/000312240406900405.

Hopi Tribal Council, Barbara. "Letter to the Department of Energy [Public Comment #550976]." September 10, 2001.

Hunt, Kathleen P., Nicholas S. Paliewicz, and Danielle Endres. "The Radical Potential of Public Participation Processes: Using Indecorous Voice and Resistance to Expand the Scope of Public Participation." In *Breaking Boundaries: Innovative Practices in Environmental Communication and Public Participation*, edited by Kathleen P. Hunt, Gregg B. Walker, and Stephen P. Depoe, 149–72. Albany: SUNY Press, 2019.

Indigenous Environmental Network. "Indigenous Anti-Nuclear Statement: Yucca Mountain and Private Fuel Storage at Skull Valley." August 12, 2002. http://www.ienearth.org/indigenous-anti-nuclear-statement-yucca-mountain-and-private-fuel-storage-at-skull-valley/.

———. "Yucca Mountain Nuclear Waste Storage Infringes on Native Rights: Risks for Tribes Could Endanger Future Generations." May 9, 2002. https://www.corpwatch.org/article/yucca-mountain-nuclear-waste-storage-infringes-native-rights.

Indigenous Environmental Network, and Oil Change International. *Indigenous Resistance against Carbon*. Washington, DC: Oil Change International, August 2021. https://www.ienearth.org/indigenous-resistance-against-carbon/.

International Atomic Energy Agency. "Managing Spent Nuclear Fuel: Global Overview" (issue brief). 2022. http://www.iaea.org/NewsCenter/Focus/RadWaste/nuclfueloverview.html.

Ishiyama, Noriko. "Environmental Justice and American Indian Tribal Sovereignty: Case Study of a Land-Use Conflict in Skull Valley, Utah." *Antipode* 35, no. 1 (2003): 119–39. https://doi.org/10.1111/1467-8330.00305.

Jacob, Michelle M. *Yakama Rising: Indigenous Cultural Revitalization, Activism, and Healing*. Tucson: University of Arizona Press, 2014.

Jacobs, Margaret D. *White Mother to a Dark Race: Settler Colonialism, Maternalism, and the Removal of Indigenous Children in the American West and Australia, 1880–1940*. Lincoln: University of Nebraska Press, 2009.

Jacobs, Robert. "Nuclear Conquistadors: Military Colonialism in Nuclear Test Site Selection during the Cold War." *Asian Journal of Peacebuilding* 1, no. 2 (2013): 157–77. SNU Open Repository, http://s-space.snu.ac.kr/handle/10371/90857.

Jacobs, Robert, and Mick Broderick. "United Nations Report Reveals the Ongoing Legacy of Nuclear Colonialism in the Marshall Islands." *The Asia-Pacific Journal* 10, no. 47 (2012): 1.

Johnson & Graham's Lessee v. McIntosh, no. 21 US 543 (US Supreme Court 1823).

Johnson, Daniel Morley. "Reflections on Historical and Contemporary Indigenist Approaches to Environmental Ethics in a Comparative Context." *Wicazo Sa Review* 22, no. 2 (2007): 23–55.

Johnson, Geneviève Fuji. *Deliberative Democracy for the Future: The Case of Nuclear Waste Management in Canada*. Toronto: University of Toronto Press, 2008.

Johnson, Taylor N. "The Dakota Access Pipeline and the Breakdown of Participatory Processes in Environmental Decision-Making." *Environmental Communication* 13, no. 3 (2019): 335–52. https://doi.org/10.1080/17524032.2019.1569544.

———. "Indigenous Publicity in American Public Lands Controversies: Environmental Participation in the Fight for Bears Ears National Monument." *Frontiers in Communication* 6 (2021). https://www.frontiersin.org/articles/10.3389/fcomm.2021.673115.

———. "'The Most Bombed Nation on Earth': Western Shoshone Resistance to the Nevada National Security Site." *Atlantic Journal of Communication* 26, no. 4 (2018): 224–39. https://doi.org/10.1080/15456870.2018.1494177.

Johnson, Taylor N., Kensey I. Dressler, Nicolas Hernandez, and Danielle Endres. "Environmental Justice: A Third Pillar of Environmental Communication Research." In *The Routledge Handbook of Environment and Communication*, edited by Anders Hansen and Robert Cox, 63–81. London: Routledge, 2023. https://www.routledge.com/The-Routledge-Handbook-of-Environment-and-Communication/Hansen-Cox/p/book/9780367634483.

Johnson, Taylor N., and Danielle Endres. "Decolonizing Settler Public Address: The Role of Settler Scholars." *Rhetoric and Public Affairs* 24, no. 1–2 (2021): 333–48. https://doi.org/10.14321/rhetpublaffa.24.1-2.0333.

Johnson, Troy, Duane Champagne, and Joane Nagel. "American Indian Activism and Transformation: Lessons from Alcatraz." In *American Indian Activism: Alcatraz to the Longest Walk*, edited by Troy Johnson, Duane Champagne, and Joane Nagel, 9–44. Urbana: University of Illinois Press, 1997.

Johnston, Barbara Rose. "Nuclear Disaster: The Marshall Islands Experience and Lessons for a Post-Fukushima World." In *Global Ecologies and the Environmental Humanities: Postcolonial Approaches*, 22. Routledge Interdisciplinary Perspectives on Literature. New York: Routledge, 2015.

Josephy, Alvin, Troy Johnson, and Joane Nagel, eds. *Red Power: The American Indians Fight for Freedom*. 2nd ed. Lincoln: University of Nebraska Press, 1999.

Keeler, Jacqueline, ed. *Edge of Morning: Native Voices Speak for the Bears Ears*. Salt Lake City, UT: Torrey House Press, 2017.

Kelly, Casey Ryan. "Détournement, Decolonization, and the American Indian Occupation of Alcatraz Island (1969–1971)." *Rhetoric Society Quarterly* 44, no. 2 (2014): 168–90.

———. "Orwellian Language and the Politics of Tribal Termination (1953–1960)." *Western Journal of Communication* 74, no. 4 (2010): 351–71. https://doi.org/10.1080/10570314.2010.492821.

———. "'We Are Not Free': The Meaning of in American Indian Resistance to President Johnson's War on Poverty." *Communication Quarterly* 62, no. 4 (2014): 455–73.

Kennedy, Dane. *Decolonization: A Very Short Introduction.* New York: Oxford University Press, 2016.

Kennedy, George A. "North American Indian Rhetoric." In *Comparative Rhetoric: An Historical and Cross-Cultural Introduction,* 83–111. New York: Oxford University Press, 1998.

Kennedy, Joe. Native American Forum on Nuclear Issues, April 10, 2008. Nevada Test Site Oral History Project.

Keown, Michelle. "Waves of Destruction: Nuclear Imperialism and Anti-Nuclear Protest in the Indigenous Literatures of the Pacific." *Journal of Postcolonial Writing* 54, no. 5 (2018): 585–600. https://doi.org/10.1080/17449855.2018.1538660.

Kidwell, Clara Sue, Homer Noley, and George E. Tinker. *A Native American Theology.* Maryknoll, NY: Orbis Books, 2001.

Kimmerer, Robin Wall. *Braiding Sweetgrass: Indigenous Wisdom, Scientific Knowledge and the Teachings of Plants.* Minneapolis: Milkweed Editions, 2013.

The Kino-nda-niimi Collective. *The Winter We Danced.* Winnipeg: Arbeiter Ring Publishing, 2014.

Kinsella, William J. "Nuclear Boundaries: Material and Discursive Containment at the Hanford Nuclear Reservation." *Science as Culture* 10, no. 2 (2001): 163–94. https://doi.org/10.1080/09505430120052284.

———. "One Hundred Years of Nuclear Discourse: Four Master Themes and Their Implications for Environmental Communication." In *The Environmental Communication Yearbook,* edited by Susan L. Senecah, 2:49–71. Mahwah, NJ: Lawrence Erlbaum Associates, 2005.

Kinsella, William J., Dorothy Collins Andreas, and Danielle Endres. "Communicating Nuclear Power: A Programmatic Review." In *Communication Yearbook,* 39:277–309. New York: Routledge, 2015.

Knack, Martha C. *Boundaries Between: The Southern Paiutes, 1775–1995.* Illustrated ed. Lincoln: University of Nebraska Press, 2004.

Kovach, Margaret. *Indigenous Methodologies: Characteristics, Conversations, and Contexts.* Illustrated ed. Toronto: University of Toronto Press, 2010.

Kretch, Shephard, III. *The Ecological Indian: Myth and History.* New York: W. W. Norton & Company, 1999.

Kuletz, Valerie L. "Invisible Spaces, Violent Places: Cold War Nuclear and Militarized Landscapes." In *Violent Environments,* edited by Nancy Lee Peluso and Michael Watts, 237–60. Ithaca, NY: Cornell University Press, 2001.

———. *The Tainted Desert: Environmental and Social Ruin in the American West.* New York: Routledge, 1998.

La Duque, Winona. "Native America: The Economics of Radioactive Colonization." *Review of Radical Political Economics* 15, no. 3 (1983): 9–19. https://doi.org/10.1177/048661348301500303.

la paperson. *A Third University Is Possible.* Minneapolis: University of Minnesota Press, 2017.

LaDuke, Winona. *All Our Relations: Native Struggles for Land and Life.* Cambridge, MA: South End Press, 1999.

———. "Commentary: Is It Sacred Enough?." *Minnesota Public Radio,* August 20, 2003. http://news.minnesota.publicradio.org/features/2003/08/18_gundersond_spiritladuke/.

———. *Recovering the Sacred: The Power of Naming and Claiming.* Cambridge, MA: South End Press, 2005.

———. *The Winona LaDuke Chronicles: Stories from the Front Lines in the Battle for Environmental Justice.* Illustrated ed. Ponsford, MN: Fernwood Publishing, 2017.

LaDuke, Winona, and Ward Churchill. "Native America: The Political Economy of Radioactive Colonialism." *Critical Sociology* 13, no. 3 (1986): 51.

———. "Native America: The Political Economy of Radioactive Colonialism." *The Journal of Ethnic Studies* 13, no. 3 (1985): 107.

Lake, Randall A. "Between Myth and History: Enacting Time in Native American Protest Rhetoric." *Quarterly Journal of Speech* 77, no. 2 (1991): 123–51.

———. "Enacting Red Power: The Consummatory Function in Native American Protest Rhetoric." *Quarterly Journal of Speech* 69, no. 2 (1983): 127–42. https://doi.org/10.1080/00335638309383642.

Lechuga, Michael. "An Anticolonial Future: Reassembling the Way We Do Rhetoric." *Communication & Critical/Cultural Studies* 17, no. 4 (2020): 378–85. https://doi.org/10.1080/14791420.2020.1829659.

Leonard, Louis G. "Sovereignty, Self-Determination, and Environmental Justice in the Mescalero Apache's Decision to Store Nuclear Waste." *Boston College Environmental Affairs Law Review* 24, no. 3 (1997): 651–93.

Liboiron, Max. *Pollution Is Colonialism*. Durham, NC: Duke University Press Books, 2021.

"Limited Appearance Hearing in the Matter of Private Fuel Storage L.L.C.: Volume 3." Salt Lake City, UT: Nuclear Regulatory Commission, June 24, 2000.

Livingston, Dalaki. "An Upward Journey and Sunwise Path." In *Communication Theory: Racially Diverse and Inclusive Perspectives,* edited by Mark P. Orbe, Jeanetta D. Sims, and Jasmine T. Austin, 62–63 Solana Beach, CA: Cognella Academic Publishing, 2021.

Lomawaima, K. Tsianina. "Tribal Sovereigns: Reframing Research in American Indian Education." *Harvard Educational Review* 70, no. 1 (2009): 1–23. https://doi.org/10.17763/haer.70.1.b133t0976714n73r.

Lowan, Greg. "Exploring Place from an Aboriginal Perspective: Considerations for Outdoor and Environmental Education." *Canadian Journal of Environmental Education* 14 (2009): 42–58.

Luebben, Thomas E., and Cathy Nelson. "Indian Wars: Efforts to Resolve Western Shoshone Land and Treaty Issues and to Distribute the Indian Claims Commission Judgement Fund." *Natural Resources Journal* 42 (2002): 801.

Lyons, Scott Richard. "Rhetorical Sovereignty: What Do American Indians Want from Writing?" *College Composition and Communication* 51, no. 3 (2000): 447–68. https://doi.org/10.2307/358744.

Mackey, Eva. *Unsettled Expectations: Uncertainty, Land and Settler Decolonization*. Halifax: Fernwood Publishing, 2016.

Makhijani, Arjun. "A Readiness to Harm." In *Nuclear Wastelands: A Global Guide to Nuclear Weapons Production and Its Health and Environmental Effects,* edited by Arjun Makhijani, Howard Hu, and Katherine Yih, 1–10. Cambridge, MA: The MIT Press, 2000.

Makhijani, Arjun, Howard Hu, and Katherine Yih, eds. *Nuclear Wastelands: A Global Guide to Nuclear Weapons Production and Its Health and Environmental Effects*. Cambridge, MA: The MIT Press, 2000.

Makhijani, Arjun, David Sumner, Howard Hu, and Alistair Woodward. "Health Hazards of Nuclear Weapons Production." In *Nuclear Wastelands: A Global Guide to Nuclear Weapons Production and Its Health and Environmental Effects,* edited by Arjun Makhijani, Howard Hu, and Katherine Yih, 65–104. Cambridge, MA: The MIT Press, 2000.

Masco, Joseph. *The Nuclear Borderlands: The Manhattan Project in Post–Cold War New Mexico*. Princeton, NJ: Princeton University Press, 2006.

Mathur, Piyush. "Nuclearism: The Contours of a Political Ecology." *Social Text* 19, no. 1 (2001): 1–18.

Mays, Kyle T. "Decolonial Hip Hop: Indigenous Hip Hop and the Disruption of Settler Colonialism." *Cultural Studies* 33, no. 3 (2019): 460–79. https://doi.org/10.1080/09502386.2019.1584908.

McCombs, Brady, and Ellen Knickmeyer. "Trump Proposal Triggers Rush of Uranium Mining Plans, Including in Southern Utah." *Deseret News*, February 23, 2020, sec. Utah. https://www.deseret.com/utah/2020/2/23/21138406/uranium-mines-trump-energy-fuels-energy-environment.

McCue-Enser, Margret. "Genocide in the Sculpture Garden and Talking Back to Settler Colonialism." *Quarterly Journal of Speech* 106, no. 2 (2020): 179–204. https://doi.org/10.1080/00335630.2020.1744181.

McGee, Michael Calvin. "The 'Ideograph': A Link between Rhetoric and Ideology." *Quarterly Journal of Speech* 66, no. 1 (1980): 1–16.

McGinty, Ellie I. Leydsman. "Land Ownership of Utah." In *Rangeland Resources of Utah*, edited by Utah Public Lands Policy Coordination Office, 9–23. Utah State University Cooperative Extension, 2009. https://extension.usu.edu/rangelands/ou-files/RRU_Introduction.pdf.

McKinnon, Sara L., Robert Asen, Karma R. Chávez, and Robert Glenn Howard, eds. *Text + Field: Innovations in Rhetorical Method*. University Park, PA: Penn State University Press, 2016.

"Memorandum of Understanding between the Seneca Nation and the US Department of Energy." 2017. https://www.wv.doe.gov/Document_Index/Seneca_Nation_Spent_Nuclear_Fuel_Agreement%202017.pdf.

"Memorandum of Understanding between the Ute Indian Tribe and the University of Utah." 2020. https://admin.utah.edu/ute-mou/.

Middleton, Michael, Aaron Hess, Danielle Endres, and Samantha Senda-Cook. *Participatory Critical Rhetoric: Theoretical and Methodological Foundations for Studying Rhetoric in Situ*. Lanham, MD: Lexington Books, 2015.

Middleton, Michael K., Samantha Senda-Cook, and Danielle Endres. "Articulating Rhetorical Field Methods: Challenges and Tensions." *Western Journal of Communication* 75, no. 4 (2011): 386–406. https://doi.org/10.1080/10570314.2011.586969.

Mignolo, Walter D. "Delinking: The Rhetoric of Modernity, the Logic of Coloniality and the Grammar of de-Coloniality." *Cultural Studies* 21, no. 2–3 (2007): 449–514.

———. "Epistemic Disobedience, Independent Thought and Decolonial Freedom." *Theory, Culture & Society* 26, no. 7–8 (2009): 159–81.

Mihesuah, Devon Abbott. *So You Want to Write about American Indians?: A Guide for Writers, Students, and Scholars*. Lincoln: University of Nebraska Press, 2005.

Mims, B. "Different Views: For the Goshutes, a Test of Tradition." *Salt Lake Tribune*, July 16, 2000.

Moreton-Robinson, Aileen. *Talkin' up to the White Woman: Aboriginal Women and Feminism*. Queensland: University of Queensland Press, 2000.

———. *The White Possessive: Property, Power, and Indigenous Sovereignty*. Minneapolis: University of Minnesota Press, 2015.

Morgensen, Scott Lauria. "Destabilizing the Settler Academy: The Decolonial Effects of Indigenous Methodologies." *American Quarterly* 64, no. 4 (2012): 805–8. https://doi.org/10.1353/aq.2012.0050.

Morris, Glen T. "International Law and Politics: Toward a Right to Self-Determination for Indigenous Peoples." In *The State of Native America: Genocide, Colonization, and Resistance*, edited by M. Annette Jaimes, 55–86. Boston, MA: South End Press, 1992.

Morris, Richard, and Mary E. Stuckey. "'More Rain and Less Thunder': Substitute Vocabularies, Richard Nixon, and the Construction of Political Reality." *Communication Monographs* 64, no. 2 (1997): 140–60.

Morris, Richard, and Philip Wander. "Native American Rhetoric: Dancing in the Shadows of the Ghost Dance." *Quarterly Journal of Speech* 76, no. 2 (1990): 164–91. https://doi.org/10.1080/00335639009383912.

Moulton, Kristen. "NRC Lets Utah, Indian Tribes Intervene in Proposed Nuclear Waste Site." *Associated Press*, April 23, 1998. http://www.energy-net.org/NUZ/NAT-AMER/9842334.TXT.

Nadasdy, Paul. "Transcending the Debate over the Ecologically Noble Indian: Indigenous Peoples and Environmentalism." *Ethnohistory* 52, no. 2 (2005): 291–331. https://doi.org/10.1215/00141801-52-2-291.

Na'puti, Tiara R. "Archipelagic Rhetoric: Remapping the Marianas and Challenging Militarization from 'A Stirring Place.'" *Communication and Critical/Cultural Studies* 16, no. 1 (2019): 4–25. https://doi.org/10.1080/14791420.2019.1572905.

———. "Disaster Militarism and Indigenous Responses to Super Typhoon Yutu in the Mariana Islands." *Environmental Communication* 16, no. 5 (2022): 612–29. https://doi.org/10.1080/17524032.2022.2026798.

———. "From Guåhan and Back: Navigating a Both/Neither Analytic for Rhetorical Field Methods." In *Text + Field: Innovations in Rhetorical Method*, edited by Sara L. McKinnon, Robert Asen, Karma R. Chávez, and Robert Glenn Howard, 56–71. University Park, PA: Penn State University Press, 2016.

———. "Oceanic Possibilities for Communication Studies." *Communication and Critical/Cultural Studies* 17, no. 1 (2020): 95–103. https://doi.org/10.1080/14791420.2020.1723802.

———. "Rhetorical Contexts of Colonization and Decolonization." In *Oxford Research Encyclopedia of Communication*, 2020. https://www.researchgate.net/publication/344352338_Rhetorical_Contexts_of_Colonization_Decolonization.

———. "Speaking of Indigeneity: Navigating Genealogies against Erasure and #RhetoricSoWhite." *Quarterly Journal of Speech* 105, no. 4 (2019): 495–501. https://doi.org/10.1080/00335630.2019.1669895.

Na'puti, Tiara R., and T. Jake Dionne. "Settler Colonialism on Display: Touring On-Campus Places of Public Memory to Teach Ideological Rhetorical Criticism." *Communication Teacher* 35, no. 2 (2020): 1–8. https://doi.org/10.1080/17404622.2020.1857420.

NECONA. "National Environmental Coalition of Native Americans." Accessed May 27, 2020. http://necona.indigenousnative.org/.

———. "Nuclear Free Zones." Accessed May 27, 2020. http://necona.indigenousnative.org/nfz.html.

Nelson, Melissa K., and Daniel Shilling, eds. *Traditional Ecological Knowledge: Learning from Indigenous Practices for Environmental Sustainability*. Cambridge: Cambridge University Press, 2018.

Newcomb, Steven. "Perspectives: Healing, Restoration, and Rematriation." *News & Notes*, Spring/Summer 1995.

Nijdam, Elizabeth "Biz." "Recentering Indigenous Epistemologies through Digital Games: Sámi Perspectives on Nature in Rievssat (2018)." *Games & Culture* 18, no. 1 (2023): 27–41. https://doi.org/10.1177/15554120211068086.

Nuclear Information and Resource Service. "Beware of 'Private Fuel Storage': New Report Criticizes Industry Plan for Nuclear Waste" (press release). July 26, 2001. http://www.nirs.org/press/07-26-2001/1.

———. "Environmental Racism, Tribal Sovereignty and Nuclear Waste." February 15, 2001. https://www.nirs.org/environmental-racism-tribal-sovereignty-and-nuclear-waste-nirs-factsheet/.

———. "Nuclear Waste + Native Lands= Environmental Racism" (press release). October 24, 2000. https://www.nirs.org/alerts/10-24-2000/.

———. "Opposition to Private Fuel Storage Mounts from Public Interest Groups and Tribes: Citing National Security and Environmental Justice Concerns, Groups Urge Nuclear Agency to Listen to Utah's Appeal" (press release). April 4, 2005. http://www.nirs.org/press/04-04-2005/1.

Obama, Barack. "Memorandum for the Secretary of Energy: Blue Ribbon Commission on America's Nuclear Future." The White House Office of the Press Secretary, January 29, 2010. http://brc.gov/index.php?q=page/executive-order.

"Ohngo Gaudadeh Devia's Contentions Regarding the Materials License Application of Private Fuel Storage in an Independent Spent Fuel Storage Installation." Nuclear Regulatory Commission, November 24, 1997. http://pbadupws.nrc.gov/docs/ML0037/ML003728301.pdf.

Olaniyan, O. M. "Know Your History: Toward an Eternally Displaceable Strategic Essentialism." *Journal of International and Intercultural Communication* 14, no. 4 (2021): 1–15. https://doi.org/10.1080/17513057.2021.1957139.

Olson, Christa J., and Rubén Casas. "Felipe Guaman Poma de Ayala's Primer Nueva Corónica y Buen Gobierno and the Practice of Rhetorical Theory in Colonial Peru." *Quarterly Journal of Speech* 101, no. 3 (2015): 459–84. https://doi.org/10.1080/00335630.2015.1056747.

Ono, Kent A. *Contemporary Media Culture and the Remnants of a Colonial Past.* New York: Peter Lang Publishing, 2009.

Peeples, Jennifer A., Richard S. Krannich, and Jesse Weiss. "Arguments for What No One Wants: The Narratives of Waste Storage Proponents." *Environmental Communication: A Journal of Nature and Culture* 2, no. 1 (2008): 40–58. https://doi.org/10.1080/17524030701642751.

Pezzullo, Phaedra C. "Environment." *Oxford Research Encyclopedia of Communication,* October 26, 2017. https://doi.org/10.1093/acrefore/9780190228613.013.575.

———. *Toxic Tourism: Rhetorics of Pollution, Travel, and Environmental Justice.* Tuscaloosa: University of Alabama Press, 2007.

Pezzullo, Phaedra C., and Catalina M. de Onís. "Rethinking Rhetorical Field Methods on a Precarious Planet." *Communication Monographs* 85, no. 1 (2018): 103–22. https://doi.org/10.1080/03637751.2017.1336780.

Pezzullo, Phaedra C., and Ronald Sandler. "Introduction: Revisiting the Environmental Justice Challenge to Environmentalism." In *Environmental Justice and Environmentalism: The Social Justice Challenge to the Environmental Movement,* 1–24. Cambridge, MA: MIT Press, 2007.

Powell, Malea. "Rhetorics of Survivance: How American Indians Use Writing." *College Composition and Communication* 53, no. 3 (2002): 396–434. https://doi.org/10.2307/1512132.

Powell, Malea, Daisy Levy, Andrea Riley-Mukavetz, Marilee Brooks-Gillies, Maria Novotny, Jennifer Fisch-Ferguson, and The Cultural Rhetorics Theory Lab. "Our Story Begins Here: Constellating Cultural Rhetorics." *Enculturation: A Journal of Rhetoric, Writing, and Culture* (2014). http://enculturation.net/our-story-begins-here.

Pritzker, Barry M. "The Great Basin." In *A Native American Encyclopedia,* 220–48. Oxford: Oxford University Press, 2000.

Private Fuel Storage. "The PFS Project Benefits the Nation," 2004. http://www.privatefuelstorage.com/benefit/nation.html.

———. "Voices: Leon Bear." 2004. http://www.privatefuelstorage.com/voices/bear.html.

———. "Voices: Mary Allen." 2004. http://www.privatefuelstorage.com/voices/allen.html.

———. "Who Will Benefit." 2004. http://www.privatefuelstorage.com/benefit/benefit.html.

"Private Fuel Storage, LLC Limited Appearance Session." Nuclear Regulatory Commission, Salt Lake City, UT, April 2, 2002.

Privott, Meredith. "An Ethos of Responsibility and Indigenous Women Water Protectors in the #NoDAPL Movement." *American Indian Quarterly* 43, no. 1 (2019): 74–100. https://doi.org/10.5250/amerindiquar.43.1.0074.

Public Citizen, and Nuclear Information and Resource Service. "On Verge of Approval, Private Fuel Storage Site Is Not a Safe or Just Solution for Nuclear Waste" (press release). March 31, 2005.

"Public Comments on Site Recommendation for the Yucca Mountain Project." Hawthorne, NV, October 12, 2001.

"Public Hearing Session for a Geologic Repository for the Disposal of Spent Nuclear Waste and High-Level Radioactive Waste at Yucca Mountain, Nye County, Nevada." Statham Hall, Lone Pine, CA, October 10, 2001.

"Public Meeting on the P Draft Environmental Impact Statement for the Private Fuel Storage Facility." Nuclear Regulatory Commission, Salt Lake City, UT, July 27, 2000.

———. Nuclear Regulatory Commission, Salt Lake City, UT, July 28, 2000.

Rai, Candice, and Caroline Gottschalk Druschke, eds. *Field Rhetoric: Ethnography, Ecology, and Engagement in the Places of Persuasion*. Tuscaloosa: University Alabama Press, 2018.

The Red Nation. *The Red Deal: Indigenous Action to Save Our Earth*. Brooklyn, NY: Common Notions, 2021.

Reilly, Bennie, Sr. Nevada Test Site Oral History Project, University of Nevada Las Vegas, May 10, 2004. http://digital.library.unlv.edu/ntsohp/.

Richter, Jennifer. "Energopolitics and Nuclear Waste: Containing the Threat of Radioactivity." *Energy Research & Social Science* 30 (2017): 61–70. https://doi.org/10.1016/j.erss.2017.06.019.

Riley, Michael. "Trainload of Debate on Nuke Storage." *Denver Post*, June 11, 2006.

Riley-Mukavetz, Andrea. "Developing a Relational Scholarly Practice: Snakes, Dreams, and Grandmothers." *College Composition and Communication* 71, no. 4 (2020): 545–65.

Rott, Nathan. "New Mexico Is Divided over the 'Perfect Site' to Store Nation's Nuclear Waste." *NPR*, April 11, 2019. https://www.npr.org/2019/04/11/709600915/new-mexico-is-divided-over-the-perfect-site-to-store-nation-s-nuclear-waste.

Runyan, Anne Sisson. "Disposable Waste, Lands and Bodies under Canada's Gendered Nuclear Colonialism." *International Feminist Journal of Politics* 20, no. 1 (2018): 24–38. https://doi.org/10.1080/14616742.2017.1419824.

Russell, Caskey. "Language, Violence, and Indian Mis-Education." *American Indian Culture and Research Journal* 26, no. 4 (2002): 97–112.

Sailiata, Kristina. "Decolonization." In *Native Studies Keywords*, edited by Stephanie Nohelani Teves, Andrea Smith, and Michelle Raheja, 301–8. Tucson: University of Arizona Press, 2015.

Schmitt, Casey. "Invoking the Ecological Indian: Rhetoric, Culture, and the Environment." In *Voice and Environmental Communication*, 66–87. New York: Palgrave MacMillan, 2014.

Schneider, Keith. "Dying Nuclear Plants Give Birth to New Problems." *New York Times*, October 31, 1988. http://www.nytimes.com/1988/10/31/us/dying-nuclear-plants-give-birth-to-new-problems.html?pagewanted=all&src=pm.

Schwartz, Jessica A. "Matters of Empathy and Nuclear Colonialism: Marshallese Voices Marked in Story, Song, and Illustration." *Music and Politics* 10, no. 2 (2016). http://dx.doi.org/10.3998/mp.9460447.0010.206.

Schwartz-DuPre, Rae Lynn, and Shelby Scott. "Postcolonial Globalized Communication and Rapping the Kufiyya." *Communication, Culture & Critique* 8, no. 3 (2015): 335–55. https://doi.org/10.1111/cccr.12085.

"Science and Engineering Report for a Geologic Repository for the Disposal of Spent Nuclear Fuel and High-Level Radioactive Waste at Yucca Mountain, Nye County, Nevada." Elko Convention and Visitors Authority, Elko, NV, September 5, 2001.

"Scoping Meeting for Preparation of an EIS for the Private Fuel Storage Facility." Nuclear Regulatory Commission, Salt Lake City, UT, June 2, 1998.

Sheridan, Joe, and Roronhiakewen "He Clears the Sky" Dan Longboat. "The Haudenosaunee Imagination and the Ecology of the Sacred." *Space and Culture* 9, no. 4 (2006): 365–81. https://doi.org/10.1177/1206331206292503.

Shome, Raka. *Diana and Beyond: White Femininity, National Identity, and Contemporary Media Culture.* Chicago: University of Illinois Press, 2014.

———. "Postcolonial Approaches to Communication: Charting the Terrain, Engaging the Intersections." *Communication Theory (10503293)* 12, no. 3 (2002): 249.

———. "Postcolonial Interventions in the Rhetorical Canon: An 'Other' View." *Communication Theory* 6, no. 1 (1996): 40–59. https://doi.org/10.1111/j.1468-2885.1996.tb00119.x.

Shome, Raka, and Radha Hegde. "Culture, Communication, and the Challenge of Globalization." *Critical Studies in Media Communication* 19, no. 2 (2002): 172–89. https://doi.org/10.1080/07393180216560.

Shrader-Frechette, Kristin. *Environmental Justice: Creating Equality, Reclaiming Democracy.* New York: Oxford University Press, 2002.

Simpson, Audra. *Mohawk Interruptus: Political Life across the Borders of Settler States.* Durham, NC: Duke University Press, 2014.

———. "On Ethnographic Refusal: Indigeneity, 'Voice' and Colonial Citizenship." *Junctures: The Journal for Thematic Dialogue*, no. 9 (2007): 67–80.

Simpson, Leanne Betasamosake. *As We Have Always Done: Indigenous Freedom through Radical Resistance.* Minneapolis: University of Minnesota Press, 2017.

Skull Valley. Documentary. KUED, 2001.

Skull Valley Band of Goshutes. "The Skull Valley Goshutes." Skull Valley Goshute. Accessed February 20, 2003. http://www.skullvalleygoshutes.org/main.html.

Smith, Chad. "Letter to the Department of Energy [Public Comment #551117]." September 21, 2001. http://www.ymp.gov/documents/sr_comm/sr_pdf/551117.pdf.

Smith, John, and Sean Gleason. "'Knowledge Is Like Food': Qanruyutet on Change and Subsistence from John Smith." *Text & Performance Quarterly* 41, no. 1/2 (2021): 37–60. https://doi.org/10.1080/10462937.2021.1916583.

Smith, Linda Tuhiwai. *Decolonizing Methodologies: Research and Indigenous Peoples.* London: Zed Books, 1999.

Smoak, Gregory. "Great Basin." In *The Oxford Handbook of American Indian History*, edited by Frederick E. Hoxie, 377–93. New York: Oxford University Press, 2016.

Solnit, Rebecca. *Hope in the Dark: Untold Histories, Wild Possibilities.* Chicago: Haymarket Books, 2016.

Solomon, Barry D., and Fei Li. "Environmental Equity and Nuclear Waste Repository Siting in East Asia." In *Development Studies in Regional Science: Essays in Honor of Kingsley E.*

Haynes, edited by Zhenhua Chen, William M. Bowen, and Dale Whittington, 147–66. New Frontiers in Regional Science: Asian Perspectives. Singapore: Springer, 2020. https://doi.org/10.1007/978-981-15-1435-7_10.

Southwest Research and Information Center. "Navajo Nation President Joe Shirley, Jr. Signs Diné Natural Resources Protection Act of 2005: New Law Bans Uranium Mining, Processing throughout Navajo Nation." April 29, 2005. http://www.sric.org/voices/2005/v6n2/navajo_pr_dnrpa.php.

Sowards, Stacey K. "#RhetoricSoEnglishOnly: Decolonizing Rhetorical Studies through Multilingualism." *Quarterly Journal of Speech* 105, no. 4 (2019): 477–83. https://doi.org/10.1080/00335630.2019.1669891.

Spangler, J. "Foes of Goshute Nuclear Waste Plan Take Case to D.C." *Deseret News*, April 5, 2005. https://www.deseret.com/2005/4/5/19885534/foes-of-goshute-nuclear-waste-plan-take-case-to-d-c.

Spivak, Gayatri C. "Can the Subaltern Speak?" In *Marxism and the Interpretation of Culture*, edited by Lawrence Grossberg, 217–313. Chicago: University of Illinois Press, 1988.

Stanley, B. Liahnna. "Pubic Scarves and Earthworm Sex: Storying Indigenous Eroticisms and Futures." *Review of Communication* 22, no. 4 (2022): 351–63.

———. "Returning Home." In *Communication Theory: Racially Diverse and Inclusive Perspectives*, edited by Mark P. Orbe, Jeanetta D. Sims, and Jasmine T. Austin, 215–19. Solana Beach, CA: Cognella Academic Publishing, 2021.

Steward, Julian H. "Some Western Shoshoni Myths." *Smithsonian Institution Bureau of American Ethnology* 136, no. 31 (1943): 249–99.

Stoffle, Richard W. "Native Americans and Nuclear Waste Storage at Yucca Mountain, Nevada: Potential Impacts of Site Characterization Activities." Ann Arbor, MI: Institute for Social Research, 1987.

Stoffle, Richard W., Richard Arnold, and Angelita Bullets. "Talking with Nature: Southern Paiute Epistemology and the Double Hermeneutic with a Living Planet." In *Talking with Nature: Southern Paiute Epistemology and the Double Hermeneutic with a Living Planet*, 75–100. Piscataway, NJ: Gorgias Press, 2016. https://doi.org/10.31826/9781463236892-005.

Stoffle, Richard W., and Michael J. Evans. "American Indians and Nuclear Waste Storage: The Debate at Yucca Mountain, Nevada." *Policy Studies Journal* 16, no. 4 (1988): 751–67.

Stoffle, Richard W., David B. Halmo, John E. Olmsted, and Michael J. Evans. *Native American Cultural Resource Studies at Yucca Mountain, Nevada*. Ann Arbor: University of Michigan, Institute for Social Research, 1990.

Stoffle, Richard W., and Maria Nieves Zedeno. "Historical Memory and Ethnographic Perspectives on the Southern Paiute Homeland." *Journal of California and Great Basin Anthropology* 23, no. 2 (2001): 229–48. https://escholarship.org/uc/item/7rq7b58g.

Stoffle, Richard, Kathleen Van Vlack, Sean O'Meara, Richard Arnold, and Betty Cornelius. "Incised Stones and Southern Paiute Cultural Continuity." *Journal of California and Great Basin Anthropology* 41, no. 1 (2021): 19–36.

Stone, Richard. "Near Miss at Fukushima Is a Warning for U.S., Panel Says." *Science,* May 20, 2016. https://www.science.org/content/article/near-miss-fukushima-warning-us-panel-says.

Stuckey, Mary E., and John M. Murphy. "By Any Other Name: Rhetorical Colonialism in North America." *American Indian Culture and Research Journal* 25, no. 4 (2001): 73–98.

Styres, Sandra, and Dawn Zinga. "The Community-First Land-Centred Theoretical Framework: Bringing a 'Good Mind' to Indigenous Education Research?" *Canadian Journal of Education* 16 (2013): 284–413.

Sutton, Anthony. "Farming, Fieldwork, and Sovereignty: Addressing Colonialist Systems with Participatory Critical Rhetoric." In *Decolonizing Native American Rhetoric: Communicating Self Determination*, edited by Casey Ryan Kelly and Jason Edward Black, 324–42. New York: Peter Lang, 2018. https://doi.org/10.3726/b13447/29.

Tarin, Carlos A. "Buen Vivir: Indigeneity, Environmental Activism, and Decolonial Organizing." In *Latina/o/x Communication Studies: Theories, Methods, and Practice*, 209–27. Lanham, MD: Lexington Books, 2019.

Taylor, Bryan C. "Nuclear Waste and Communication Studies." *Review of Communication* 3, no. 3 (2003): 286–92. https://doi.org/10.1080/0308399.

———. "Nuclear Weapons and Communication Studies: A Review Essay." *Western Journal of Communication* 62, no. 3 (1998): 300–315.

Taylor, Bryan C., and William J. Kinsella. "Introduction: Linking Nuclear Legacies and Communication Studies." In *Nuclear Legacies: Communication, Controversy, and the U.S. Nuclear Weapons Complex*, edited by Bryan C. Taylor, William J. Kinsella, and Stephen P. Depoe, 1–37. Lanham, MD: Lexington Books, 2007.

Taylor, Bryan C., William J. Kinsella, and Stephen P. Depoe, eds. *Nuclear Legacies: Communication, Controversy, and the U.S. Nuclear Weapons Complex*. Lanham, MD: Lexington Books, 2007.

Thompson, Joshua. "The Green Metal Mining Boom Is On." *High Country News*, October 13, 2022. https://www.hcn.org/articles/landline-the-green-metal-mining-boom-is-on.

Thorpe, Grace. "Our Homes Are Not Dumps: Creating Nuclear Free Zones." *Natural Resources Journal* 36, no. 4 (1996): 955–64.

———. "Statement of Grace Thorpe to the National Congress of American Indians." December 1, 1993. http://necona.indigenousnative.org/ncai.html.

Todd, Zoe. "An Indigenous Feminist's Take on the Ontological Turn: 'Ontology' Is Just Another Word for Colonialism." *Journal of Historical Sociology* 29, no. 1 (2016): 4–22. https://doi.org/10.1111/johs.12124.

Torre, Joaquin. "Tattooing Decolonial and Indigenous Futurity." Paper presented at the National Communication Association Convention, New Orleans, LA, November, 2022.

Tuck, Eve. "Suspending Damage: A Letter to Communities." *Harvard Educational Review* 79, no. 3 (October 6, 2009): 409–28. https://doi.org/10.17763/haer.79.3.n0016675661t3n15.

Tuck, Eve, Marcia McKenzie, and Kate McCoy. "Land Education: Indigenous, Post-Colonial, and Decolonizing Perspectives on Place and Environmental Education Research." *Environmental Education Research* 20, no. 1 (January 2, 2014): 1–23. https://doi.org/10.1080/13504622.2013.877708.

Tuck, Eve, and K. Wayne Yang. "Decolonization Is Not a Metaphor." *Decolonization: Indigeneity, Education & Society* 1, no. 1 (2012): 1–40.

Twain, Mark. *Roughing It*. American Publishing Company, 1873.

UN Committee for the Elimination of Racial Discrimination. "Early Warning and Urgent Action Procedure: Decision 1(68): United States of America." 2006. https://digitallibrary.un.org/record/573142?ln=en.

UN Inter-American Commission on Humans Rights. *Report No. 75/02, Case 11.140, Mary and Carrie Dann, United States*. December 27, 2002. http://www1.umn.edu/humanrts/cases/75-02a.html.

United Church of Christ Commission for Racial Justice. *Toxic Wastes and Race in the United States: A National Report on the Racial and Socio-Economic Characteristics of Communities with Hazardous Waste Sites*. 1987. https://www.nrc.gov/docs/ML1310/ML13109A339.pdf.

University of Colorado Boulder. *Report of the Investigative Committee of the Standing Committee on Research Misconduct at the University of Colorado at Boulder Concerning Allegations of Academic Misconduct against Professor Ward Churchill.* May 9, 2006. https://www.law.du.edu/documents/corporate-governance/churchill/WardChurchillReport.pdf.

University of Utah. "Indigenous Land Acknowledgement." @theU, October 9, 2020. https://attheu.utah.edu/facultystaff/indigenous-land-acknowledgement/.

"Uranium Mine Hearing: Foreign Ownership Issue." *Lakota Times,* March 19, 2009. https://www.lakotatimes.com/articles/uranium-mine-hearing-foreign-ownership-issue/.

Urban Environmental Research, and Ian Zabarte. *Tribal Concerns about the Yucca Mountain Repository: An Ethnographic Investigation of the Moapa Band of Paiutes and the Las Vegas Paiute Colony.* Clark County Department of Comprehensive Planning, Nuclear Waste Division, October 20, 2002. https://www.nirs.org/wp-content/uploads/ejustice/nativelands/tribalconcerns1102.pdf.

US Department of Energy. *Battlefield of the Cold War: Atmospheric Nuclear Weapons Testing, 1951–1963.* Vol. 1. Washington DC: US Department of Energy, 2006.

———. "Department of Energy's Tribal Program: Hanford Site." Hanford Site, December 14, 2022. https://www.hanford.gov/page.cfm/inp.

———. "Nuclear Waste Policy Act as Amended with Appropriations Acts Appended." March 2004. https://www.energy.gov/sites/prod/files/edg/media/nwpa_2004.pdf.

———. "Site Recommendation Comment Summary Document." US Department of Energy Office of Civilian Radioactive Waste Management, 2002.

US Department of Energy, Office of Civilian Radioactive Waste Management. "Preservation through Cooperation Fact Sheet [YMP-0340]." US Department of Energy, June 2000.

US Department of Energy, Office of Nuclear Energy. "5 Fast Facts about Nuclear Waste." Energy.gov, July 30, 2019. https://www.energy.gov/ne/articles/5-fast-facts-about-nuclear-waste.

"US Department of Energy Public Hearing on the Possible Site Recommendation of Yucca Mountain." 232 Energy Way, North Las Vegas, NV, September 5, 2001.

———. Bob Rudd Community Center, Pahrump, NV, October 12, 2001.

———. Bob Rudd Community Center, Pahrump, NV, December 5, 2001.

———. Longstreet Inn and Casino, Amargosa Valley, NV, October 10, 2001.

———. Town Center, Crescent Valley, NV, October 10, 2001.

US Department of Energy, Waste Isolation Pilot Plant. "Regulatory Background." Accessed January 28, 2020. https://wipp.energy.gov/regulatory-background.asp.

US Energy Information Administration. "Nuclear Explained: US Nuclear Industry." April 18, 2022. https://www.eia.gov/energyexplained/nuclear/us-nuclear-industry.php.

———. "The Nuclear Fuel Cycle." July 12, 2022. https://www.eia.gov/energyexplained/nuclear/the-nuclear-fuel-cycle.php.

US Environmental Protection Agency. "40 CFR Part 197: Public Health and Environmental Radiation Protection Standards for Yucca Mountain, NV; Final Rule." *Federal Register* 66, no. 114 (June 13, 2001): 32074–135.

US Government Accountability Office. "Commercial Spent Nuclear Fuel: Congressional Action Needed to Break Impasse and Develop a Permanent Disposal Solution." September 23, 2021. https://www.gao.gov/products/gao-21-603.

———. "Disposal of High-Level Nuclear Waste." Accessed January 29, 2020. https://www.gao.gov/key_issues/disposal_of_highlevel_nuclear_waste/issue_summary.

US Nuclear Regulatory Commission. "NRC: Backgrounder on Radioactive Waste." July 23, 2019. https://www.nrc.gov/reading-rm/doc-collections/fact-sheets/radwaste.html.

———. "NRC: High-Level Waste." August 3, 2017. https://www.nrc.gov/waste/high-level-waste.html.

———. "NRC Issues License to Holtec International for Consolidated Spent Nuclear Fuel Interim Storage Facility in New Mexico." May 9, 2023. https://www.nrc.gov/cdn/doc-collection-news/2023/23-031.pdf.

———. "NRC: Radioactive Waste." August 14, 2017. https://www.nrc.gov/waste.html.

Utah American Indian Digital Archive. "The Paiutes: History." Accessed January 17, 2022. https://utahindians.org/archives/paiutes/history.html.

Valaskakis, Gail Guthrie. *Indian Country: Essays on Contemporary Native Culture.* Waterloo, ON: Wilfrid Laurier University Press, 2005.

Vandenbosch, Robert, and Susanne E. Vandenbosch. *Nuclear Waste Stalemate: Political and Scientific Controversies.* Salt Lake City: University of Utah Press, 2007.

Vats, Anjali. "(Dis)Owning Bikram: Decolonizing Vernacular and Dewesternizing Restructuring in the Yoga Wars." *Communication and Critical/Cultural Studies* 13, no. 4 (2016): 325–45. https://doi.org/10.1080/14791420.2016.1151536.

Vizenor, Gerald. "Aesthetics of Survivance: Literary Theory and Practice." In *Survivance: Narratives of Presence,* edited by Gerald Vizenor, 1–24. Lincoln: University of Nebraska Press, 2008.

———. *Manifest Manners: Narratives on Postindian Survivance.* Lincoln: University of Nebraska Press, 1999.

———. *Survivance: Narratives of Native Presence.* Lincoln: University of Nebraska Press, 2008.

Voyles, Traci Brynne. *Wastelanding: Legacies of Uranium Mining in Navajo Country.* Minneapolis: University of Minnesota Press, 2015.

Walker, J. Samuel. *The Road to Yucca Mountain: The Development of Radioactive Waste Policy in the United States.* Oakland: University of California Press, 2009.

Walker, Mark. "Flooding and Nuclear Waste Endanger a Tribe's Ancestral Land." *Minneapolis / St. Paul Business Journal,* November 15, 2021. https://www.bizjournals.com/twincities/news/2021/11/15/flooding-and-nuclear-waste-endanger-a-tribe-s.html.

Wanzer, Darrel Allan. "Delinking Rhetoric, or Revisiting McGee's Fragmentation Thesis through Decoloniality." *Rhetoric & Public Affairs* 15, no. 4 (2012): 647–57.

Wanzer-Serrano, Darrel. *The New York Young Lords and the Struggle for Liberation.* Philadelphia: Temple University Press, 2015.

Watts, Vanessa. "Indigenous Place-Thought and Agency Amongst Humans and Non Humans (First Woman and Sky Woman Go On a European World Tour!)." *Decolonization: Indigeneity, Education & Society* 2, no. 1 (2013). https://jps.library.utoronto.ca/index.php/des/article/view/19145.

Weaver, Jace. "Introduction: Notes from a Miner's Canary." In *Defending Mother Earth: Native American Perspectives on Environmental Justice,* edited by Jace Weaver, 1–28. Maryknoll, NY: Orbis Books, 1996.

Whyte, Kyle. "Indigenous Environmental Movements and the Function of Governance Institutions." In *Oxford Handbook of Environmental Political Theory,* edited by Teena Gabrielson, Cheryl Hall, John M. Meyer, and David Schlosberg, in press. https://www.academia.edu/13152743/Indigenous_Environmental_Movements_and_the_Function_of_Governance_Institutions.

———. "Indigenous Experience, Environmental Justice and Settler Colonialism." In *Nature and Experience: Phenomenology and the Environment,* edited by Bryan E. Bannon, 157–74. Lanham, MD: Rowman & Littlefield International, 2016.

———. "What Do Indigenous Knowledges Do for Indigenous Peoples?" In *Traditional Ecological Knowledge: Learning from Indigenous Practices for Environmental Sustainability,* edited by Melissa K. Nelson and Daniel Shilling, 57–84. Cambridge: Cambridge University Press, 2018.

Wieskamp, Valerie N., and Cortney Smith. "'What to Do When You're Raped': Indigenous Women Critiquing and Coping through a Rhetoric of Survivance." *Quarterly Journal of Speech* 106, no. 1 (2020): 72–94. https://doi.org/10.1080/00335630.2019.1706189.

Wilkins, David E., and K. Tsianina Lomawaima. *Uneven Ground: American Indian Sovereignty and Federal Law.* Tulsa: University of Oklahoma Press, 2002.

Wilkins, David E., and Heidi Kiiwetinepinesiik Stark. *American Indian Politics and the American Political System.* 3rd ed. Lanham, MD: Rowman & Littlefield Publishers, 2010.

Wilkinson, Charles. *Indian Tribes as Sovereign Governments: A Sourcebook on Federal-Tribal History, Law, and Policy.* Oakland, CA: American Indian Resources Institute, 1991.

Wilson, Shawn. *Research Is Ceremony: Indigenous Research Methods.* Black Point, NS: Fernwood Publishing, 2008.

Wolfe, Patrick. "Corpus Nullius: The Exception of Indians and Other Aliens in US Constitutional Discourse." *Postcolonial Studies* 10, no. 2 (2007): 127–51. https://doi.org/10.1080/13688790701348540.

———. "Settler Colonialism and the Elimination of the Native." *Journal of Genocide Research* 8, no. 4 (2006): 387–409. https://doi.org/10.1080/14623520601056240.

Woods, Lucas Brady. "A U.S. Uranium Mill Is Near This Tribe. A Study May Reveal If It Poses a Health Risk." *NPR,* July 6, 2022, sec. Environment. https://www.npr.org/2022/07/06/1109518597/native-tribe-utah-u-s-uranium-mill-affects-health.

Worchester v. Georgia, no. 31 US 515 (US Supreme Court 1832).

Yagelski, Robert. "A Rhetoric of Contact: Tecumseh and the Native American Confederacy." *Rhetoric Review* 14, no. 1 (1995): 64–77.

Yih, Katherine, Albert Donnay, Annalee Yassi, A. James Ruttenber, and Scott Saleska. "Uranium Mining and Milling for Military Purposes." In *Nuclear Wastelands: A Global Guide to Nuclear Weapons Production and Its Health and Environmental Effects,* edited by Arjun Makhijani, Howard Hu, and Katherine Yih, 105–68. Cambridge, MA: The MIT Press, 2000.

Younging, Gregory. *Elements of Indigenous Style: A Guide for Writing by and about Indigenous Peoples.* Edmonton, AB: Brush Education, 2018.

"Yucca Mountain Project Comments." Fiesta Hotel, Las Vegas, NV, October 5, 2001.

"Yucca Mountain Public Hearing White Pine." Bristlecone Convention Center, Ely, NV, October 10, 2001.

"Yucca Mountain: Serpent Swimming Westward—Indigenous Action Media." Accessed January 24, 2022. https://www.indigenousaction.org/yucca-mountain-serpent-swimming-westward/.

Yurth, Cindy. "Uranium Mining Claims Pile up outside Rez Borders, Industry Reps Speculate about the Market." *Navajo Times,* March 19, 2009. https://www.navajotimes.com/news/2009/0309/031909uranium.php.

Zabarte, Ian. Nuclear Technology in the American West Oral History Project, April 12, 2008. Tape No. U-1927. Everett L. Cooley Collection, University of Utah Marriott Library Special Collections Department.

———. "View of the Western Shoshone Nation Relating to the Yucca Mountain Socioeconomic Studies." October 16, 1990.

Zalasiewicz, Jan, Colin N. Waters, Mark Williams, Anthony D. Barnosky, Alejandro Cearreta, Paul Crutzen, Erle Ellis, et al. "When Did the Anthropocene Begin? A Mid-Twentieth Century Boundary Level Is Stratigraphically Optimal." *Quaternary International* 383 (2015): 196–203. https://doi.org/10.1016/j.quaint.2014.11.045.

INDEX

Abraham, Spencer, 54, 131, 142, 145–46, 156–57
All Pueblo Council of Governors, 57
Allen, Mary, 159
allotments, land, 68, 140
American Indian, as term, xiii–xiv
American Indian Citizenship Act (1924), 132, 139–40
American Indian Religious Freedom Act (1978), 58, 77, 111–12
Andrews, James, 135
animacy of more-than-human beings, 123–24
anthropology, as field, 31
anticolonial inductive fieldwork, 181
anticolonialisms, 178. *See also* decoloniality; decolonization; neocolonialism; nuclear decolonization; postcolonialism
antinuclear movement, mainstream vs. Indigenous, 20–21, 183–84
Apache peoples and nations, 122–23
Argonne National Lab West, 57
Arnold, Richard, 112–13, 124–25, 150
Ash Meadows-Southern Paiute district, 78
assimilation, 108, 114, 131–32, 137, 139–40

Atomic Energy Commission, 46, 49

Bacoch, Alan, 151
Bacoch, Jessica, 123–24, 130–31
BANANA (Build-Absolutely-Nothing-Anywhere-Near-Anyone), 7
Bare Mountain, 76
Bear, Iby, 74
Bear, Lawrence, 119, 161
Bear, Leon: criticism of, 117, 160, 161, 163; economic development rhetoric, 107–8, 118–19, 128, 132, 167; Indigenous Lands rhetoric, 106, 119, 128; sovereignty and national interest rhetorics, 120, 159, 161–62; and tensions in Skull Valley Goshute nation, 1–2; on toxic waste in Skull Valley, 11
Bear, Richard, 74
Beck, John, 143
Begay, Marlene, 126
BIA (Bureau of Indian Affairs): establishment of reservations, 68, 71, 74, 101; leases on uranium mining, 46; and Skull Valley PFS site, 11n25, 109, 133, 162, 164, 168–69
Biden, Joe, 56

Big Pine Paiute Tribe, 104, 123–24, 130–31, 151
Blackbear, Sammy, 11, 118, 160, 161, 162
Blackfeet peoples and nations, 122
Blackhawk, Ned, 176n2
BLM (Bureau of Land Management), 11n25, 139
Blue Ribbon Commission on America's Nuclear Future, 56, 144, 185, 186
Borrows, John, 138
Brayboy, Bryan, 35
Bruyneel, Kevin, 25, 132, 140–41
Bullcreek, Margene: formation of Ohngo Gaudadeh Devia, 11, 132–33; home Lands rhetoric, 106, 108–9; mentioned, 40, 61, 75; relationality with Lands rhetoric, 127–28; sacred Lands rhetoric, 116–18, 120; sovereignty and national interest rhetorics, 160–61, 162; and tensions in Skull Valley Goshute nation, 1–2
Bureau of Indian Affairs. *See* BIA
Bureau of Land Management (BLM), 11n25, 139
Bush, George W., 8, 49, 55, 114, 116, 144
Byrd, Jodi, xi–xii, 20, 34, 41n50, 137, 164

Cajete, Gregory, 94, 95, 96, 111
Cameco Resources, 47
cancer rates, 47, 49
Carbaugh, Donal, 122–23
Caron-Jake, Vivienne, 83, 103
ceremonies, spiritual, 88–89, 112, 117, 127
Certeau, Michel de, 3n5
CGTO (Consolidated Group of Tribes and Organizations), 150n67, 152
Chaplain, Jessica, 179n8
Chavez, Lee, 150
Chemehuevi Indian Tribe, 8, 71, 104, 115, 125, 148
Church of Jesus Christ of Latter-day Saints (LDS), 67, 70, 118
Churchill, Ward, ix–x note 2, 41n50
citizenship. *See* Indigenous nationhood; US citizenship
Clifford, James, 100
Coffey, Wallace, 137–38, 173–74

colonialism, defined, 41. *See also* decolonization; nuclear colonization; nuclear decolonization; settler colonialism
communication, with more-than-human beings, 122–23, 124–25
communication studies, research paradigm shift, xii–xiii
compensation, for nuclear testing victims, 49
Comprehensive Test Ban Treaty, 49
comradeship, 182–83
Confederated Tribes of the Goshute Reservation, 72
Confederated Tribes of the Yakama Nation, 57
consent-based siting process, 186
Consolidated Group of Tribes and Organizations (CGTO), 150n67, 152
Coulthard, Glen, 153
creation stories, 62–64, 78, 105
Creator-given rights, 103, 110, 115
Crescent Valley, 88, 90 fig. 9
Crow Butte Uranium mine, 47
Crum, Steven, 67, 68, 72–73, 84
culture. *See* spiritual and cultural beliefs

Dann, Carrie, 83, 88n2, 113, 122, 125, 126, 149
Dann, Mary, 83, 88n2
Davis, Mike, 85
decide-announce-defend model of participation, 151–52
decoloniality, 34, 35
decolonization: defined, 32–34; in Indigenous Lands rhetorics, 97–98. *See also* nuclear decolonization
Deep Creek (Ibapah), 72, 73, 74, 106
Defa, Dennis, 72, 127
Deloria, Vine, Jr., 96, 122, 141
Department of Energy. *See* DOE
Department of the Interior, 11, 109
Dhillon, Jaskiran, 182, 183
Diné Lands (Navajo Reservation), 4, 46–47
Diné peoples, 70
DOE (Department of Energy): consent-based siting process, 186; and INEEL, 57–58; lack of government-to-government

negotiations, 131–32, 150–53, 156; and "national sacrifice zones," 144; and Yucca Mountain site authorization, 12, 55–56, 82, 105
domestic dependent nations, 137–38, 173
Dominguez, Atanasio, 65
dual citizenship, 132, 139
Duck Valley Reservation, 68, 69
Duckwater Shoshone people and nation, 8, 80
Dugway Proving Grounds, 85
Durham, Barbara, 154

Eastern Shoshone peoples and nations, 68
ecological effects: environmental impact concerns in Indigenous national interest rhetorics, 154–55; of uranium mining, 46–47; of weapons testing, 49–50
ecological Indian stereotype, 23, 30n6, 96n31, 121
ecology/ecological system, as term, 52n99
economic development: in Indigenous Lands rhetorics, 85–86, 107–8, 118–19, 120, 128; in Indigenous national interest rhetorics, 158–59, 162, 164, 166–68
Ely Shoshone Tribe, 125–26
Elzeflawy, Atef, 150
Energy Research and Development Administration, 54
Envirocare Low-Level Radioactive Disposal Site, 85–86
environmental effects. *See* ecological effects
environmental (in)justice, 7, 20–23, 42, 115, 120, 129, 183–84. *See also* nuclear colonization
environmental movement: mainstream vs. Indigenous, 21–23, 183–84; US vs. Indigenous national interests, 171–72
Environmental Protection Agency (EPA), 53n101, 55
Environmental Protection Agency Super Fund sites, 48
Escalante, Silvestre Vélez de, 65
Eso district (White Rock Spring-Western Shoshone), 78
Estevez, Pauline, 83, 152–53
ethnographic refusal, 16, 141

ethnology, as field, 31
Evans, Michael, 77

Fanon, Frantz, 32, 97
Farrar, Michael, 169
Fernald site, 145
Fort Hall Indian Reservation, 57
Fort Mojave Indian Tribe, 150
Fowler, Catherine, 76, 77, 79
free and prior informed consent model for decision-making, 186
Fukushima Daiichi nuclear disaster, 51

Gilio-Whitaker, Dina, 21, 42, 100, 110, 111, 121–22, 164, 184
Glass, Matthew, 142
Goldtooth, Tom, 109, 163
Goshute peoples, 72. *See also* Skull Valley Goshute people and nation
Government Accountability Office, 186
government-to-government relations, 150–54, 156, 185
gradual encroachment, 33
Great Basin: colonization and reduction of Indigenous Lands in, 65–68, 69, 70, 71, 72–75, 84, 101–2, 105–6; diversity of Indigenous peoples in, 65; in Indigenous creation stories, 62–64; landscape, 61–62; map of traditional Indigenous territories of, 66 fig. 4; as "national sacrifice zone," 143–44, 155. *See also* Skull Valley Goshute Reservation; Yucca Mountain
Grossman, Zoltan, 22

half-lives, 52, 54
Hanford site, 48, 57, 145
Hansen, Jim, 170
Harney, Corbin: on NTS, 27–28, 49–50; opposition to Yucca Mountain site, 40, 82; relationality with Lands rhetoric, 123, 124; sacred Lands rhetoric, 113; on Shoshone peoples and territory, 65, 68–69, 148; as spiritual leader, 88–89
health effects: of uranium mining, 46–47; of weapons testing, 49
Hecht, Gabriel, 44n61

Hegde, Radha, 34

Helmer, Bill, 130, 154

high-level nuclear waste: classification of, 6, 53; crisis of, 7–8, 53–55, 184–85; disproportionate location within Indigenous Lands, 56–58; on-site storage of, 51, 56, 166. *See also* Skull Valley PFS high-level nuclear waste site; Yucca Mountain high-level nuclear waste site

Hiroshima and Nagasaki bombing, 48

Holtec site, 57

home Lands: as concept, 93, 100–102; Skull Valley as, 105–10; Yucca Mountain as, 102–5. *See also* relationality with Lands; sacred Lands

Honor the Earth, 11, 22, 109

Hoopiiana, Cory, 118

Hopi Tribal Council, 154–55

human effects. *See* ecological effects; health effects

Ibapah (Deep Creek), 72, 73, 74, 106

Idaho National Engineering and Environmental Lab (INEEL), 57–58

Idle No More movement, 36

Indian, as term, xiii–xiv

Indian Reorganization Act (1934), 68, 74

Indigenous, as term, xiii–xiv, 94

Indigenous communication methods, 179

Indigenous environmental and antinuclear movements: Honor the Earth, 11, 22, 109; and Indigenized environmental justice framework, 20–23, 42, 120, 129, 183–84; vs. mainstream movements, 20–23, 183–84; NECONA, 11, 40, 57, 58–59; and relationality with Lands, 96–97. *See also* Indigenous Environmental Network

Indigenous Environmental Network: calls for halting nuclear waste production, 51–52; calls for uranium mining bans, 47; mentioned, 11, 22; national interest rhetorics, 148–49, 163; sacred Lands rhetoric, 114, 115–16; statements on nuclear colonialism, 37–38, 40, 102; on successful decolonization, 187

Indigenous environmentalisms, as term, 11n27, 97

Indigenous knowledges: defined, 30–31; and Indigenous rhetorics, 177–83; material dimension of, 13–14, 23; public texts as forms of, 17, 180; and radical resurgence, 36; supported through decolonization efforts, 33. *See also* Indigenous Lands rhetorics; Indigenous national interest rhetorics; spiritual and cultural beliefs

Indigenous Lands rhetorics: defined, 91, 92; topoi, 93–99. *See also* home Lands; Lands; relationality with Lands; sacred Lands

Indigenous national interest rhetorics, as concept, 134–35. *See also* Indigenous nationhood; sovereignty; US national interest

Indigenous nationhood: domestic dependent status, 137–38, 173; environmental protection concerns, 154–55; overview, 139; and US citizenship status, 138–39, 155–58, 165, 169–70. *See also* sovereignty

Indigenous peoples and nations, as term, xiv

Indigenous rhetorics, 19–20, 177–83

Indigenous sciences, 178

INEEL (Idaho National Engineering and Environmental Lab), 57–58

Intermountain Power Project, 85

internal colonialism, as term, 41n50. *See also* settler colonialism

International Atomic Energy Agency, 53n103

Ishiyama, Noriko, 12

Johnson, Rachel, 104

Johnson, Taylor N., 20, 34, 179n8

Kaibab Band of Paiutes, 71, 103

Kamps, Kevin, 162–63

Kennedy, Joe, 126

Kimmerer, Robin Wall, 94, 100, 122

Kinsella, William, 44

kinship groups, 64–65, 67

Knack, Martha, 70

knowledge practices. *See* Indigenous knowledges

Kuletz, Valerie, 40, 114

LaDuke, Winona: on NECONA, 58; on radioactive colonization, ix–x note 2, 39, 40, 41n50, 57, 108; on relationality with

Lands, 97, 121; on sacred Lands, 111, 112; on uranium mining, 46, 47
Lake, Randall, 19
Lakota peoples, 47
Lands: in environmental (in)justice rhetoric, 20–23, 42, 120, 129, 183–84; in Indigenous Lands rhetorics, 93–94; repatriation in decolonization efforts, 33, 97; as term, ix note 1, 90–91, 93. *See also* home Lands; Indigenous Lands rhetorics; relationality with Lands; sacred Lands
Las Vegas Paiute Tribe, 71, 80, 104, 115, 150
LDS (Church of Jesus Christ of Latter-day Saints), 67, 70, 118
Lechuga, Michael, xii, 36, 177–78, 181
Liboiron, Max, ix note 1, 35, 90, 91
Lomawaima, K. Tsianina, 136
Lone Pine Paiute Shoshone Tribe, 104
Longboat, Roronhiakewen "He Clears the Sky" Dan, 95
low-level nuclear waste storage sites, x note 3, 58, 85–86
Lyons, Scott, 19, 34

Magnesium Corporation plant, 86
Makhijani, Arjun, 48
Marshall, John, 137
Marshall Islands, 48
Masco, Joseph, 44
Mason, Alberta, 118
material rhetoric, 13–14, 23
McGee, Michael, 142
Mdewakanton Band of Eastern Dakota, 51
Mescalero Apache Lands, 4, 48
Meyers, Calvin, 104, 126, 149–50, 152
mining: settler, 67, 78; uranium, 4, 45–47, 125
Moapa Band of Paiutes and Reservation, 8, 71, 80, 122, 152
Moon, Ennis, 74
Moon, Little, 74
Moon, Sam, 74
Moon Neck, Lisa, 74
Mount Charleston, 76
MRS (monitored retrievable storage) program, 7–8, 10, 56–57, 58, 167–68

Murphy, John, 42
Muskogee Tribal Town Confederacy, 58

Nadasdy, Paul, 22–23
Na'puti, Tiara, 14, 20, 93n17, 179
National Cancer Institute, 49
National Congress of American Indians (NCAI), 111
National Council of Muskogee Creek, 58
National Environmental Coalition of Native Americans (NECONA), 11, 40, 57, 58–59
National Environmental Policy Act (1970), 12, 151
National Historic Preservation Act (1966), 58
national identity. *See* Indigenous nationhood; sovereignty; US citizenship
national interests, as rhetorical construct, 135. *See also* Indigenous national interest rhetorics; US national interest
national sacrifice rhetoric, 142–44, 155, 160
national sacrifice zones, 143–44, 155
national security rhetoric, 142–43, 170
National Wildlife Refuge sites, 48
Native, as term, xiii–xiv
Native American, as term, xiii–xiv
Native American and Indigenous studies, xii, 31. *See also* Indigenous rhetorics
Native American Graves Protection and Resources Act (1990), 58, 77
Native peoples and nations, as term, xiv
Navajo Nation, 47
Navajo Reservation (Diné Lands), 4, 46–47
NCAI (National Congress of American Indians), 111
NECONA (National Environmental Coalition of Native Americans), 11, 40, 57, 58–59
Nellis Airforce Range, 77, 79 fig. 7
neocolonialism, 20, 34, 35
Nevada National Security Site. *See* NTS
new materialisms, 13, 23
Newe, as term, xiv, 62–63. *See also* Skull Valley Goshute people and nation; Western Shoshone peoples and nations
Nez Perce people and nation, 57

NIMBY (Not-In-My-Back-Yard), 7

Northern Paiute peoples and nations, 69, 101

Northern Shoshone peoples and nations, 68

Northwestern Shoshone peoples and nations, 68

NRC (Nuclear Regulatory Commission): government-to-government negotiations, 150, 169; and Holtec site, 57; on nuclear waste, 54–55; and Skull Valley PFS site, 10, 11, 56, 106, 132, 133, 164–65, 168, 169–70; and Yucca Mountain site, 12, 55–56

NTS (Nevada Test Site), 79 fig. 7; anthropological studies of, 78; as colonized space, 49–50; location in Western Shoshone territory, 27–28; mentioned, 48; protests against, 27, 28, 29 fig. 2, 50; restricted access to, 77, 79. See also Yucca Mountain high-level nuclear waste site

nuclear accidents, 51, 107, 116

nuclear colonization: as convergence of settler colonialism and nuclearism, 41–45; disproportionate Indigenous relationship to, 37–38, 56–58; rhetorical shift to decolonization, xi–xii, 2–3, 4–5, 59; scholarship on, ix–x note 2, 39–41; as term, ix, 37, 39

nuclear decolonization: defined, 2; as form of Indigenized environmental justice movement, 20–23, 183–84; as Indigenous theoretical framework, 30–34, 35–37; research methods, 14–18, 179–83; as rhetorical phenomenon, 13–14, 18, 20–23, 34, 177–78; rhetorical shift to, xi–xii, 2–3, 4–5, 59; successes, overview of, 3–4, 187. See also Indigenous Lands rhetorics; Indigenous national interest rhetorics

nuclear-free zones, 4, 57, 58–59, 130

Nuclear Information Resource Service, 108

nuclear power: as nuclear colonization, 50–51; in US national interest rhetoric, 143, 144

Nuclear Regulatory Commission. See NRC

Nuclear Research and Information Service, 171–72

nuclear technological production: justification of, 43–44; as nuclear colonization, 45–51; uranium mining and milling, 4, 45–47, 125; in US national interest rhetoric, 143–44; weapons, 4, 48–50, 143, 144. See also NTS

nuclear waste: crisis of, 53–55, 184–85; low-level storage sites, x note 3, 58, 85–86; siting policy suggestions, 185–86; types of, 6, 52–53; in US national interest rhetoric, 144–46, 160, 166, 170–71. See also high-level nuclear waste

Nuclear Waste Policy Act (1982), 8, 12, 55, 56, 77, 145, 156, 168

nuclear weapons, 4, 48–50, 143, 144

nuclearism: as ideology, 43–44, 143; and settler colonialism, 37–38, 44

nuclearity, defined, 44n61

Nuwuvi, as term, xiv, 63. See also Southern Paiute peoples and nations

OAS (Organization of American States), 149

Obama, Barack, 56, 145, 185

object-oriented ontologies, 13, 23

Office of the Nuclear Waste Negotiator, 10, 56, 167, 185

Ogwe'pi district (Oasis Valley–Western Shoshone), 78

Ohngo Gaudadeh Devia (OGD): goals of, 11, 132–33; home Lands rhetoric, 106–10; mentioned, 40, 84; sacred Lands rhetoric, 116–17; sovereignty and national interest rhetorics, 86, 165, 169

Ohte, Eunice, 122

ontological turn, 13, 23

Operations Crossroads and Sandstone, 48

Organization of American States (OAS), 149

origin stories, 62–64, 78, 105

Owens Valley Bishop Paiute peoples, 104, 150

Pahrump Paiute Tribe, 80–82, 112–13, 149–50

Paiute peoples, 69–70. See also specific groups

Paiute Tribes of Utah, 104

paternalism, 137

Pezzullo, Phaedra, 23

PFS (Private Fuel Storage): collaboration with Skull Valley Goshute government, 1, 9–10, 158–59, 162–63; criticism of, 162–63, 168; national interest rhetoric, 146, 165–67; withdrawal from Skull Valley PFS site plan, 11. See also Skull Valley PFS high-level nuclear waste site

place, in Indigenous Lands rhetorics, 94–96

Place-Thought, 95, 96
political sovereignty, 137–38, 169, 173–74
politics of recognition, 153
Polynesian communities, 118
postcolonialism, 20, 34–35
posthumanisms, 23
Powell, J. W., 71
Prairie Island Indian Community, 51
Prairie Island Nuclear Generating Plant (Xcel Energy), 51
Pritzker, Barry, 66
Public Citizen and Nuclear Resource and Information Service, 170–71
public hearings/comment periods, 103–4, 153–54, 156–58, 165, 169–70
public texts, as source, 17, 180
Pueblo Lands, 57
puha (spiritual power), 75, 112–13

Quintana, Danny, 160

race: and colonization, 20, 184; stereotypes, 23, 30n6, 64, 96n31, 121
Radiation Exposure Compensation Act (1990), 49
radical resurgence: decolonization as mode of, 36; in Indigenous Lands rhetorics, 98–99. *See also* survivance
radioactive colonization, as term, ix, 37, 39. *See also* nuclear colonization
reciprocal relationships, 95, 121, 123
recognition, politics of, 153
reflexivity, 181–83
Reid, Harry, 9
Reilly, Bennie, Sr., 124
relationality with Lands: as concept, 94, 95, 96–97, 121–23; and Skull Valley, 127–28; and Yucca Mountain, 123–26. *See also* home Lands; sacred Lands
religion. *See* spiritual and cultural beliefs
repatriation, 33, 97
reprocessed nuclear fuel, 53, 144n52
rhetorical colonialism, 42–43
rhetorical fieldwork, 14–15, 180

rhetorical sovereignty, 19, 34
rhetorical studies: categories, 18–20; as field, 13–14, 23
Riley-Mukavetz, Andrea, 93
Rio Grande Valley, 66
Rocky Flats, 48, 145
Ruby Valley Treaty (1863), 9, 27, 49–50, 68, 82, 103, 130, 148–49
Rush Valley, 85

Sac and Fox Nation, 57, 58
sacred Lands: as concept, 93–94, 96, 110–12; Skull Valley as, 116–20; Yucca Mountain as, 112–16. *See also* home Lands; relationality with Lands
sacrifice rhetoric, 142–44, 155, 160
Sailiata, Kristina, 33
Sam, Lorinda, 125–26
Sanchez, Virginia, 49
Savannah River, 57, 58
Schrader-Frechette, Kristin, 41
scientific-based rhetoric, 178
self-determination and self-governance: decolonization as mode of, 33; in Indigenous national interest rhetorics, 149–50, 158–59, 164; recognition of, 185–86. *See also* sovereignty
Senda-Cook, Samantha, 15n36
Seneca Lands, 58
settler colonial rhetorics, 18–19
settler colonialism: and assimilation, 108, 114, 131–32, 137, 139–40; decolonization as resistance to, 32–34, 35–37; defined, 41; as incomplete, 98, 176; and Indigenous spirituality, 111–12, 115; and nuclearism, 37–38, 44; and race, 20, 184; scholarly critiques of, 4–5, 20, 21, 31, 34–35, 179; and sovereignty, 136–38, 164, 169, 173–74; in US context, 41–42; and US-Indigenous trust relationship, 133n11, 134n13, 168, 173; and violence, 42–43, 70
Sheridan, Joe, 95
Shivwits Reservation, 71
Shome, Raka, 34
Shoshone-Bannock peoples and nations, 57–58, 68

Shoshone peoples, 68–69. *See also specific groups*

Simpson, Audra, 16, 34, 98, 140, 141

Simpson, Leanne, 3, 36, 94, 98–99

Skull Valley Goshute people and nation: creation stories, 63, 105; kinship groups, 64–65; and Newe term, xiv, 62–63; opposition to PFS site, home Lands rhetoric, 106–7, 108–10; opposition to PFS site, Indigenous national interest rhetorics, 86, 160–65, 169–70; opposition to PFS site, relationality with Lands rhetoric, 127–28; opposition to PFS site, sacred Lands rhetoric, 116–18, 119–20; population, 72n43, 75; reduction/relocation of Lands, 72–75, 84, 101–2, 105–6; support for PFS site, economic development and Indigenous Lands rhetorics, 85–86, 107–8, 118–19, 120, 128; support for PFS site, economic development and Indigenous national interest rhetorics, 158–59, 162, 164, 167

Skull Valley Goshute Reservation, 61 fig. 3, 73 fig. 5, 74 fig. 6; establishment, 72–73; as home Lands, 105–10; location and landscape, 60–61, 84, 101; in relationality with Lands rhetoric, 127–28; as sacred Lands, 116–20; and Termination era, 74–75; toxic waste surrounding, 84–86, 107, 108

Skull Valley PFS high-level nuclear waste site: as interim site, 56; licensing process, 133, 168–69; location, 84, 106; opposition to, home Lands rhetoric, 106–7, 108–10; opposition to, Indigenous national interest rhetorics, 86, 160–65, 169–70; opposition to, relationality with Lands rhetoric, 127–28; opposition to, sacred Lands rhetoric, 116–18, 119–20; opposition to, US national interest rhetoric, 170–72; overview, 9–13; successful prevention of, 11, 109–10; support for, economic development and Indigenous Lands rhetorics, 85–86, 107–8, 118–19, 120, 128; support for, economic development and Indigenous national interest rhetorics, 158–59, 162, 164, 166–68; support for, mutually beneficial US-Indigenous national interest rhetorics, 160, 166–67; support for, US national interest rhetoric, 146

slavery, 70

Smith, Chad, 150, 151

Smith, Edward, 8–9, 83–84, 104, 115, 125

Smith, Linda Tuhiwai, 35

Solnit, Rebecca, 4, 187

Southern Paiute Lands: colonization of and federal control over, 70, 71, 79–80, 101; traditional location of, 66 fig. 4, 69–70, 81 fig. 8. *See also* Yucca Mountain

Southern Paiute peoples and nations: creation stories, 64, 78; kinship groups and political structures, 64–65, 70–71; and Nuwuvi term, xiv, 63; opposition to Yucca Mountain site, home Lands rhetoric, 102–5; opposition to Yucca Mountain site, Indigenous national interest rhetorics, 148–58; opposition to Yucca Mountain site, relationality with Lands rhetoric, 123–26; opposition to Yucca Mountain site, sacred Lands rhetoric, 112–16; reduction/relocation of Lands, 71, 101; relations with Yucca Mountain, overview of, 83–84

sovereignty: and government-to-government relations, 150–54, 185; Land visitation permits as affirmation of, 27–28, 28 fig. 1; misuse of, 160–65; political vs. inherent, 136–38, 169, 173–74; and politics of recognition, 153; rhetorical, 19, 34; self-determination and governance, 149–50, 158–59, 164, 185–86; third space of, 132, 140–41, 155; treaty-based, 148–49; and US-Indigenous trust relationship, 133n11, 134n13, 168, 173. *See also* Indigenous nationhood

Spanish colonialism, 65, 66, 70

spent nuclear fuel, 51, 53

spiritual and cultural beliefs: ceremonies, 88–89, 112, 117, 127; creation stories, 62–64, 78, 105; and limited focus of anthropological studies, 77; mountains as sacred sites, 8, 75–76, 113; puha, 75, 112–13; traditionalist values, 89, 107, 108, 113–14, 117. *See also* home Lands; Indigenous knowledges; relationality with Lands; sacred Lands

Stark, Heidi, xiv–xv

Steele, Rupert, 85

stereotypes, racial, 23, 30n6, 64, 96n31, 121

Steward, Julian, 64

Stoffle, Richard, 77, 78–79, 80, 125

Stuckey, Mary, 42

Supreme Court, 133n11, 137
survivance: decolonization as mode of, 3, 36; defined, 35–36; and Indigenous national interest rhetorics, 153; relationality with Lands as essential to, 94, 123; and sacred Lands rhetoric, 114, 115, 117; sovereignty as essential to, 136. *See also* radical resurgence

Taylor, Bryan, 44
Telescope Peak, 76
Termination era (1945–1961), 74–75, 140
Thorpe, Grace, 40, 57, 58–59
Timber Mountain, 76
Timbisha Shoshone Tribe, 80, 126, 130, 148, 150, 154
Todd, Zoe, 14
Tonopah Bombing Range, 77
Tourtellotte, J. E., 73
traditionalist values, 89, 107, 108, 113–14, 117
Trail of Tears, 93n18
Treaty of Guadalupe Hidalgo (1848), 65, 68
Treaty of Ruby Valley (1863), 9, 27, 49–50, 68, 82, 103, 130, 148–49
tribe, as term, xiv–xv
Trinity test, 48
Truman, Harry S., 48–49
Trump, Donald, 56
trust relationship, 133n11, 134n13, 168, 173
Tsosie, Rebecca, 137–38, 173–74
Tuck, Eve, 32, 33, 97, 129
Twain, Mark, 61

Uintah and Ouray Reservation, 73, 101–2
Umatilla people and nation, 57
UN Committee for the Elimination of Racial Discrimination, 83
uranium mining and milling, 4, 45–47, 125
Urban Environmental Research, 77, 80, 151
US citizenship: and assimilation, 132, 139–40; Indigenous tactical use of, 138–39, 155–58, 165, 169–70
US national interest: alignment with Indigenous national interests, 160, 166–67; inconsistent departmental prioritization of, 133–34, 168–69; national security and sacrifice rhetoric, 142–44, 160, 170; and nuclear waste storage, 144–46, 160, 166, 170–71; prioritized over Indigenous national interests, 131–32, 145, 170–72; as rhetorical construct, 135, 141–42
US Supreme Court, 133n11, 137
Utah, opposition to Skull Valley PFS site, 170, 171 fig. 10
Ute peoples and nations, 47, 70, 73, 101–2

Vandenbosch, Robert and Susan, 55n114, 167–68
violence, and settler colonialism, 42–43, 70
Vizenor, Gerald, 35–36

Walker River Paiutes, 126
Walla Walla Lands, 57
Wanapum people and nation, 57
Wash, Tom, 74
Waste Isolation Pilot Plant, 53n101, 58
wasteland rhetoric, 75, 84–85, 106–7, 117. *See also* national sacrifice zones
Waters, as term, 93
Watts, Vanessa, 95, 96
weapons, nuclear, 4, 48–50, 143, 144. *See also* NTS
Wells, John, 151
West Valley Demonstration Project, 57, 58
Western Shoshone Lands, 90 fig. 9; colonization of and federal control over, 27–28, 67–68, 79–80, 82, 101, 148; traditional location of, 66 fig. 4, 67–68, 81 fig. 8. *See also* Yucca Mountain
Western Shoshone National Council, 8, 27, 69, 82, 104, 151, 153
Western Shoshone peoples and nations: creation stories, 63, 78; kinship groups and political structures, 64–65, 68–69; and Newe term, xiv, 62–63; opposition to Yucca Mountain site, home Lands rhetoric, 102–5; opposition to Yucca Mountain site, Indigenous national interest rhetorics, 148–58; opposition to Yucca Mountain site, relationality with Lands rhetoric, 123–26; opposition to Yucca Mountain site, sacred Lands rhetoric, 112–16; protests against federal occupa-

tion, 27–28, 29 fig. 2; reduction/relocation of Lands, 68, 69, 101; relations with Yucca Mountain, overview of, 82–83

White Sands Proving Ground, 48

Whitney, Lois, 104

Whyte, Kyle, 11n27, 21, 30, 129

Wilkins, David, xiv–xv

Wilkinson, Charles, 110

Wilson, Shawn, 182

Wolf, Karen, 122–23

Wolfe, Patrick, 41

Yakama people and nation, 57

Yakima Lands, 57

Yang, K. Wayne, 32, 33, 97, 129

Yomba Shoshone people and nation, 80

Yowell, Raymond, 8, 103, 114

Yucca Mountain: anthropological studies of, 76–78, 114; federal control over, 79–80, 79 fig. 7, 102–3, 105; as home Lands, 102–5; Indigenous access to and occupation of, 77, 78–79, 80–82, 81 fig. 8; in relationality with Lands rhetoric, 123–26; as sacred Lands, 8, 75–76, 112–16; Southern Paiute relations with, overview of, 83–84; Western Shoshone relations with, overview of, 82–83

Yucca Mountain high-level nuclear waste site: authorization and licensing process, 55–56, 145, 156–57; opposition to, home Lands rhetoric, 102–5; opposition to, Indigenous national interest rhetorics, 148–58; opposition to, relationality with Lands rhetoric, 123–26; opposition to, sacred Lands rhetoric, 112–16; overview, 8–9, 12; proposal and research process, 55, 76–78, 114; support for, US national interest rhetoric, 144–46

Yuchi Tribal Organization, 58

Zabarte, Ian, 77, 80, 82, 115, 151, 153

NEW DIRECTIONS IN RHETORIC AND MATERIALITY
WENDY S. HESFORD, CHRISTA TESTON, AND SHUI-YIN SHARON YAM,
SERIES EDITORS

Current conversations about rhetoric signal ongoing attentiveness to and critical appraisal of material-discursive phenomena. New Directions in Rhetoric and Materiality provides a forum for responding to and extending such conversations, but also asks that books published in the series attend to social events of consequence unfolding around the world—such as violence based on misinformation, continued police brutality, immigration legislation and migration crises, and more. The series therefore seeks to amplify books that examine rhetoric's relationship to materiality while also confronting material-rhetorical forces of oppression, power imbalances, and differential vulnerabilities.

Nuclear Decolonization: Indigenous Resistance to High-Level Nuclear Waste Siting
DANIELLE ENDRES

Decolonial Conversations in Posthuman and New Material Rhetorics
EDITED BY JENNIFER CLARY-LEMON AND DAVID M. GRANT

Untimely Women: Radically Recasting Feminist Rhetorical History
JASON BARRETT-FOX

Violent Exceptions: Children's Human Rights and Humanitarian Rhetorics
WENDY S. HESFORD

Zoetropes and the Politics of Humanhood
ALLISON L. ROWLAND

Ecologies of Harm: Rhetorics of Violence in the United States
MEGAN EATMAN

Raveling the Brain: Toward a Transdisciplinary Neurorhetoric
JORDYNN JACK

Post-Digital Rhetoric and the New Aesthetic
JUSTIN HODGSON

Not One More! Feminicidio on the Border
NINA MARIA LOZANO

Visualizing Posthuman Conservation in the Age of the Anthropocene
AMY D. PROPEN

Precarious Rhetorics
EDITED BY WENDY S. HESFORD, ADELA C. LICONA, AND CHRISTA TESTON

www.ingramcontent.com/pod-product-compliance
Lightning Source LLC
Chambersburg PA
CBHW020650230426
43665CB00008B/379